HOPE

HOPE

Healing Our People & Earth

DR JUDE CURRIVAN

HAY HOUSE

Australia • Canada • Hong Kong • India
South Africa • United Kingdom • United States

First published and distributed in the United Kingdom by:
Hay House UK Ltd, 292B Kensal Rd, London W10 5BE. Tel.: (44) 20 8962 1230;
Fax: (44) 20 8962 1239. www.hayhouse.co.uk

Published and distributed in the United States of America by:
Hay House, Inc., PO Box 5100, Carlsbad, CA 92018-5100. Tel.: (1) 760 431
7695 or (800) 654 5126; Fax: (1) 760 431 6948 or (800) 650 5115.
www.hayhouse.com

Published and distributed in Australia by:
Hay House Australia Ltd, 18/36 Ralph St, Alexandria NSW 2015.
Tel.: (61) 2 9669 4299; Fax: (61) 2 9669 4144. www.hayhouse.com.au

Published and distributed in the Republic of South Africa by:
Hay House SA (Pty), Ltd, PO Box 990, Witkoppen 2068.
Tel./Fax: (27) 11 467 8904. www.hayhouse.co.za

Published and distributed in India by:
Hay House Publishers India, Muskaan Complex, Plot No.3, B-2, Vasant Kunj,
New Delhi – 110 070. Tel.: (91) 11 4176 1620; Fax: (91) 11 4176 1630.
www.hayhouse.co.in

Distributed in Canada by:
Raincoast, 9050 Shaughnessy St, Vancouver, BC V6P 6E5.
Tel.: (1) 604 323 7100; Fax: (1) 604 323 2600

© Jude Currivan, 2011

The moral rights of the author have been asserted.

The author of this book does not dispense medical advice or prescribe the use of
any technique as a form of treatment for physical or medical problems without the
advice of a physician, either directly or indirectly. The intent of the author is only
to offer information of a general nature to help you in your quest for emotional and
spiritual well-being. In the event you use any of the information in this book for
yourself, which is your constitutional right, the author and the publisher assume
no responsibility for your actions.

A catalogue record for this book is available from the British Library.

Every effort has been made to obtain permission to print the poem 'Now That We
Have Tasted Hope' on page 184; the publishers will be pleased to include any
necessary credits when the book is reprinted.

ISBN 978-1-84850-373-1

Printed and bound in Great Britain by
TJ International, Padstow, Cornwall.

MIX
Paper from
responsible sources
FSC® C013056

HOPE is dedicated to all of us — everyone who is living on Earth at this crucial moment of potential global breakthrough.

As the Hopi elders have said,
'We are the ones we've been waiting for.'

The future of the whole-world lies in our hands, and minds — and hearts.

Contents

Acknowledgements   *ix*

Introducing HOPE   *xi*

The Beginning of HOPE…   *xv*

Part I: Re-membering Who We Really Are

Chapter 1: Our Origins: Ethiopia   3
Chapter 2: Our Hidden Heritage   15
Chapter 3: Our New Start   37
Chapter 4: Hope, Healing and Love   51
Chapter 5: Healing Archetypal Patterns   61
Chapter 6: The Cosmic Hologram   75
Chapter 7: Re-membering Ourselves   83
Chapter 8: Spiral Evolution   89
Chapter 9: The Bigger Picture   97

Part II: Nations

Chapter 10: USA   115
Chapter 11: Russia and Poland   135
Chapter 12: Old to New Covenant   145
Chapter 13: Atonement to At-One-Ment   155

CONTENTS

Chapter 14: The Power of One   177
Chapter 15: China and Tibet   187
Chapter 16: India, Pakistan and Afghanistan   203
Chapter 17: Japan   219
Chapter 18: UK   235

Part III: Healing the Whole-World

Chapter 19: Peace and Resoulution   251
Chapter 20: Nuclear Non-proliferation and Disarmament   261
Chapter 21: W(h)ealth   273
Chapter 22: Me to We   285
Chapter 23: Healing our Real-ationship with Gaia   291
Chapter 24: Our Cosmic Destiny: 2012 and Beyond   309

Continuing to HOPE...   317

Resources   319

Index   321

Acknowledgements

HOPE is the outcome of many years of experience and research, during which I've enjoyed the privilege and pleasure of being guided, taught, helped along, accompanied and sometimes shoved forward by wonderful beings, both incarnate and discarnate.

Space and my memory render a complete list impossible. So I ask all those who've done so to forgive me for not mentioning them by name and to accept my heart-felt gratitude for all they've contributed to deepening my understanding of the whole-world.

Here, though, I would like to name and wholeheartedly thank those without whose involvement *HOPE* could not have been realized:

My dear fellow travellers and healers Sarah Bisby, Laura Payne and Justina Pettifer, who've organized, supported and encouraged me through many journeys, both inner and outer.

My Hay House family, especially my marvellous publisher Michelle Pilley and extraordinarily good editors Lizzie Hutchins and Joanna Lincoln.

And, whilst in India, Jhoshi, a kind guesthouse owner in Jodphur, whose remarkable efforts with intermittent internet connection and a recalcitrant and aged printer enabled me to download and print an edited version of the book to work with.

As always, my life and work have been enormously enriched by my darling husband Tony, who every day, by his gentle presence and support, embodies what love is really about.

And my marvellous step-children William and Alice, of whom we're both so proud and who continually validate our hopes.

The spirit of my beloved mum, who remains ever-present with me and a continuing inspiration.

And my wonderful mentor and guide Thoth, whose wisdom and love have sustained me throughout my life.

Introducing *HOPE*

As a cosmologist and healer, and before that as an international businesswoman, I've journeyed to nearly 70 countries around the world and explored numerous cities, sacred sites, places of conflict and genocide, regions of natural and man-made disaster and landscapes of soaring natural beauty and profound indigenous wisdom. *HOPE* shares my understanding and experiences of the energetic connections between people and places.

When asked, 'What's a cosmologist?' I reply that it's someone who wants to understand the entire Cosmos. This is not just about understanding the physical universe but the totality of what we call reality.

Wisdom traditions of the past have tended to emphasize one way of knowing through our human experience. Over the years, I've come to describe these as the spiritual paths of the shaman, the sage and the seer. These three focus in turn on our perception of the world through the compassion of our hearts, the clarity of our minds and the creativity of our purpose. But after millennia during which these different routes to enlightenment have been trod, at this momentous and unique time, by bringing all three into balance, we're able to expand our awareness beyond the limitations of the past. In *HOPE* I'll explain how we all have the ability to do this and awaken the divine potential within ourselves.

I've also directly experienced multi-dimensional realities for over 55 years and, like primary peoples around the world, see myself as part of an interconnected web of life and the Earth as a living being whom the ancient Greeks knew as Gaia. The profound interconnection between us and 'all our relations' is at the heart of the wisdom teachings of many traditions, with our 'relations' including the Sun, Moon, Earth and all her children and the wider Cosmos. In *HOPE*, I not only share the spiritual understanding of our cosmic connections and purpose but also how leading-edge science and spirit are coming together to reveal the greater reality of the whole-world.

This emerging vision describes the entire Cosmos as a unified cosmic hologram where consciousness explores itself by holographically co-creating realities on all scales of existence and myriad and multi-dimensional levels of awareness.

Every human being who has ever lived is a unique microcosm of the oneness of All That Is. And yet we're also integral aspects of the experiences played out through the larger groups that comprise our collective consciousness. At each level, from the personal to the collective, we exhibit patterns of behaviour based on our beliefs, emotions and thoughts.

So, in *HOPE*, we'll explore too how different groups and indeed countries reflect and embody, on larger scales, the same themes and issues, emotional/mental and psychic wounds and behaviour patterns that we experience and play out on personal levels. We'll investigate how different areas of conflict around the world are based on historical trauma and collective fear-based behaviour that we've energetically continued to resonate with over the years. Crucially, we'll see how to heal and release these, and in doing so, how these nations, all unique members of the family of humanity, can offer essential gifts to further our collective cosmic destiny.

As both an astronomer and an astrologer, I've found my understanding of the bigger picture of what is unfolding at this incredible time has been deepened by the cosmic connections between astronomical cycles and the astrological influences of the matrix of consciousness that is our Solar/Soular System. So we'll also see how powerful planetary influences are supporting us on a collective level and how such alignments help explain why 2012 is so synchronistically destined to offer us the breakthrough of a Shift of collective consciousness.

As I've discovered, and directly experienced for over half a century, we have enormous spiritual help from other dimensions of existence. At this crucial moment, as we go through the birthing process of a new way of being, the veils between the worlds are becoming ever thinner. Our ancestors, angels, spiritual masters and the elemental and devic realms of Gaia are all working with our higher selves to help us expand our awareness. But, as they and the Mayan elders who prophesied the significance of 2012 say, the choice is up to us!

We can't have hope for the future, however, unless we undertake the healing of our people and planet. This fundamentally is what *HOPE* is about. If we're to achieve an evolutionary world Shift, we need to release our collective trauma, liberate ourselves from the limitations, fragmented perceptions and fear-based behaviour of the past and fundamentally heal our real-ationships with each other and with Gaia.

Gaia is undertaking her own Shift. And I profoundly believe that the more we're in harmony with her and all the beings who are our brothers and sisters in our collective Earth walk, the greater the grace with which she will undertake the adjustments within her own planetary field of consciousness.

As Albert Einstein once famously said, we can't solve a problem from the same level of awareness that created it. Over the last 13 years, I've experienced how our collective awareness is expanding beyond the limits of our personality – the ego-based level of consciousness that has engendered such patterns.

In my earlier books, *The 8th Chakra* and *The 13th Step*, I've described how the 8th chakra of the universal heart, positioned midway between our heart and throat chakras, is the energetic portal to our transpersonal awareness. Activating the 8th chakra, and the further transpersonal chakras that comprise the unity awareness of our higher selves, is essential to achieve what Einstein would have recognized as a quantum leap in our evolutionary journey.

As we approach 2012 and beyond, a key aspect of *HOPE* is to inspire and empower *you* to contribute what you can to make a difference. Through understanding what's *really* going on and re-membering who you *really* are, you can participate in envisaging, co-creating and embodying a planetary community at a higher level of consciousness than ever before.

The Beginning of HOPE...

As I began to write *HOPE* in August 2010, I'd just heard that a group of 33 miners who were thought to have died when the roof of the San José copper-gold mine in northern Chile collapsed several weeks before, had been discovered alive. But they were trapped and told they could not be rescued for possibly a further four months.

With great courage and pragmatism, supported by the entire nation, engineers and experts from around the world began the huge challenge to rescue them.

Keeping hope alive in this desperate situation was crucial.

The miners' families set up Camp Hope at the pithead.

When miner Ariel Ticona's wife Elizabeth gave birth to a baby girl on 14 September, they changed her name from the one they'd planned, Carolina, to Esperanza, which means 'hope' in Spanish.

And when miner Victor Zamora wrote a short letter to his mother, delivered via the five foot long capsules that had been nicknamed *palomas*, doves, he told her, 'Even in the deepest part of the Earth, there shines light.'

Though he was still trapped deep within the womb of Gaia, his mother Nelly nonetheless felt that he had been reborn. And she smiled with pride and hope when he and his wife Jesica, who were due to have a baby in six months, chose her name: *Pax Victoria*, Peace Victory.

Soon after 8 a.m. on the ninth day of the tenth month of 2010, the sixty-ninth day since the miners' ordeal had started, the drill broke through to them. From that point, as the Chilean Mining Minister Laurence Golborne noted, it began taking symbolically 33 days to reach the 33 miners...

At midnight on 12 October, a heroic rescuer, Manuel Gonzales, climbed into the metal rescue hatch called Phoenix and took the immensely lonely journey down through almost half a mile of solid rock to reach the miners. Over the next 22 hours, throughout 13 October, Manuel and another five rescuers who had joined him helped each miner in turn to climb into the Phoenix for the journey to the surface.

As each one was freed after their long ordeal it was as if they were reborn.

The final miner to leave was Luis Urzua, the quiet foreman his men called Don Lucho, 'Mr Fighter', whose leadership had sustained them throughout. And as he returned to the surface, knowing that all the men in his care had been saved, with powerful humility he told the waiting world that they had never given up hope.

As the daughter and granddaughter of miners myself, I felt, as did many others around the world, profoundly moved by the plight of these brave men and their families, and enormously relieved and inspired by their story.

And as Manuel, their intrepid rescuer and the last man to leave the underground cavern that had been both their prison and their sanctuary, emerged into the light, I knew that these brave and humble men were ambassadors of hope for us all.

PART I
RE-MEMBERING WHO WE REALLY ARE

It's time to re-member who we really are. That means re-membering the hidden heritage of our human family and healing the traumas of our past that we continue to embody and play out in fear-based behaviour. And in doing so, we will perceive the potential of our cosmic destiny and ultimately real-ize and embody the wholeness of our divine selves and experience the oneness of the Cosmos.

At the level of our higher selves, the consciousness that continues life after life, we choose the circumstances of our birth. Through the choice of time and place we embody a personality that is uniquely ours, based on the corresponding planetary influences, and is the emotional and mental 'lens' through which we perceive our lives. We also choose the circumstances into which we incarnate, and thus the family, ethnic, religious and national lineage that interconnects us with larger group experiences. And thirdly, we undertake our higher self's or soul's purpose for this lifetime.

At this crucial time of the Shift, we're undertaking the primordial healing of our entire collective consciousness from the very first moment that our Soular System originated. So more and more of us are re-membering not only past human lives but, as our awareness expands through the 8th chakra of the universal heart, many other non-human experiences, a perception that is offering us the opportunity to heal at the most fundamental level.

So, to heal and release the personal and collective patterns of human behaviour that no longer serve our higher purpose, let's begin by going back to their seed-point, their energetic origin, the very beginning of our human journey...

CHAPTER 1
Our Origins: Ethiopia

'Hope is like a track in the countryside. When many people
walk along it, it becomes a road.'

LIN YUTANG

Looking out of the window of the Ethiopian Airlines plane, I
gazed down through the heat haze onto a parched landscape of
sun-baked scrub speckled with occasional trees. Peering into
the distance from north to south, I could see the land far below
cleaved by a huge gash, the Great Rift Valley that had formed
millions of years before as a result of the grinding apart of the
Earth's crust along an ancient scarline, and where, far into the
future, the landmass of Africa will likely split into two massive
regions separated by the infill of a future sea.

On that February day in 2010, if we'd been flying the
nearly 4,000-mile length of the Great Rift Valley rather than
across it, we could have, politics permitting, begun our journey
at its northern point in Lebanon's Baqaa Valley near its border
with Syria. We would have then flown south along the Jordan
Valley, marking the border between Israel and Jordan, over the
salt-laden Dead Sea, down the Red Sea and across the narrow
strait of water that separates Yemen and the southern tip of
Saudi Arabia from Africa. Continuing south through Ethiopia
along the Rift's enormous span, the longest on our planet, we

3

would have passed through Kenya, Tanzania, Rwanda, Uganda and the Democratic Republic of Congo and finally headed into northern Mozambique before losing sight of it.

It's along the length of the Rift in Ethiopia, Kenya and Tanzania that some of the earliest remains of our human ancestors have been discovered. These ancient remains have led to Ethiopia often being called the cradle of humanity.

As we'll see as we explore our human heritage and destiny throughout *HOPE*, our history and psyche on personal and collective levels are inherently resonant with the Earth; we truly are co-creative and co-evolutionary partners. And so from the very beginning of what it has meant to be human, our collective psyche has not only connected with that of Gaia but also signalled that deep within us there may be a psychic rift, a profound schism whose influence has played out in a multitude of ways from the earliest times.

A fundamental aspect of the schism has been our progressive separation of 'right' and 'left'-brain perception. The rift between intuitive, heart-centred and feminine-aspected awareness and rational, mind-based and masculine focus has grown over recent millennia and resulted in many of the collective issues that now challenge us and need to be re-soulved on an urgent basis.

Many of the African countries along the Rift continue to play out such deep patterns of trauma to the present day. And in the Middle East, conflicts not only between the Israelis and Palestinians but also involving the Syrians and Lebanese, all of whose lands lie on or border the Rift, have persisted in scarring our collective psyche.

Recent genetic studies have not only confirmed that our entire human family traces its lineage back to an African genesis on the Rift Valley but shown that all of us – the entire world population of some 6.7 billion people – can be traced back to an amazingly tiny population of modern humans, estimated at around 200 people. Between 70,000 and 90,000 years ago these courageous folk journeyed from Ethiopia across the narrow strait that joins Africa to Yemen and the Arabian peninsula, and from there their descendants went on to populate the entire globe. The name of the strait they braved is known in Arabic as Bab-el-Mandeb, in English the 'Gate of Tears'.

So, not only are we literally one tribe, but in an archetypal way, on some energetic level, our human family was conceived in schism and born in sorrow.

As the pace of the world Shift accelerates, just as for personal healing, we now need to heal on a collective basis the remaining schisms and traumas that limit us and hold us in fear-based patterns. And, again as for personal healing, to do so we need to go back to the beginning, the seed-point of such traumas.

So, the reason for our expedition to Ethiopia was to understand the primordial psychic wounds of our entire race and be in service to their healing. Our purpose was to return to their seed-points to energetically transform the Rift into a place of rebirth and the Gate of Tears into a Portal of Hope.

* * * *

In a wonderful synchronicity, only a few months before our journey in February 2010 archaeologists had announced the discovery of the earliest hominid yet found that was able to walk upright, dating back some 4.4 million years. They had called her Ardi, which means 'ground' in the Afar language of Ethiopia.

It was here on the Rift, at a place called the Afar Triangle, an enormously powerful tectonic hotspot, near to where a more recent forebear, Lucy, and her kin, some 3.2 million years old, had been found, that Ardi and her tribe first left the security of the trees that had been our ancestral environment for millions of years.

Archaeologists are hugely intrigued by Ardi's skeletal structure and that of the other members of her type they've since found. Not only was Ardi's upright stance a revolutionary development, but evidence as apparently innocuous as the equivalence in the size of teeth between her and the males of her type also revealed to the scientists that something dramatic happened at this critical juncture in our human story. The equality in the teeth size strongly suggests that instead of the male dominance over a harem of females that we see in the great apes of today, Ardi's tribe formed closer pair-bonds, a development that also ties into a greater investment in child-rearing.

Ardi is the first moment in our collective past when perhaps we can sense that the relationship between male and female evolved beyond the basic needs of security and sex to become something deeper, with a greater degree of emotional awareness and involvement.

We know that some animals and birds mate for life, exhibit grief at the loss of one of their own and even care for members of different species. But with Ardi we may be seeing the origin of intimate love.

Wider empathy and compassion also seem to have had early roots. In October 2009, archaeologists from the University of York, led by Dr Penny Sipkins, recounted examples of deep compassion dating back at least half a million years. The material evidence included the remains of a child with a congenital brain abnormality who wasn't abandoned but cared for, and who lived to five or six years old. And a later Neanderthal who was blind in one eye and had deformed feet and a withered arm was looked after by the community for as long as 20 years.

Such love is the heart of what makes us human.

* * * *

Flying high above the now sparsely wooded terrain, I envisaged how it would have been when Ardi and her tribe made their home there. I suddenly felt incredibly sad at the loss of the rich environment that had nurtured them and at how over the last few millennia we have come close to destroying the abundance that surrounded Ardi so many years ago.

Two-thirds of Ethiopia was once covered by trees. Now it is a meagre 3 per cent.

The travel company we'd chosen to work with, Travel Ethiopia, offers a wonderful gift to their fellow Ethiopians. For some years, they've undertaken a tree-planting project and every visitor is invited to plant a tree. Almost our first act on arriving was to make the short trip outside Addis Ababa with our hosts Samrawit and her husband Thomas, the owners of the company, and their staff to plant our own saplings in the rich red earth of this ancient land.

As we did so, I immediately felt balanced and grounded and understood not only the practical benefits of the tree-planting projects that are springing up around the world, but the emotional and spiritual benefits they bring.

****

Earlier, as I'd mulled over the trip to come, I'd also sensed that, like previous sacred journeys, it would take on archetypal attributes that would connect the personal experiences of the travellers to the bigger picture of what is collectively unfolding.

I've also learned from many previous occurrences that whilst offering amazing opportunities for personal growth and for being in service to collective healing, such spiritual journeys do, as all initiations, take people to the very depths of themselves. Often they do so in unexpected and challenging ways. But in my experience it's usually when we're willing to meet the shadow aspects of ourselves and face our inner fears that we are able to receive deeper life lessons and healing.

So, in the days and weeks before we left, I wasn't too surprised to encounter signs and synchronicities unfolding.

And past familiarity with them as way-showers ensured I paid them attention.

* * * *

Just over three years before travelling to Ethiopia, I'd stood at the Canaanite high altar at Megiddo in what is now Israel at the completion of the 13 global healing journeys that I describe in *The 13th Step*. At that place of ancient sacrifice, I'd gazed over the Plain of Megiddo, the biblical Armageddon, far below and seen a vision of hope.

Instead of the biblical prophecy of a final battle there between the forces of good and evil, my vision was of a congress of peace, a wonderful coming together of the rainbow tribes of our human family in reconciliation and harmony. As I wrote in *The 13th Step*, I'd felt that this was 'an apocalypse of peace, the revelation of the Heaven on Mother Earth that we can co-create together'. At that moment and in that incredible place I became aware that the purpose of the 13 pilgrimages had been realized. I felt that the planetary unity grid had been activated and the divine feminine had been re-energized in our collective consciousness. But it took much longer to appreciate that in the culmination of those journeys and in that perfect location lay the seed of the next step of my life journey.

Earlier that day we had stood at the Golden Gate of Jerusalem and, at dawn, sensed the powerful essence of the divine feminine energetically returning to her sanctuary in the Holy of Holies on Temple Mount. But despite recognizing the archetypal yearning for communion between the feminine and masculine aspects of our collective psyche, it took some time for me to understand that the masculine was still too wounded to do so. As I should have realized standing on the sacrificial altar at Megiddo in October 2006, one of the deepest behaviour patterns which has played out on a collective level has been that of sacrifice.

So, when only a few days before we were due to fly to Ethiopia's capital Addis Ababa, I heard the tragic news of the crash of Ethiopian Airlines Flight 409 from Beirut in Lebanon, at the top of the Rift, I was deeply saddened but not shocked.

Taking off in the early hours of 25 January for the same destination that we ourselves were bound for, the pilot, for still unknown reasons, failed to follow instructions to avoid an oncoming storm, and only a few minutes later the plane was seen to be on fire as it crashed into the sea off Lebanon, killing all 90 people on board.

The archetypal elements of the tragedy – Fire and Water – were already familiar to me from my global journeys of more than a decade. At their highest vibrations, these embody the Fire of spirit and the Water of unconditional love that flow through our collective Shift of consciousness. But at other levels, from prehistory onwards, their resonant energies have been invoked in the burning Fire and Water-blood of sacrifice.

Their symbolic, energetic and physical presence would return yet again in an incredibly powerful and poignant way a few months later. But now, as I pondered the crash, I was also reminded to go behind the appearance of events and delve more deeply for the purpose behind such an apparent 'accident'. I wholeheartedly believe that there are *no* accidents. Everything, however tragic and catastrophic, happens for a higher reason, whether we are able to perceive it or not.

And as I attuned to the sad loss of the 90 people on Flight 409, I was acutely conscious of their 'sacrifice' amidst Fire and Water.

* * * *

From the moment we reached Ethiopia, though, we felt uplifted. We felt wonderfully welcomed by the kindness of everyone we met.

Soon after we arrived, we headed for Ethiopia's National Museum in Addis, where Ardi's remains were being looked after. Her later descendant, the famous 3.2 million-year-old Lucy, was also there. Our aim was to energetically attune with Ardi, Lucy and all our ancestors. And, in the energies of the 8th chakra of the universal heart, to return to the seed-point of our human origins, to intend and envisage that all the rifts that have emanated from those beginnings be opened to healing and release.

Standing in a small room in the museum near to the remains of Ardi and Lucy but connecting at the same time with many others around the Earth, we anchored the global attunement by our physical presence.

In a very simple way, we energetically attuned to the unconditionally loving energies of the universal heart and, grounding our connection with the highest level of Spirit and connecting with all the realms of Gaia through the transpersonal 9th chakra, a hand's length beneath our feet, we opened ourselves to the flow of divine love to heal our original collective seed-point.

* * * *

As we journeyed onward through the primordial landscape of Ethiopia, our experiences showed us that the key to transforming the primal rift of our origins into a rebirth was going to be our inclusion and healing of all the polarized perceptions that we have personally and collectively held for so long.

The judgements that arise from such polarization have separated 'me' from 'you' and 'us' from 'them'. Differences have been feared rather than celebrated and 'the other' has been excluded rather than included.

As we continued to explore this polarization and its healing, we came to understand that healing in the non-judgemental love of the universal heart formed the crucial basis of resolving the remaining conflicts in all their manifestations around the world.

Three further experiences during our amazing journey showed us this.

The first was when we visited the ancient Seilassie church near the town of Gondar, dedicated to the Holy Trinity. As we entered, I took a seat at the side as our wonderful local guide Assefa began to describe how on the church walls the story is shown of the '99 angels and the fallen angel Lucifer'. I was half-listening as he continued to point out the Bible stories depicted on the walls. Looking up to my right, I saw high above me, almost hidden in shadow, a beautiful fresco of Mary looking down with a lovingly serene radiance. Then, as my gaze was drawn to the wall opposite, I saw a human-sized portrayal of Lucifer, depicted to be as frightening as possible.

I suddenly felt profound compassion for Lucifer, whose name means 'light-bringer' and who is said to have been the highest of the angelic realm. I felt the profound courage it had taken at the soul level for such a being to enter the shadow to consciously explore its polarization – and perhaps ultimately lead the way to the transcendence of such perceived polarity. And deep within myself, I felt the judgement and outcasting of that luciferic spark which those angelic beings who did not 'fall' had in some sense made – and then a profound feeling of hope for a possible reconcilation.

When Assefa had finished his description of the church, our group came into a circle and I explained what I'd felt and suggested we might choose to be in the universal heart and welcome back the 'hundredth angel' within ourselves. Everyone enthusiatically agreed and our attunement was wonderfully powerful.

When I walked outside a little while later, one of the group came up to me and asked me to follow her. A small circle of people had gathered round something. Entering the circle, I came upon an incredible sight: on the ground was a young and clearly damaged vulture – another outcast!

As we all opened our hearts to him, the dying vulture allowed me to walk up to him and hold him and even for us to get some water to him. Finally he allowed us to carry him into the shade of a nearby tree. We asked the priest nearby to watch over him as he passed. We needed to move on, but before we did, we envisaged the young vulture flying free and liberated in all his glory – another angel journeying home that day.

Later, right at the end of our journey, we spent a night at the town of Harar and had the extraordinary opportunity to feed wild hyenas on a short stick from our outstretched hands!

Hyenas, too, are generally perceived as outcasts, yet they perform an indispensible service. In Harar each night they enter the town and eat the edible trash that litters the streets. For many years, a so-called hyena man has met them as night falls and fed them. His acceptance of them and them of him meant that as strangers accepted by him, we were also accepted by them. Without fighting or snarling, for an amazing few moments they took food from us before sloping off into the darkness to continue their nightly clean-up of the town.

This sense of re-membering and resolving into our personal and collective psyche all those we have outcast, and the outcast aspects of ourselves, is fundamental as the basis for healing the schsims within and between us and for the transcendence of our polarity-based awareness. We cannot, however, do this from the level of our personality – our ego-selves – where such traumas are energetically held, but only from the transpersonal and unconditionally loving universal heart.

Every time we choose to be loving, kind, forgiving and non-judgemental – but still, importantly, discerning of what feels right or wrong – we take another step into the universal heart and into the unity awareness that is our divine reality. We take another step along our journey home – to Heaven On Mother Earth.

* * * *

Energetically, our birth on the Rift Valley and our migration through the Gate of Tears can now be healed: the Rift can be a rebirth and the Gate of Tears a rainbow bridge of *HOPE*.

The Rift Valley also reflects on Earth the dark axis of dust known to the Mayans as the 'Black Road' or 'road of rebirth' which reaches across our Milky Way Galaxy and which the Sun, now aligned with the Galactic Centre, is crossing as we approach 2012.

The ancient hermetic dictum of 'as above, so below' sums up this Earthly and cosmic mirroring. As we walk our path for HOPE together, we'll discover how profoundly this universal interconnectivity joins all scales of existence and experience. We'll dance a journey of healing that meshes the 'ordinary' practicalities of our everyday lives with the 'extraordinary' re-membering of our cosmic heritage and invites us all to embody our own unique highest purpose in being here at this axial moment in the unfolding of the divine plan.

CHAPTER 2
Our Hidden Heritage

'Hope is faith holding out its hand in the dark.'
GEORGE ILES

As we approach the cusp of the December solstice of 2012, the Mayan elders and their thirteenth-generation leader Don Alejandro Perez Oxlaj understand that this isn't simply a moment in time but a significant part of an immense process, the ending of a great cosmic cycle and the beginning of a new one.

Due to the slight wobble of the Earth about her axis, over a 26,000-year period the path of the Sun against the backdrop of our Galaxy traces a wave that now aligns with the Galactic Centre, or GC. The Sun is at a crossing-point where his path through the sky – the ecliptic – now intersects the dark band of dust that trails across the plane of our Milky Way Galaxy that the Mayans call the Black Road.

Whilst astronomically such cycles repeat themselves over vast epochs of time, this crossing-point comes at a critical juncture in our evolution. With our Sun, and indeed our entire Solar/Soular System, attuned with the massive black hole at the centre of our Galaxy, the Black Road both symbolizes the death of the old epoch and energizes the birth canal and the dawning of a new era.

This process of emergence is rather like that of a butterfly coming out of a chrysalis. Within the darkness of the cocoon, the caterpillar gradually dissolves its old body before re-forming into a higher level of its being.

Individually and collectively, we are in this transformational era of breakdown and breakthrough, where the old paradigm must fall away for us to emerge with a more coherent state of consciousness.

So it is a time to consider the three fundamental questions that define our being:

Where do we come from?

Who are we?

And where are we going?

In *HOPE*, I'm posing the question 'Where do we come from?' first. I'm doing so because as a healer I've found that unless we understand, come to terms with and release the past, especially its limiting and limited perspectives, it's very difficult to expand our awareness to seek answers to the questions of who we are and where we are going.

To heal and let go of the past, we first need to be aware of and understand it.

* * * *

As I'm writing, the progressive release of up to quarter of a million pieces of secret correspondence by WikiLeaks is revealing a tiny part of the secrecy that has surrounded the decisions of governments. Often in the past such secrets have never been uncovered. And if this has been true of recent history, how much better hidden have been the truths of more ancient times?

The passing of time itself also means that the further back we go, the less material evidence has survived for us to examine. But much that was unknown or thought to be lost is now being rediscovered. Advancing technologies are opening up the possibility of uncovering finds that now lie below desert sands or beneath the sea. And a deeper tide of awakening consciousness is bringing a greater understanding of things that have been hidden from us.

Over the last century or so, discoveries such as the Dead Sea Scrolls in Israel, the Gnostic gospels of the Nag Hammadi library in Egypt and, more recently, the Gospel of Judas, have rewritten our understanding of early Christianity. And the retrieval and translation of much earlier Sumerian texts engraved on clay tablets have given us far more of an understanding of the genesis of modern humanity.

Excavations, especially in the Near East, are now beginning to unearth sites so old they are revolutionizing archaeologists' views of the distant past. And enigmatic structures beneath the sea that are only just starting to be investigated may well completely overturn current mainstream views of our communal history.

On personal and collective levels throughout our long journey to the present time we've energetically dis-membered our psyche in many ways. And by our progressively prevalent illusion that the material world is all that there is, we have imprisoned ourselves in the sense of isolation that arises from such limited perception.

As biologists are starting to confirm, what we 'believe' we literally 'see', and so experience. And hence by defining ourselves through limiting beliefs – whether 'true' or not – we also embody the attachments that anchor us in self-limiting behaviour patterns, emotions and thoughts.

Such perspectives don't of course just restrict our understanding of the past, but of the nature of reality itself.

Their hold on us, and so how we see ourselves, each other and the wider world, is rooted there.

As we'll explore throughout *HOPE*, the transformation of our consciousness is occurring on many different levels. And so to begin to release the roots of the limited beliefs that have held us captive and the fears and fear-based behaviour patterns that have arisen from them, our process of re-membering calls us to know and understand our heritage – including those aspects that have been hidden. For in becoming more aware of our past we can more clearly appreciate the schisms within our psyche and heal and release them at their causative levels.

So we'll take our next steps in our journey of *HOPE* by exploring our hidden heritage and a number of key seed-points whose trauma has lain deep within us.

* * * *

Over the last 13 years or so, as I've journeyed around the world, on an energetic level I've become ever more aware of the presence of our ancestors. To my initial surprise, it has not been as though I've been going back in time to attune with them but as though their consciousness has been travelling into their future to intersect our timeline now.

I have gradually come to understand that what is happening at this momentous time is a Shift of our *entire* collective consciousness – not only that of those of us who've chosen to incarnate at this moment but also that of the ancestors who have chosen to support that process from other realms.

The wisdom and courage of those who trod this Earth before us and whose voices we're becoming able to hear once more can offer us guidance, spiritual sustenance and a deeper revelation of our hidden heritage. Their experiences and insights can also guide us to make better choices than they sometimes did.

Some lived in eras of huge Earth changes. And some resided in periods of peace and harmony. They experienced conflict and turmoil, epochs of great loss and of new beginnings, times of devastating fear and tumultuous hope.

We'll begin our exploration of our past with a time of extraordinary change.

* * * *

Between around 13,000 and 11,000 years ago the last ice age came to an end. As the ice melted, sea levels around the Earth rose by hundreds of feet, drowning enormous areas of coastal lands. Currently, some 50 per cent of the world's population lives within 60 miles of the sea. As researcher Graham Hancock has written in his groundbreaking book *Underworld*, the likelihood is that many if not most of our ancestors did too, and so, as the sea levels rose, a vast amount of evidence of their way of life was progressively lost beneath the waves.

As Hancock and other researchers have reported, over the last few years the discoveries of underwater ruins off the coasts of Japan, Malta, north-west India and the western tip of Cuba, to name but a few, are now beginning to offer intriguing glimpses into such ancient cultures. Some of these apparently man-made structures potentially date back to an era when mainstream archaeology declares no such sophisticated societies existed.

Excitement about what may be revealed about our ancient past from beneath the waters is growing. And our ability to make such discoveries is being enhanced by continuing improvements in marine archaeological technology. I personally hope that such discoveries will enable the legendary lands of Atlantis in the Atlantic Ocean and Lemuria, or Mu, the Mother Land in the Pacific, to resurface in our collective awareness.

* * * *

Whilst the investigation of underwater archaeological features is still in its infancy and their interpretation is still contentious, recent discoveries above water in what is now south-eastern Turkey are also providing astounding evidence of very early sophistication.

Along the summit of an elongated ridge some nine miles north-east of the ancient town of Sanliurfa is a site that archaeologist Professor David Lewis-Williams has called 'the most important archaeological dig anywhere in the world'.

Gobleckli Tepe, with its massive T-shaped stone columns etched with vivid scenes of animals, dates back at least an estimated 11,500 years and possibly, in its earliest phase, an incredible 13,000 years. As archaeologists have generally maintained that at that time our forebears were simple hunter-gatherers, this enormous ritual centre is completely overturning their view of our distant past.

Whilst the conventional dating of Egyptian monuments such as the Sphinx, the monolithic Oseirion at Abydos and even perhaps the pyramids may well yet be moved much further back in time, at the moment they are deemed to have been constructed around 4,500 years ago. That makes the earliest structures at Gobleckli Tepe already some 8,500 years old by the time the Egyptian monuments are purported to have been built!

When my husband Tony and I visited the site in early 2003, we did so just before sunset and to our great excitement had it virtually to ourselves. Scrambling over the rough ground around the excavation, we had a wonderful view of the surrounding plain far below. Then, carefully walking down into this most ancient of temples, we were awestruck by its scale and grandeur, especially when we appreciated that archaeologists have estimated that so far only about a meagre 5 per cent of the entire site has been investigated.

* * * *

As I stood next to the great stone columns that towered over me, I felt the long ages fall away. In the hush of the evening amidst this ancient temple I attuned to those who had constructed it so long ago and, as the light faded around me, I began to sense its purpose.

After so long, the voices of the past were merely whispers. But I got a deep feeling of well-being and that the monument had been raised to express gratitude for abundance and to symbolize the builders' coming together in a new form of community. My inner vision gave me a vista of a changing relationship between the people of Gobleckli Tepe and their world. Instead of roaming the landscape in hunter-gatherer lifestyles, they were starting to form larger extended groups in this place of plenty and security and become more settled. And even if, as yet, the ideas of domesticating animals and growing crops were still inchoate, I could sense their beginnings here.

* * * *

But Gobleckli Tepe isn't unique. Another ritual site in the area called Karahan Tepe, also with the characteristic T-shaped pillars, may date to the same distant era.

The presence of these two incredible monumental sites and the potential of a number of as yet uninvestigated mounds, allied to historical reports, folklore and environmental evidence, are exciting archaeologists. For they are providing increasing support for the idea that this region of south-eastern Turkey, lying between the headwaters of the two great rivers of the Tigris and the Euphrates and extending to northern Syria, northern Iraq and north-western Iran, may be the physical location of the Garden of Eden.

Written evidence from the biblical writers of Genesis, Near East historical commentators and the much earlier Sumerian texts tells a similar story – of civilization originating on a high plain called *E.din* in the Sumerian tongue. Even Klaus Schmidt, the German archaeologist who is leading the excavation at Gobleckli Tepe, calls the site a 'Temple in Eden'.

Paleo-botanical evidence, too, is showing that the environment would once have been a paradise. With low rolling hills, abundant water and plains which would then have been lush and teeming with life, the region was indeed the cradle of agriculture. DNA analysis has shown that the earliest domesticated pigs came from only 60 miles away. Cattle, sheep and goats began to be domesticated in this area of eastern Turkey too. The best match of existing wild einkorn wheat to the oldest domesticated variety was made only 20 miles away, and oats and rye were first grown here.

The archaeological proof is accumulating and ties in with ancient Sumerian records that tell of animal husbandry, agriculture and other attributes of civilization being brought to humankind from the sacred mountain Du-ku, where the Annunaki 'gods' – literally 'those who came down from heaven' – lived.

But where do the Sumerians themselves say they come from? It turns out it's the high plain of *E.din*. Historian David Rohl, basing his work on an initial analysis by researcher R. A. Walker in the 1980s, has come to the conclusion that *E.din* is to be found beyond the Zagros Mountains in the land the Sumerians called Urartu, the Bible calls the Mountains of Ararat and later peoples called Armenia.

Both the Bible writers and the much earlier Sumerians also maintain that the sacred mountain of the gods, the Du-ku where the Annunaki resided, which they called the Mountain of Assembly, was here. Whilst there are a number of possibilities for this mountain of origin, Rohl's research has convinced him that the volcanic dome of Sahand near Tabriz in northern Iran is the best candidate.

So, if this region was Eden, were the Annunaki 'gods' legendary or did they really live here?

Before we go on to consider that question and take the story of our origins forward in time, there are two further intriguing aspects of Gobleckli Tepe to ponder.

The first mystery is that around 10,000 years ago, after millennia of use, the entire site was deliberately buried under thousands of tons of earth. This enormous effort created artificial hills that entombed this most ancient of sites until its accidental rediscovery by a local shepherd and excavations, some years later in 1994, began to uncover this amazing place.

The as yet unanswered questions are, why did our ancestors take so much trouble to hide their temple? And what synchronicity is at work in revealing it to the eyes of our generation as we approach 2012?

The second mystery of Gobleckli Tepe is the discovery of human remains at the base of its great stone columns. Archaeologist Klaus Schmidt thinks that more remains may be found once the floor of the temple is dug up. If they are, they may culturally link in with a nearby but later site at Cayonu Tepesi, which dates back around 9,000 years, where some 70 human skulls and an altar-like stone slab with remnants of blood have been found.

The big and as yet unanswered question here is whether the human remains at Gobleckli Tepe and Cayonu Tepesi represent funerary rites or the earliest evidence of human sacrifice? That human sacrifice subsequently took place further south in Canaan and in many cultures throughout the ancient world is unambiguous – and something we'll return to later.

****

Since by far the earliest account of Genesis and Eden comes to us from Sumerian scribes, what more do we know of them and their culture? And how does that tie into the unfolding history of humankind?

The Sumerians are named after the land the Bible calls Shinar, where it states the descendants of Adam first settled after the Flood. It was here in what is now southern Iraq that the Sumerians established the earliest pre-Flood cities over 6,000 years ago, including Eridu, Uruk and Ur, from which the much later patriarch Abraham is said to have hailed.

Two eminent scholars of Sumer, Arno Poebel, in 1941, and S. M. Kramer, considered to be the greatest Sumerologist of the twentieth century, in his seminal 1963 book *The Sumerians*, postulated that Sumer was essentially the Land of Shem, the name of the eldest son of Noah. In other words, in their expert view, the Sumerians are the ancestors of the Hebrews.

So it seems that if we are to understand the genesis of our hidden heritage we must look to the area that is now Iraq, Iran, Syria and south-eastern Turkey. I find it fascinating – and somewhat frustrating – that many of the locations that are key to our deeper understanding of our past are currently no-go areas for westerners. So much lies under the sands and mounds of these now mainly desolate landscapes that could potentially chart an earlier progression for the Sumerians and bridge the gap between Gobleckli Tepe and the oldest cities on the plains to the south.

Up until now, the evidence we have of the Sumerians' earliest cities shows a high level of sophistication that seems to have erupted fully formed. Their records indeed claim that their civilization was brought fully fashioned to the first city of Eridu by the Annunaki 'god' Enki.

The list of Sumerian innovations and its concentrated timescale are extraordinary. The Sumerians produced the first writing system and a system of numbers, based on 60 and dividing a circle into 360 degrees, that still forms the basis of the geometry we use today. They also partitioned the day into 24 hours, made the first astronomical records and devised the earliest detailed calendars. And although not responsible for the invention of the wheel, they took the idea further than anyone had hitherto and constructed the earliest wheeled vehicles known.

And at the centres of their cities they built stepped pyramids. These mighty ziggurats must have been an awesome sight, artificial mountains towering above the flat plains of

Mesopotamia and symbolizing the mountains of origin of both the Sumerians themselves and their gods.

＊＊＊＊

Given that the Sumerian civilization, with its incredible accomplishments, seems to have emerged out of nowhere, and that the Sumerians maintain that it was all the gift of the gods they referred to as the Annunaki, 'those who from heaven to Earth came', perhaps it's time for us to take the Sumerians at their word and explore who those 'gods' might have been and where they might have come from.

In one of my earlier books, *The 13th Step*, I wrote:

Ancient Sumerian myths refer to a race of extraterrestrial reptilian beings, the Annunaki, arriving on Earth from their home planet, Nibiru, in the outer reaches of our Soular System. Research into the myths, together with channelled and guided information, suggests that they were here initially to mine for gold, which was apparently needed to stabilize the Nibiruan atmosphere that was degrading dangerously.

Though initially carrying out the mining themselves, at some point the Annunaki decided to create the race of human beings to carry out the hard labour of extracting the gold. Both the Sumerian myths and the Bible reference the mating of such 'gods' with the 'daughters of men', and researchers have considered this to be a genetic modification of hominids some 200 millennia ago to form modern humans.

The recent genome project that has traced our collective ancestry back through our mitochondrial DNA to a very few 'Eves' in this same time-frame lends additional support to these ancient myths.

*The two leaders of the reptilian Annunaki are referred
to as the brothers Enki and Enlil. And each had a
very different agenda for this genetic modification of
humanity. Enlil's agenda was the creation of a slave race,
whereas Enki's was ultimately to manifest the enormous
potential embodied in the hybrid human–Annunaki
being – including the physical embodiment of emotion,
which we humans fully express and which it appears the
Annunaki cannot.*

Most archaeologists consider the Sumerian writings to be purely mythic and the stories of the Annunaki gods mere legends. But unfolding discoveries and a willingness to go where the evidence leads are beginning to open up the possibility that such accounts are historically based.

The Sumerians were clever people. I wondered why – unless it was true – rather than take the credit for their amazing accomplishments, they would attribute such advances to 'gifts' of the 'gods'.

Manetho, the third-century BCE Egyptian priest and historian whose king list of the dynasties of ancient Egypt is still the one most referenced by Egyptologists, also viewed the Annunaki as real. He wrote, 'The Watchers [the Annunaki], who had descended to Earth in the cosmic year 1000, held converse with men and taught them that the orbits of the two luminaries, being marked by the 12 signs of the zodiac, are composed of 360 parts.'

Some researchers who acknowledge the reality of the Annunaki consider them to be merely advanced shamans. But, if so, I asked myself, then where did the knowledge they bequeathed to the Sumerians emanate from? For their knowledge was way ahead of any shamanic perception for which we have any evidence.

Over many years I've sought to find satisfying answers to the mystery of the Sumerians and the Annunaki. And so I've researched, albeit in translation, much of the Sumerian material that has been uncovered over the last 150 years. I've read many other authors' accounts and conclusions. And I've also had direct experiences that have led me to the personal perspective that the extraterrestrial Annunaki are real. I fully recognize there is much we don't yet understand about their continuing existence or contact with humanity. I do feel, however, that acknowledging at least the possibility of their reality opens up a profound mystery of our previously hidden heritage. And then a deep and as yet unacknowledged schism in our psyche can begin to be understood and healed.

For, if the Sumerians are correct, it was the Annunaki who attempted to wipe out humanity by bringing the catastrophic deluge of a great Flood.

* * * *

Initially it seems that the Annunaki, especially Enlil, were content to have humanity remain in innocence and ignorance, as portrayed by Adam and Eve in the biblical Eden.

But, as depicted by the Sumerians, some of the Annunaki, including Enlil's half-brother Enki, wished humanity to begin to evolve and offered the gifts of civilized knowledge and eventually the appointment of the first human priest-kings – a moment when the Sumerian history said kingship first 'descended from heaven'.

According to their accounts, and traced back by a number of researchers to sometime around 3100 BCE, humanity began to expand in numbers and their new-found freedoms and authority began to concern the Annunaki, especially Enlil. So 'weary of the noise' did he and his fellows become that the texts say he unleashed cataclysmic destruction on humankind.

But the texts also depict how Enki, the friend of humanity, surreptitiously warned a man called Ziusudra in the earliest Sumerian stories, and instructed him to build a great ark that could survive the coming inundation.

In 1872, British Museum archaeologist George Smith caused a sensation when he translated the writing on a clay tablet recovered from the library of the much later Assyrian king Ashurbanipal II at Ninevah in northern Iraq. For in it, the king declares: 'I have read the artistic script of Sumer ... [and I now] take pleasure in the reading of the stone inscriptions from before the Flood...'

There are well over 100 Flood traditions from around the world. Their unanimity and widespread nature, as well as Ashurbanipal's claims, suggest that a catastrophic incident with a global impact really did happen.

In the Sumerian version of the Flood, thanks to Enki's warning, the hero Ziusudra escapes the inundation in an ark. To the amazement of scholars and Britain's Victorian society, who were the first to hear of the newly translated accounts, Ziusudra's chronicle is virtually the same as the much later biblical story of Noah.

And, again like the Bible, the Sumerian story depicts how, when the floodwaters abated, the ark alighted on the summit of a mountain.

****

But if the Flood really happened, what material evidence is there other than this small and visibly insignificant clay tablet?

First, let's see whether we can identify a possible date for the deluge.

From 1928 to 1934 the British archaeologist Sir Leonard Woolley excavated the Sumerian city of Ur, where the Bible says the patriarch Abraham came from, in what is now southern Iraq. Digging an enormous shaft down over 40 feet beneath the present-day ground level, he and his workers found an 11-foot deep layer of silt. Continuing to dig deeper still, beneath the silt layer, they discovered the pottery and houses of an earlier era.

Woolley was immediately convinced that in the layer of silt he'd uncovered evidence for the biblical deluge, and hit the newspaper headlines of the day when he sent an electronic wire to London that read: 'We have found the Flood.'

Soon afterwards, however, from the conventional relative dating of the pottery Woolley unearthed under and atop the silt layer, it seemed that the sediment at around 4000 BCE was too old to be a relic of the Flood, given that the Hebrew version of the Bible, from which the English version derives, suggests a Flood date of around 2300 BCE. And so Woolley's claim was discarded.

But more recently, a reassessment of the dating of both pottery and textual sources has closed the apparent gap from both sides.

To begin with, the absolute dating for the pottery that Woolley unearthed may need to be significantly amended. With no dateable organic material yet found to give a reliable time-frame, the conventional dating is only based on estimates for the rate of cultural development. So if that development was more rapid than archaeologists have currently considered, the absolute dates of its associated earlier pottery need to be revised to a later era.

And the earlier Aramaic version of the Old Testament of the Bible and other texts also suggest an earlier date for the Flood than the Hebraic account.

Again it is historian David Rohl who is leading the scholarly argument for such revisions. He maintains that the archaeology and texts point to an amended dating of both Woolley's silt layer at Ur and the Flood to around 3100 BCE.

And he points out that the Mayan long count calendar, which begins according to their tradition after the destruction of an earlier civilization by flood, starts in the year 3114 BCE.

* * * *

Given that both the Sumerian and biblical accounts of the Flood have a hero who is told to build an ark to save himself, his family and animals, and that ark eventually coming to rest on the summit of a mountain, our next quest is to see what evidence there is for both ark and mountain.

The Sumerians, the later Classical writers, the Jewish chroniclers and even the early Christian scribes all stated that the ark landed not on Mount Ararat, where later Christian commentators and more recent searchers have focused, but in the much more extensive area to the south, covered by the (plural) Mountains of Ararat.

Indeed, there's a very ancient and well-attested tradition in those parts that the landing was in what are now called the Zagros Mountains, specifically on the peak of Judi Dagh to the south of Lake Van.

Rohl, in his book *Legend: The Genesis of Civilization*, sets out persuasive evidence for this. He cites a number of examples of writers and explorers on which to base the case for Judi Dagh being the mountain of Noah's ark.

Ancient Jewish legends tell of the seventh-century BCE Assyrian ruler Sennacherib who, during his military campaigns in the region, came across a wooden plank which he idolized as part of the ark. The discovery of an enormous carving of Sennacherib at the base of Judi Dagh suggests that this was the mountain where the plank was found.

The third-century BCE Babylonian historian Berossus wrote that in his day the local mountain people scraped bits of bitumen from the ark and wore them as charms. Intriguingly, bitumen – the oil-based pitch that the Bible says was used to seal the wooden ark – originates in the Iraqi lowlands hundreds of miles to the south of Judi Dagh – which is where Ziusudra, the Sumerian Noah, could have obtained it.

Most recently, in the 1920s William Wigram and his son Edgar, in their book *The Cradle of Mankind*, wrote of exploring the area of Judi Dagh and of joining a large crowd of pilgrims climbing to the summit altar to witness animal sacrifices at the place where they believed Noah had also sacrificed, some 5,000 years before, in gratitude for his deliverance.

And as Judi Dagh lies at the threshold of the mountainous region where the Sumerians stated their ancestors originated before travelling to the southern lowlands to build their first cities, it seems that the prehistoric jigsaw pieces are coming together.

* * * *

So, if the time-frame of 3100 BCE correlates with the Flood, is there any environmental evidence for it, other than Woolley's reassessed flood layer at Ur?

The apparent lack of sudden Earth-based climate change, major volcanism or earthquake activity around that time suggests that if we are to find confirmation of a real event or events we may need to look at an astronomical cause. With no on-land meteoritic cratering visible from that era either, we are left to consider the possibility of either an ocean impact – which, given that over 70 per cent of the Earth is covered by oceans, is a statistical likelihood – or the near miss of a comet or other similar body. Either a near miss or an object crashing into the ocean would cause enormous atmospheric upheaval, torrential rain and tsunamis – which are all described in many of the Flood stories.

Indeed, the various Flood stories portray the unfolding horror as being caused by an unremitting deluge of rain, rather than rising water *per se* – again pointing to a possible astronomical cause.

If either astronomical option I've suggested was the basis of the Flood, whilst catastrophic at the time, it would leave relatively few environmental signatures some five millennia later. In fact very few short-duration events, even when originating on land, leave an identifiable long-term mark. Just think of a modern-day disaster such as the underwater earthquake of 26 December 2006, which caused the massive tsunami that wreaked havoc in Indonesia and throughout the Indian Ocean and killed over 230,000 people in 14 countries. In only a relatively few years, without modern technology and communications to record its effects for future generations, only memory and word-of-mouth tales of its horror would remain.

So if indeed the Flood did occur around 3100 BCE and had an astronomical cause, what bodies are the likely culprits?

A prime suspect is a comet/meteor swarm of near-Earth objects called the Taurid Complex. Believed to be the remnants of a much larger comet, this is made up of a vast number of bodies, the largest of which so far discovered is the short-period comet Encke. The Complex intersects the Earth's orbit and is the source of the annual Taurid meteor showers, named after the constellation of Taurus from which they appear to emanate. And whilst Encke is the biggest object yet found within the swarm, other dark bodies could be lurking in its midst.

****

I first came across Encke as part of an extraordinary journey to Egypt in 1999 that I've written about in greater length in *The 13th Step*. It's worth summarizing that experience here, as now, some 11 years afterwards, further insights have come forward.

Just before leaving for Egypt I'd woken from a vivid dream with a clear symbol in my inner vision and the clairaudient message 'This is the symbol of Enki' echoing in my mind. The symbol depicted three vertically converging lines, the left and right being red and white respectively and the centre line black. At their upper points, they were met by a black horizontal line and above this emerged the rays of a radiant light.

At the time, the only 'Enki' of whom I was aware was the Sumerian Annunaki being and I had no idea why this was his symbol or what it meant.

During that journey, though, the group I was co-leading attuned with the symbol of my dream and, as we travelled, gradually came to perceive that it represented the coming together and balancing of the three cosmic principles of 'male', 'female' and 'child', and that these were somehow, through darkness, to activate a form of light. How this connected with Enki, however, neither I nor any of my companions had any idea.

Perceiving that the three pyramids at Giza embodied this cosmic trinity – the Great Pyramid of Khufu the 'male' principle; the second largest pyramid, attributed to his son Khafre, the 'female'; and the smallest of the three, his grandson Menkaure's pyramid, the 'child' – we decided to envisage the symbol and connect the cosmic energies together at the site of Menkaure's pyramid.

As we walked up onto the Giza Plateau that morning, the scene that met us was unbelievable. In celebration of the end of Ramadan, the entire population of Cairo seemed to be here – men, women and children. The black robes of the women predominated, transforming the plateau into a dark seething mass of people. Virtually no other tourists were present and as we slowly made our way through the crowd to Menkaure's pyramid, I realized that we were encountering the symbolic darkness of my dream.

As we attuned to our purpose I felt an incredible power suddenly surge through me and up through the pyramid. Looking up, in both my inner *and* outer vision I saw an intense column of golden light emerge from its summit. Shooting up into the sky, it appeared to explode, a beautiful starburst, to form a golden net of light stretching beyond the horizon. Later, as we shared our experiences, it became apparent that two others of the group had vividly experienced the same vision. We three would also endure the same aftermath, when on our return home we were all utterly drained of energy for several weeks.

It was only months later that I found out about the Taurid Complex and was amazed to read that the largest body within it was the comet Encke. Suddenly remembering our vision of the vast golden web of light, I wondered whether our work had been to reactivate an energetic net of protection for the Earth.

Months later still, as I looked up a reference in a book on the crop circle phenomenon, I happened to skip a few pages, and there was the symbol that I had seen in my dream. The caption, which related to Sumerian myths, stated: 'This is the symbol of the *Nin Gur*, the leader of whom was Enki'!

But now, as I've been researching the Sumerian story of the Flood and the possibility of the deluge being caused by Encke and its associated swarm, I wonder: is it too much to consider that Enlil, Enki's Annunaki adversary, was behind the intentional destruction of humanity, as the Sumerian texts maintain, and that in some way his intentions were thwarted by Enki, who not only warned us of our impending doom but also somehow created an energetic shield to protect us and the Earth from total annihilation?

Very recently, I read a Sumerian hymn to Ningishzidda, the son of Enki, who is considered by a number of researchers to equate with Thoth, the Egyptian god of wisdom. It exalts his 'pyramid house in Egypt' and goes on to describe how, 'In the land of the shield, your pedestal is closely knit as a fine-mesh net.' Was it referring to the energy shield, the net of light that, following Enki's guidance and working with his symbol, we reactivated in 1999?

We may never know. But a while afterwards I read an account of the airburst of a meteor over the city of Auckland, New Zealand. Commentators were amazed that the large meteor had been almost miraculously destroyed in mid-air rather than obliterating the city below.

* * * *

But, after the devastation of the Flood, what was happening around 3100 BCE? And what was it that was soon to energize embryonic civilization around the world, taking it to a completely new level of complexity?

CHAPTER 3
Our New Start

*'The natural flights of the human mind are not from
pleasure to pleasure but from hope to hope.'*
SAMUEL JOHNSON

The Sumerian texts describe how after the Flood, with the survival of the hero Ziusudra and his people, Enlil changed his view of humanity and resigned himself to allowing us to live. And intriguingly, with the texts stating that Enki continued to champion humanity's aspirations, civilization across a broad sweep of cultures did indeed surge forward.

Whilst few detailed records of specific events remain from that far distant era, the archaeological records of many cultures show that something very significant, perhaps *the* most significant to date in the history of civilization, was happening.

This marks the Early Dynastic period of Sumer, with its flowering of technological innovations, led by priest-kings who answered directly to the Annunaki 'gods'.

This period also saw the unification of Upper and Lower Egypt under the pharaoh Menes that led within a few centuries to the most magnificent of all ancient monuments, the Great Pyramid. The location, precision and astronomical and geomantic alignments of this pyramid, flanked by its two superb partner pyramids, are testimony to the genius and sophistication of its builders.

It was at this time too that in Britain and Ireland and on the Atlantic coast of Europe stone circles and other megalithic monuments began to be constructed in large numbers.

In the Indus Valley of the north-western region of the Indian subcontinent, an advanced urban culture thrived.

And in Japan, the already ancient Jomon culture that we'll encounter in greater depth later may have ventured on epic ocean voyages over thousands of miles to the Pacific coast of Ecuador in South America, where pottery that closely resembles the characteristic Jomon pottery of that era has been discovered.

So, around the world, civilization was on the move.

* * * *

Perhaps the most famous of the societies that undertook a major leap forward at this epic moment was ancient Egypt, which saw the beginning of a 3,000-year dynastic history.

In a similar way to the earlier emergence of Sumer, Egyptian civilization seemed to arrive fully formed. Whilst most Egyptologists acknowledge this enigma, relatively few are willing to consider outside influences as its possible cause. And yet the evidence for such influences – specifically Sumerian at this earliest dynastic period – is significant.

Running between the Nile Valley and the coast of the Red Sea is Egypt's Eastern Desert. A number of rocky river-bed valleys called wadis transect this now arid region. In modern times, they are usually dry except after a rainstorm, when flash floods can surge dangerously along these ancient watercourses. But in pre-dynastic times, the weather was wetter and the wadis may well have held water for much if not all of the year.

Rock art of that era along the walls of a number of wadis depicts large seafaring boats with high prows and sterns, the same boats made from reeds and coated in bitumen that the Sumerian seafarers of that time used to journey far afield from their Persian Gulf origins. And the solar boats depicting the gods and pharaohs of the Egyptians, famous from their many temple and tomb walls, and the enormous boat excavated from the boat pit at the side of the Great Pyramid are of the same design.

By the early dynastic era of Egypt, the trading expeditions and exploratory voyages of the seafaring Sumerians were, it seems, already extensive, with archaeological evidence pointing to an operational base on the island of Bahrain in the Persian Gulf. A route that then took the boats south, west around the coast of what is now Yemen and Saudi Arabia and north up the Red Sea would have enabled them to enter the wadi valleys and proceed westwards through them to reach the Nile valley itself.

It is not only the presence and depiction of Sumerian-looking boats that suggests their influence in Egypt. Early Egyptian dynastic burial monuments, or mastabas, and the Third Dynasty funerary complex of Pharaoh Djoser at Saqqara also powerfully advocate Sumerian sway, with the surreally modern-looking niched façade of their walls exhibiting the same design as that of the earlier ritual centre of Eridu in Sumer.

And Djoser's massive stepped pyramid also echoes the earlier ziggurats of Sumer, the pyramid-like temples whose steps raised Earth to heaven and invited the gods to visit.

Even Egyptian writing – the hieroglyphics that emerged seemingly fully structured and idiosyncratic to Egypt – can be shown to have Sumerian likenesses. Both the Sumerians and Egyptians were exceptionally pragmatic and used the most easily available materials when introducing writing. Both used reed pens or styluses. But the Sumerians wrote by engraving signs into damp clay tablets, whilst the Egyptians made paper-like sheets of the papyrus reeds that grew along the edges of the Nile river.

Whereas papyrus encouraged the Egyptians' artistic flow and the development of pictographic hieroglyphs, engraving into clay – rapidly before it dried in the heat – led naturally to the more abstract writing of the Sumerians. But by ethnographically tracking back the development of both cultural forms, Sumerian influence may well be discerned in Egyptian hieroglyphs.

In a pre-dynastic cemetery at Naqada in southern Egypt, a group of internments called Naqada II exhibits many Sumerian cultural features. And the ivory handle of a flint dagger discovered at Gebel el-Arak near the western end of Wadi Hammamat, one of the wadis leading from the Red Sea to the Nile Valley, and now in the Louvre museum, depicts scenes that are indisputably Sumerian.

But perhaps one of the most intriguing references to the early influences on Egypt's great culture is to be seen at Abydos in southern Egypt. On the wall of the so-called King's Gallery of the temple of Seti I is inscribed a chronological list of almost all the pharaohs of dynastic Egypt. But the list goes back even further, to the leaders of Egypt before the pharaonic line, the Shemsu Hor, or Followers of Horus, and an even earlier epoch when the gods lived amongst humanity.

Were the mysterious Shemsu Hor Sumerian incomers who brought ideas and technologies that enabled the glory of Egypt to arise? And from even earlier did indeed the 'gods' walk on Earth?

* * * *

Whilst much remains to be discovered, the period from the long-ago time of Gobleckli Tepe to the putative Flood of around 3100 BCE and then onwards seems to have been an era of harmony for many of our ancestors. I felt this particularly strongly when I led a group hosted by my friends Robin and Cody Johnson of the Prophets Conferences to Malta in May 2009.

Even before the onset of dynastic Egypt, some five and a half millennia ago – and perhaps for very much longer – the ancient women and men of Malta came together in the sacred precincts of their temples to revere the glory of the Cosmos and the fertility of the Earth. They appear to have venerated the complementary balance of the divine feminine and masculine in a sacred marriage through which cosmic harmony was celebrated and energized and all abundance could flow.

The many statues, small and large, they left behind are testament to their understanding of divine relationship. Once thought to represent the Mother Goddess, many of these are now understood to be androgynous, symbolizing the merging of female and male attributes.

These early people seem to have honoured the balancing of these cosmic archetypes and I believe that they realized too that only through their authentic *real*-ationship could health and harmony on both metaphysical and physical levels be sustained.

During our journey to Malta and within its temples we were offered the opportunity to reconnect with the well-spring of this ancient wisdom. As we energized the healing of the wounded masculine, we were then able to reconcile and restore the sacred marriage *within ourselves*. And so energize the healing of our collective schism too.

Not only the people of Malta but also the most profound spiritual traditions of ancient times, including those of Egypt and India, perceived the manifest world, at all scales of existence, as being generated and pervaded by a cosmic trinity of active, passive and neutral principles – the divine essence of the masculine, feminine and child. The Vedic sages of ancient India saw the male/active life-force energy they called the *pingala* and the female/passive energy they called the *ida* weaving around and through our chakras and the child/neutral energy they called the *shushumna* channelling up through them.

When these divine masculine and feminine energies are balanced and so able to give birth to the divine child energies within us, the ancient sages saw the so-called *kundalini* energy that otherwise lies dormant at the base of the spine surge through us, enabling us to fully embody our divine nature.

The purpose of the sacred marriage between the divine feminine and masculine that ancient peoples such as those of Malta enacted in their temples was thus not only to bring cosmic harmony and fertility to their land but also within themselves. For such balance enabled the energetic activation, or birth, of the divine child within and the attainment of enlightenment.

When this cosmic trinity of consciousness is harmonized and fully expressed within us, we are truly healed and whole, a state embodied by the universal symbol of the caduceus, which has been a representation of healing from the earliest times. For millennia, only the highest adepts understood and attained such wholeness. But now we have evolved to a point where we are all able to attain our inner divinity.

I believe that this is our spiritual and cosmic destiny at the dawning of the Age of Aquarius.

* * * *

As we'll see as we continue to walk the path for HOPE, our accelerating collective Shift isn't only a leap in awareness for our human family, but also for the living Earth, Gaia, and all her children.

Our sacred journey to Malta not only offered us a profound opportunity to connect with its ancient well-spring of wisdom and access the healing energies of its monumental temples, but also, in service, to reactivate their vortices of Earth energies to enable our highest intentions to flow throughout the planetary grid.

Not only the temples of Malta but the entire island holds the etheric memory of the generosity and kindness of the ancestors. Indeed, its very bedrock, a form of mellow limestone, seems to transmute light into a warm and nourishing glow, leading to Malta's name – *Melita*, the island of honey.

As a nexus point of the telluric and elemental energies of Gaia, positioned at the heart of the Mediterranean Sea, Malta, as more and more spiritual pilgrims are recognizing, is now ready to radiate its reawakening purpose to Europe, Africa, the Middle East and beyond.

For the island's role, and that of the ancestors who are so present here, is to help to heal the karmic imprint of conflict and trauma and illuminate the new resonance of peace and compassion throughout the psychic body of Gaia and so support and facilitate the Shift.

The most ancient, mysterious and magnificent relics of Malta's past are a mighty collection of megalithic temples that have stood against the ravages of time. Some, such as the temple of Mnajdra, are aligned to the Sun and Moon, and archaeologists currently assume that they were constructed around 5,500 years ago. Whilst this is even before the suggested date for the Flood, there is no real archaeological evidence to sustain this view, and intriguing pointers from their astronomical alignments and recent underwater discoveries suggest that these monolithic temples may be much, much older. For it was the rising of sea levels following the end of the last Ice Age around 13,000 years ago that caused Malta and its companions to become islands. Before that they were upland areas of an extensive land bridge to Sicily and Italy to the north. And in the coastal waters around the islands there have been exciting discoveries of what may be the ruins of other temples.

Even before I had arrived in Malta, the ancestors there were appearing in my dreams and welcoming the group's travellers and intentions.

During our journey we were joined by a local guide and author Francis Aliosio, who for many years has been researching and tuning into Malta's ancient past. Our meeting with Francis opened up an invaluable opportunity for us all to visit and share the wonderful energies of the sites that his local knowledge and

43

energy work had accessed. For me, the most significant of the places Francis guided us to was Ta Tenc on the high cliffs at the southern edge of the tiny island of Gozo. The time spent at this incredible power point, resonating with the awakening 12-fold unity chakra system that is being activated within our personal and collective energy fields, was for many of our group a very powerful experience.

Before the journey I'd felt that the energies of Malta would be gentle and their voices soft – and indeed they were. But what I realized as I experienced them directly was the profound strength within that gentleness. It's a power that emanates from the ancient ancestors who are present here still and their real-ationship with this very special place. It's a power that doesn't need to shout or be aggressive. And that embodies the higher service of *em*-powerment rather than the selfish wants of *me*-powerment.

* * * *

For nearly 1,000 years following the creative eruption of 3100 BCE, an era of peace accompanied the expansion of ideas and communities. As I attuned to the long epoch of harmony in Malta I heard the voices of the ancestors and felt the way they experienced the world. Sitting quietly in their etheric company I could feel their profound joy at being in balance and harmony with their world.

But, as we've already seen with the calamitous event of the Flood, the history of humanity can't be separated from our inter-relationship with our Earthly and cosmic environment. And around 2200 BCE another trauma engulfed humanity. The achievements of the preceding millennium were almost wiped out. And one of the societies that suddenly disappeared, never to recover, was the ancient culture of the island of Malta.

As I sat in the warm May sunshine, instead of feeling grief, anger or bitterness at the destruction wreaked upon these people, I felt their sense of continuous connection with the Cosmos and a calm acceptance that eventually, and inevitably in the physical realm, all things pass. Their love of Gaia and the evolutionary spirals of experience that are innate in our human journey sustained them and now they are ready to play their role in helping humanity rediscover that cosmic connection and undertake the next evolutionary leap.

*** *

A fairly recent and very welcome trend in archaeology is to consider the environment within which the waves of ancient cultures arose, prospered and declined. A host of technologies and a progressive willingness to cross the perceived boundaries between disciplines is now beginning to enable a much more wholistic understanding of the past.

And it is that cross-disciplinary research that has enabled that key moment of 4,200 years ago, a further seed-point of our collective trauma, to be increasingly understood.

In 1993, Harvey Weiss, Professor of Near Eastern Archaeology at Yale, was one of the first to challenge the prevailing view that the downfall of a whole swathe of cultures around that time was primarily due to social or political causes. His evidence came from combining the archaeological record with information on the climate at the time.

Weiss's first case study focused on a region of northern Mesopotamia called the Habur Plains, in today's north-eastern Syria, where a group of urban centres had arisen around 2500 BCE. Supported by abundant and well-organized agricultural hinterlands, they thrived until about 2200 BCE, when the townspeople suddenly abandoned their homes and livelihoods and migrated south.

Weiss's investigation of soil samples suggests the people fled from a blitz of dust raised by a long-term drought. As a knock-on effect, further to the south, the Mesopotamian Empire that had relied on the agricultural produce from the north was also crippled.

But the effects of the drought were even more widespread. In a broad arc, the devastation extended across the lands of the eastern Mediterranean from the Aegean and the early Minoan civilization in Crete across present-day Turkey down through Canaan and Mesopotamia and as far south as Egypt, where it correlated with the demise of the pyramid-building Old Kingdom, and then east to the Indus Valley of north-western India.

Further proof of extended drought came through samples of seabed sediments from the Gulf of Oman, 700 miles to the south-east of Mesopotamia. Climatologists modelling the movement of atmospheric circulation have been able to show how relatively minor changes can have major effects. Studies by Gerald Bond at Columbia University's Earth Observatory facility in New York state have shown that the timing of the extended drought coincided with a period of cooling in the North Atlantic that would have dried out the Mediterranean and Near East by creating a pressure gradient that pulled moisture to the north.

Once the scientists began to know where to look, the climate change prime cause of the 4,200-year-old collapse began to be discovered everywhere. Even the key ice-core data taken from Greenland as part of the GISP2 project, which records climate over the last 15,000 years, was shown by its chief scientist Paul Mayewski to record the unique signature of the 2200 BCE disaster. When he focused on the south–north movement of Atlantic air masses, he found it correlated exactly with the extent of the disaster. And archaeological author Brian Fagan has also shown how the diversion of storms from the mid-Atlantic to north of the Alps and Pyrenees brought wetter conditions to central Europe but drought to the eastern Mediterranean.

To the south of Mesopotamia, the empire of Akkad was one of the casualties. Although its collapse had been well documented, its cause had remained unknown. And yet the Akkadians did record the drought, in a lengthy composition called the *Curse of Akkad* written soon afterwards. Its passages chillingly lament that:

The large fields and acres produced no grain

The flooded fields produced no fish

The watered gardens produced no honey and wine

The heavy clouds did not rain

On its plains where grew fine plants

lamentation reeds now grow.

As we've seen, broad-based studies of history are showing more and more clearly the fundamental interaction between people and places, humanity and Gaia. It is a theme that we will return to, as its implications for our current era are crucial.

****

Before the calamity of 2200 BCE, whilst small-scale violence did exist, communities seem to have been generally peaceful. But afterwards, the world was changed forever.

Over the next few centuries, most but not all societies gradually recovered or began anew elsewhere, and the next wave of civilization saw the rise of the Mycenaean kingdoms, the Hittite Empire in Turkey and Syria, and the Middle Kingdom of pharaonic Egypt. But instead of the peace and harmony of their predecessors, this next tranche of expansion saw more hierarchical and militaristic cultures facilitated by the manufacture of bronze and the development of weapons.

Ancient myths describe the coming of war during the Bronze Age as beginning with a dispute between brothers –

both gods and men. Symbolically and literally, the aggression unleashed by this schism of the bloodline profoundly wounded the masculine psyche – a wounding that further millennia of brother fighting brother, literally and metaphorically and eventually spreading to the global brotherhood of mankind, have progressively deepened.

****

After a further millennium, it seems that another catastrophic breakdown at around 1200 BCE brought about the end of the era, an even more calamitous disintegration that Princeton historian Robert Drews, in his definitive book *The End of the Bronze Age: Changes in Warfare and the Catastrophe ca. 1200 BC*, has called 'the worst disaster in ancient history'.

This time, too, rapid and disastrous natural environmental events are becoming seen as primary triggers of the collapse, although by now increasing social stresses and man-made environmental degradation also played a role. In addition to once again widespread drought, this time the eruption of the Hekla volcano in Iceland and a series of earthquakes throughout the Near East appear to have contributed to the turmoil.

During a period of chaos and depopulation that again lasted a couple of hundred years, the transition to the Iron Age occurred, as long-distance trade in the tin needed to manufacture bronze was disrupted and the more plentiful supply of inferior but more easily mass-produced iron weapons began to be substituted.

The arms race and the widespread aggression of warfare had begun.

****

The appalling experience of the Late Bronze Age collapse and the collective memories of the earlier calamities appear to have wounded our psyche at a deep level. The relative peace of the pre- and post-Flood times gave way to ever-greater conflict. Hierarchies and the widening control and suppression of peoples and the Earth would progressively characterize the coming chapters of humanity's story.

Over the three millennia since the disintegration of the Bronze Age, the voice of the sacred feminine has gone unheeded in the clamour of 'might is right'. Aggression hasn't just been expressed through war between men, but ultimately between humanity and the Earth. This has brought us to the edge of global breakdown.

If we're to redeem ourselves and transform the potential breakdown into a transformational breakthrough, we have to heal the metaphysical wound within our collective psyche, especially the imbalance in the masculine aspect of ourselves, and restore and consummate the sacred marriage.

* * * *

The healing of the schism between masculine and feminine is crucial to our collective resoulution. And at an even deeper and more hidden level of our psyche, does the involvement of the Annunaki in our past on both energetic and physical levels perhaps explain a further rift within our psyche? For the part of us that embodies the Enki energy knows we are divine beings, eternal and extraordinary spirits and vastly more than our human experience. But another part of our psyche resonates with the Enlil agenda and is expressed in our deepest fears and the feelings of worthlessness that so often disempower us.

But what happened to the Annunaki?

The Sumerians tell that at the time of the calamity of 2200 BCE they 'flew away like birds', essentially abandoning their overt involvement with humanity and the Earth. And over the millennia since then, the memories of their encounters with humankind morphed into myth.

Other than the Sumerian texts, what evidence is there to suggest that our long-ago ancestors actually saw the Annunaki walking the Earth?

The prevalence of dragon tales from around the world continues to testify to a potent influence, for the Annunaki were it seems dragon-like in appearance. Varying traditions either depict benevolent dragon-like beings bringing the benefits of civilization or, conversely, the manipulative control of dragon rulers. Were these the Enki and Enlil agendas playing out in different cultures?

Whilst in the Sumerian records Enki is the benevolent champion of humanity, in the Bible he is personified as the serpent in the Garden of Eden, encouraging Eve, and through her Adam, to eat of the Tree of Knowledge.

Throughout South American legends, the winged serpents Kulkulkan and Quetzalcoatl likewise are bringers of wisdom, and many of the earliest rulers and dynastic lineages are described as the sons of dragons.

And now a growing number of researchers are maintaining that a hidden Enlil agenda, whether physical or energetic, lies behind millennia-long attempts to control human destiny by instilling fear and presenting ostensible solutions that support its covert aims.

Now, as we awaken from our collective amnesia of our hidden heritage, it's time for us to learn the truth. Whether energetic or physical, it's also time for the involvement of the Annunaki with humanity to re-emerge into our awareness and for our psyche to be healed.

CHAPTER 4

Hope, Healing and Love

'Once you choose hope, anything's possible.'
CHRISTOPHER REEVE

Having explored in general terms some of the most profound schisms of our collective past and the hidden heritage that is beginning to be revealed, it's now time to look at how we can start to heal those traumas and embody that understanding for the greater good.

The idea for this book first came about in late 2009, when my friend Laura and I discussed how we might continue the healing work that I'd been undertaking around the world. Laura had first met me at a talk I'd given during which she'd had a profound inner vision of our working together in service to the healing of such suffering.

As we shared our vision of the collective Shift of awareness that's speeding up, we agreed that healing the past of traumas and the present of fear-based beliefs and behaviour patterns was needed. But to break through to a communal rebirth at a higher level of consciousness, we recognized that on both personal and collective levels we also needed to understand the bigger picture and higher purpose of what was happening in the present and to envisage and consciously co-create the future.

Healing the past and releasing the deepest traumas and schisms that remain in our psyche are fundamental to our freedom to go forward. Otherwise our emotional wounds and fear-based responses will continue to imprison us in limiting and limited beliefs and behaviour patterns.

In the midst of the apparent tumult in the world, we also need to see what is happening on a higher level – not just the confusion and turmoil evident on the surface but the cosmic intention that lies above and behind that appearance.

As ever-more conscious co-creators, we also need, as Gandhi said, to 'be the change we want to see in the world' and to manifest the cosmic destiny of our collective future.

* * * *

That sense of needing to 'be the change' was apparent to me in early 2010, sitting around our kitchen table. Tony, Laura, another friend, Justina, who has organized many of our sacred journeys around the world, and I mulled over how to take the next step forward.

Initially we focused on how we could support the healing of humanity's real-ationship with the Earth and make good the damage we have imposed. From my past experiences, I knew of the intrinsic energetic connections between people and places, and appreciated that the healing of both was intimately interconnected.

As is often the case, it was my beloved Tony who provided the key to our aims when he said that what we were talking about was HOPE, standing for Healing Our People & Earth.

Our intention was to invite everyone who felt the call to join together on a path for HOPE in service to the energetic healing of the deepest emotional wounds and rifts that still fragment our collective psyche and lie at the root of the remaining conflicts and fear-based behaviour patterns around the world.

Crucially, too, we decided, HOPE would be about under-standing the bigger picture that is unfolding as the Shift accelerates.

And thirdly it would endeavour to empower people in this incredible time of transformation to expand their awareness and become ever more whole and conscious co-creators.

Thanks especially to Laura and computer-savvy friends, a Path for HOPE website, Facebook and Twitter addresses were set up to begin to spread the word.

And, as there was so much to share about HOPE, the idea of this book was also born.

* * * *

Fundamentally this book is about three things: hope, healing and love.

The first two are embodied in its title: *HOPE: Healing Our People & Earth.*

When I looked up the word 'hope,' I found the *Collins English Dictionary* defined it as 'a feeling or desire for something and *confidence in the possibility of its fulfilment.'* The emphasis is mine, as I feel that this confidence or faith in an outcome is the energy that gives hope its enduring power.

Similarly the word 'heal' can be defined as 'being restored to harmony or wholeness'. The envisaging and awareness of such intrinsic wholeness, rather than a sense of apparent dis-ease that somehow needs to be cured, is also, in my experience, enormously valuable in any healing process.

So, as we'll explore together, the aim of our journey of HOPE is the feeling, desire and confidence that we can restore ourselves and our real-ationship with our beloved Gaia to harmony and wholeness. And, as we'll also see, the only way to do that is through love.

The saying is 'Where there's life, there's hope'. But even more fundamentally I believe that 'Where there's *love*, there's hope' because love offers hope both within and *beyond* life. In our journey of HOPE we'll discover the power of love to enable us to hope and to heal – and to literally re-member who we *really* are.

Hope arises in our hearts. We *feel* rather than *think* hopeful. For love sees deeper truths and recognizes that our time here on the physical plane is only one aspect of our divine existence. Love nurtures and inspires hope when all rational thought has given up. It's then that love sustains us and calls us to acts of heroic courage, selfless compassion and extraordinary creativity that transcend all boundaries and barriers.

The worldview of the primary peoples still walking the Earth today, whose common cosmology is perhaps the closest we have to that of our distant forebears, shows that such empathy extended to and embraced the entirety of the natural world and the multi-dimensional realms beyond. Living wisdom keepers and our ancient ancestors alike have seen themselves as part of a wholly interrelated Cosmos and honoured all life as aspects of that Oneness.

In our scientific materialism, we've mislaid that sense of inclusion and respect. But our deepest roots as human beings were nurtured by that profound awareness and empathy. Compassionate connectivity with all life lies at the very core of our being. And as we heal into the wholeness of our innate divine nature, so hope, as old as our human story, will surely be rekindled within us.

****

When I was about eight years old I remember a violent thunderstorm raging above our house. Instead of staying inside, Mum called my little brother Bill and me to go with her and sit outside on our front step, watching as the lightning and thunder crashed above us and the torrential rain fell like a curtain a few feet from where we sat sheltered only by the overhang of our front porch.

As the heavens raged, with Bill and me sitting either side of her, Mum held our hands and just smiled. Any fear within me dissolved, replaced by excitement at the primordial drama unfolding before us. And later, with the storm moving on and calm returning, our smiles grew as a beautiful rainbow lit the sky.

'It's a sign of hope,' Mum told us.

She said that however dark things looked, there was always hope.

From that day, whenever I've been in darkness or at the centre of any kind of storm in my life, I've remembered the hope of that rainbow long ago and found the courage and inspiration to go forward.

A few years ago, Mum gave me the wonderful message of the rainbow of hope once again when she passed over and I was in the midst of grief. Mum had always loved Judy Garland and as I was preparing for her funeral, I sensed that she wanted to have Judy's song 'Over the Rainbow' played. So I went onto the internet and ordered a CD that included the song.

I had placed the order in good time, but the day before the funeral no CD had arrived. So that afternoon I headed to my local music shop, concerned, as I was very doubtful they'd have such a CD in stock. They did. But it wasn't the almost sad version recorded by Garland at the end of her life – the version I'd tried to obtain online. Instead it was the hopeful version she'd sung as a young girl in the film *The Wizard of Oz*. And next day, as we left my brother's home for Mum's funeral, I saw something I'd never seen before and have never seen since: whilst it wasn't raining, the air was filled with a suspension of tiny glistening water droplets – and the perfect arc of a glorious rainbow shone over us as we celebrated the life of our wonderful mother and bid her God speed on her new adventure.

And now I was sure in the knowledge that she would always be near to me and that our love for each other would go on forever.

* * * *

Hope, healing and love are a co-creative trinity on both personal and collective levels.

I've certainly needed hope and love on my own inner journey of healing. Even with Mum's constantly loving presence and support, my life has been extraordinarily full of great highs and deep lows. As I've worked through my own inner turmoil and have travelled around the world, what I've discovered, both as a cosmologist who from my earliest years has walked between multi-dimensional realms and as a healer accompanying many others to their own seed-points of trauma, is that despite the uniqueness of our own individual experiences, we all embody the same archetypal patterns based on limiting beliefs and exhibit the dysfunctional behaviour that arises from them.

We hold such beliefs and their associated traumas within our personality-based energy field. So trying to heal them at that ego-self level of awareness is rather like pulling ourselves up by our bootlaces – however strong they are, it can't be done.

And that's why over the millennia, as we've continued to play out these patterns and experience in ever-more diverse and complex ways what it means to be human, we've accumulated so much emotional 'baggage'.

But now, at this crucial moment in our evolution, our awareness is expanding beyond the apparent limitations of the past. We're beginning to access the newly available energies of the 8th chakra of the universal heart which offer us compassionate insights into the schisms of our past and enable transformational personal and planetary healing.

* * * *

As we literally and energetically wake up, the limitations that have co-created barriers and boundaries to our perception and experience are falling away. The veil between worlds is getting thinner, our collective unconscious is awakening, we're beginning to communicate with many other realms of existence and we're re-membering the ultimate oneness of ourselves and the entirety of the Cosmos.

Ever since the age of four, when I had my first contact with my spiritual guide Thoth, I've been fortunate enough to spend a lifetime 'walking between worlds'. For 55 years – and counting – I've also communicated with angels, devas, ascended masters and many other forms of spirit being. And although Mum didn't know about my non-physical friends, even on the human level she used to say I'd speak to anyone!

During my lifelong exploration of consciousness and the nature of reality I've also come to understand the Earth as a living being. And just as we've held traumas in the energy field of our personal and collective emotional bodies, so has the living Earth. So our collective journey of inner healing and re-membering also resonates throughout the energetic meridians of Gaia. As co-creative evolutionary partners, our Shift is also Hers.

* * * *

As we evolve beyond the personal to embody transpersonal awareness, so our experiences of different forms of trans-physical communications such as telepathy, remote viewing and synchronicity also increase.

Mainstream science as yet doesn't have a model of reality which encompasses such non-local phenomena that transcend all apparent limitations of space and time. But, as we'll see, a new vision is emerging that is beginning to be able to do so.

* * * *

Our ego-minds are excellent at persuading us that we are separate and individual. They are the perfect tool for the consciousness of a self-aware being to explore itself in relationship to other self-aware beings and the wider world.

What our ego-minds aren't good at – it's not their role – is enabling us to empathize with others.

That's what our hearts are for.

And allied with our hearts and minds is the third crucial aspect of the sacred trinity through which all consciousness is manifested: our sense of meaning and purpose.

Only when we bring our hearts, minds and purpose together, balancing their different but complementary perceptions, can we walk the path from loneliness – where the mind tries to convince us of our separation from the rest of creation – to the awareness of aloneness, that sense of self that our purpose empowers, and to the universal heartfelt reality of all-one-ness.

And what everyone who has ever walked this path understands is that it is an inner journey to wholeness, rather than an outer one.

The mind's aim whilst exploring the world is essentially to protect the self. Our experiences of life inevitably involve our beliefs, behaviour and associated emotions. So, depending on how powerfully our mind convinces us of the separateness of our nature, it seeks safety by attempting to fill an inner void by amassing 'stuff', keeping busy or retaining apparent control over the 'outer' world.

Trying to fill and thus heal an inner void can't be done from the outside. Yet, on a collective level we're still desperately attempting to do so. And sadly, this mental push for 'more' based on fear and loneliness has brought us emotionally and physically to the edge of social and planetary disaster.

* * * *

Wise choices require us to reintegrate our minds with our hearts. Regardless of our gender, we all embody masculine and feminine attributes whose balance is key if we're to fully express the wholeness of life and fulfil our human promise. Yet from, it seems, the breakdown of 2200 BCE, the feminine aspect of our collective psyche has been progressively marginalized.

To transform our current global emergency into a collective emergence, the return and balancing of feminine attributes is crucial, as the ancient wisdom keepers realized, to reconsecrate the sacred marriage within and between us in all aspects of our lives. The full honouring and inclusion of heart-based caring, compassion, empathy and co-operation within our collective organizations and societies is urgently needed to stand alongside and complement the mind-based masculine attributes that have prevailed for so long.

As we each 'show up' to hear and enact the guidance of the universal heart that connects us at a higher level of awareness, we embody our highest purpose in being here and now. For completion of the Shift is up to all of us. As indigenous elders around the world have said about this time and its potential for breakthrough, 'We are the ones we have been waiting for'.

HOPE is a call to action to reintegrate our personal and collective heart, mind and purpose; to fully express the divine feminine in partnership with the divine masculine within us all. It's a call for us to follow where the evidence leads: to the acknowledgement – and manifestation – of a whole-world view. And it invites, calls and empowers us to come together and to dedicate ourselves, as ever-more conscious co-creators, to envisaging and manifesting a global breakthrough.

CHAPTER 5
Healing Archetypal Patterns

'Hope never abandons you, you abandon it.'
GEORGE WEINBERG

As we re-member and heal our personal and collective heritage, we are also awakening to and re-membering a greater vision for our future.

Healing and releasing our personal and collective traumas – essentially clearing our karma, letting go of our energetic baggage and liberating our psyche – is crucial to transcending the limitations of the past and taking the leap of love into the next stage of our cosmic destiny.

Working for many years as a healer, first with thousands of people on individual levels and then progressively with larger groups and eventually on a planetary scale, I have found that there are five archetypal patterns – of abandonment, abuse, betrayal, denial and rejection. One or more predominates in all our personal lives, and between us we collectively embody them all.

Time and again, life after life, we play out these patterns in our own personal lives. They are usually triggered in early childhood, or even in the womb, by events that may seem inconsequential when rationalized as an adult. But to the child who experienced them and the inner child aspect of us that continues to resonate with them, they are profound traumas that we may spend a lifetime – or lifetimes – unable to release.

A further time in our early life when we are particularly susceptible to the triggering of such an archetype is during puberty. And so, by the time we reach adulthood, the pattern is embedded in our psyche and in the beliefs and behaviour that then form the lens through which we perceive, co-create and experience our reality.

We also often play these archetypes out in family groups, with grandparents, parents and children exhibiting different aspects of the same pattern. And collectively we have expressed all five archetypes throughout history. As we'll see, different nations, ethnic and cultural groups have a preponderance of specific patterns that they have embodied throughout their historical experiences and that are the root cause of much of the fear-based and dysfunctional behaviour that continues to hold us psychically in its thrall.

For many people, such archetypal energy patterns remain hidden in their subconscious. But their reality can eventually be seen, often first by others, in the repetitions of their life experiences.

When we begin to recognize how these archetypal patterns have persisted in manifesting on physical, emotional and mental levels, we can go to the seed-points of their various traumas to heal them and open up a future free of their associated fears and limitations.

Let's start by taking a further look at each pattern in turn and how it tends to express itself energetically in our lives.

* * * *

The abandonment pattern is fundamentally about a sense of loss. This can appear to be as trivial, at least to an adult, as a small child losing sight of a parent or spending time away from them. It can arise not only from the experience of such physical loss, however temporary, but also from emotional loss. The lack or inconsistency of family or home security, arising from myriad causes and along a spectrum of severity, engenders the abandonment pattern in childhood that lives on into adult behaviour.

The loneliness that is characteristic of this pattern is a profound sense of something or someone being missing. With such feelings, the behaviour patterns that arise are attempts at coping with the inner loneliness and sense of loss and the emotional pain that ensues.

For example, someone who is playing out this archetype, perhaps as a result of losing a loved one in their earlier life or some loss of security, may become particularly needy or controlling, including in their relationships with others. And where events make it difficult to control those around them, or such control isn't sufficient, as it never can be, to fill their inner void, they may instead attempt to maintain their security through regulating their circumstances and surroundings.

Usually, this shows in two ways. Either someone is particularly controlling about their surroundings, sometimes to the point of obsessive-compulsive behaviour, and/or they feel driven to accumulate more 'stuff' – whether it be money, power or possessions.

In all five archetypes, we impose our patterns in our behaviour towards others, we encounter others who impose the same patterns on us and, in their most insidious form, we impose them on ourselves.

So, for instance, with an abandonment pattern we might feel drawn to someone who's expressing the same sense of loss. A relationship with that person can result in a push me–pull you roller-coaster of emotions. Or, in an otherwise apparently fine relationship, at a moment when it seems ready to go to the next level of intimacy, one or the other of the partners embodying the abandonment pattern sabotages the bond – either subconsciously or consciously aiming to abandon the other rather than suffer the perceived worse pain of being abandoned.

Two and a half thousand years ago the Buddha counselled against attachment. What he intended, I believe, for us to understand was that we need to flow through life and allow it to flow through us without trying to hang on to its pleasure or avoid its pain. The danger is that to avoid the emotional hurt that comes with perceived loss, we shut ourselves off from feeling any affection and so essentially abandon ourselves.

The Buddha also spoke of the 'illusion' of the physical world. But I would rather translate his word *maya* as meaning 'partial' rather than 'illusory' reality. As spiritual beings, when we're born into human form we enter a physical experience. But the sense of individuation that is our birthright can also foster the partiality that we are separate from Spirit. It's that perception of separation – and thus inevitably loss – from which the beliefs and feelings of abandonment and loneliness arise and from which emanates the fear-based behaviour that is then played out.

Fear is a natural and healthy response to danger and our bodies have a natural way of responding to it and then releasing it. But chronic fear that persists even when the immediate danger has passed deepens within our psyche. The dread of loss and the uncertainties of change, especially as we go through the transformative processes, both inner and outer, of the Shift, have resulted in increasing levels of chronic fear and the associated stress, anxiety and depression.

Social trends have seen apparently paradoxical increases in both anxiety and self-esteem. But, as sociologists Richard Wilkinson and Kate Pickett maintain in their book *The Spirit Level*, outward self-esteem and apparent self-confidence are often a defence and security mechanism, especially in younger people, that hides deeper insecurities within. Such inauthentic self-esteem, with its added emphasis on the superiority of 'me' rather than the balance between the 'me' and the 'we', isn't just a problem for the individual but, at its extreme, a major issue for society as a whole.

The greatest levels of dysfunctional behaviour arising from such chronic fears and inauthentic esteem can be seen to manifest in unequal societies. In the USA and UK, currently two of the most unequal societies on Earth, increases in inequality over the last decade or so have gone hand in hand with a growth in social dis-ease.

However, the increasing and unsustainable cost of pharmaceutical treatment for fear-based stress, anxiety and depression has led, at least in the UK, to the dawning recognition of the benefits of physical exercise and regular meditation. Whilst my Mum, 50 years ago, could have told medical authorities that exercise and meditation – or as Mum would have said, 'quiet sitting' – worked, at last the scientific papers that 'prove' their efficacy are now starting to be recognized and the methods being put into practice.

Mum also showed me how to release my anxiety. I'd been building up more and more fear of some forthcoming school examinations that were crucial if I wanted to go on to university. Even though I'd been doing my school work, my mind had hijacked my fear. It ran it around and around until I was trapped. The day of the exams, in my bedroom my anxiety erupted. I was hyperventilating, crying and shaking uncontrollably.

Hearing me, Mum rushed up the stairs. She took one look at me and even though she must have been scared by my state, she kept calm and taught me a lesson I've never forgotten.

First she told me to begin to breathe more deeply and to focus on my breath. After a few minutes my shallow hyperventilating had eased and my anxiety began to ease. When she could see that happening, she told me to feel my body and gradually relax it from my head to my feet.

She could sense I was trying to tell my body what to do, so instructed me instead to just go with the feeling and, through my deep breathing, allow my body to do what it would naturally do, which, in the absence of danger, would be to relax.

After a few more minutes, I was much calmer and, thanks to her help, got through the exams – and passed.

After that, whenever I felt anxiety building within me, I pre-empted it rather than let it take over. And in the years to come I discovered first meditation to clear and cleanse my mind and then attunement to literally attune myself to the wisdom of our Higher Selves that directly connects us to the oneness of All That Is.

* * * *

Healing an abandonment pattern crucially involves recognizing that life involves inevitable change that incorporates loss and letting go. To feel grief at such a passing is natural. We grieve not only the consciously remembered past but the often unconsciously hoped-for future that will now not happen. And when we allow the grief to flow through us, it can release the trauma of the loss and support us in going forward.

But a deeper healing comes with our realization that love transcends all apparent separation and that we never lose anyone we love – they are always with us.

Some years ago, the husband of a friend of mine passed over. On the morning of his funeral I went to buy flowers to take with me, and as I went into the florist's I heard his voice telling me clearly to buy a single yellow rose. Looking around the shop at a number of yellow roses, I plainly heard one after the other being dismissed with a 'No, not that one' until I stopped at a beautiful creamy yellow one. Feeling a bit embarrassed at arriving with a single rose rather than a wreath, Tony and I went to the funeral. As we were welcomed, I gave our friend the rose and, prompted by her husband's spirit, told her that he'd asked me to do so. So sad a moment before, now her eyes lit up. Afterwards she told me that every Friday her husband had brought her a bouquet of red roses with one single creamy yellow rose just like the one I'd bought. So that single creamy yellow rose told her, more than anything else could have, that even though her beloved husband had passed over, he was still with her.

Over the years, I have received a number of messages in this way that have specifically helped those who are grieving and feeling abandoned by their loved ones to know they haven't been abandoned at all. And I've seen how that communication has guided them on their inner journey of healing.

* * * *

The next pattern we'll take a look at is that of abuse.

Abusing others is often used as a way of making ourselves feel better. Again, with the limited perception of separation, seeing someone else as 'other' and holding the belief that they are somehow 'lesser' has rationalized abuse throughout history.

Whether it is through conquest or slavery, rape or 'merely' intimidation, the cruelty of deliberately inflicting abuse on physical, emotional and mental levels pervades our societies. And, more than any other, the archetypal pattern of abuse continues to play out on everyday levels within families on an inter-generational basis and in schools and workplaces.

Many of the adults with whom I've worked to heal the trauma of abuse have told me that when abused as young children, they felt ashamed and at fault. Such childhood abuse is especially traumatic when it is perpetrated, as it often is, by adults who are in a position of trust or authority, deepening the sense by the abused that somehow it is they who are in the wrong.

Whether carried out by an individual or by a country or culture against its perceived enemies, abuse is a pattern where the abusers often justify – or even deny – the abuse on the basis that the abused 'deserved it'. We see this used in conflicts around the world to rationalize genocide, mass rape as a weapon of war and the asymmetric punishment of minorities.

One increasingly widespread aspect of the abuse pattern within our collective psyche is that of addiction, where essentially we are abusing ourselves. Drug addiction is increasing, often as a response to stress, and is reaching epidemic levels in some regions, such as Afghanistan and parts of India and Ethiopia.

* * * *

The treachery of betrayal, the third archetypal pattern, can often be the most emotionally painful of all to bear, because betrayal can only be carried out against someone with whom there's already been a real-ationship. The destruction of trust that the disloyalty of betrayal entails strikes deep within us.

Of the five archetypal traumas, all of which were depicted in the Bible as having being suffered by Jesus, the one that has bequeathed us a collective name is his betrayal by Judas Iscariot. So deeply has this betrayal affected us that when we call someone a 'Judas' they immediately understand what we are accusing them of.

With the betrayal pattern, there is generally a need by the betrayer to justify themselves. And usually this takes the form of having become disillusioned with a real-ationship. So, if we're to begin to understand and heal the pain of betrayal, we first need to *listen* to the self-justification of the betrayer, even when we fundamentally disagree with it.

The betrayal pattern is the one I carry. For years when I was younger I found myself being betrayed by those I'd considered close and eventually I was also able to recognize where I'd betrayed others and so was able to undertake a great deal of inner healing.

I found both for myself and for those whom I've helped that, as with all the archetypal patterns we embody, when we do understand and begin to heal this pattern, there will be fewer occurrences of it in our lives. For its energetic imprint, whose vibration resonates with others holding the same pattern, is then quietened and eventually released.

After acknowledging my own betrayal pattern, I progressively worked to heal and release it. But one day, when I was teaching a healing workshop in Austin, Texas, I encountered its deepest aspect.

The day before we'd explored the transpersonal awareness of the universal heart. And I'd spoken of how our 12-fold soul-level chakra system is gradually activating the culminating thirteenth level of unity consciousness. I'd also shared how the ancient tradition of solar – or soular – heroes such as Jesus and his 12 disciples embodied this resonance of 12 into 13.

The following morning, I woke up around 4 a.m. with tears pouring down my face. I felt my heart was breaking as I plunged into an inner vision of myself as Judas. And as the events of 2,000 years ago unfolded, I experienced a very different sense of what had happened between Jesus and Judas than that depicted in the Bible.

Instead of betraying his master for 30 pieces of silver, Judas had, I felt, deep love for him. I sensed that Jesus had known what needed to play out for the culmination of his mission on Earth and that he had asked the hardest thing possible of the man who was perhaps his closest disciple. As my vision unfolded, I saw Judas's despair at being asked to betray the messiah. But also how, instead of being disloyal, he undertook what was asked.

As I looked from Judas's eyes into the eyes of Jesus that morning, a feeling of sublime love flowed through me and I understood that Jesus' unconditional love surrounded and incorporated his 12 disciples in their communal transcendence into Christed consciousness.

A number of years later, in 2006, it was announced in the world's media that a lost Gospel of Judas had been discovered and translated. And when I managed to obtain a copy, once more I felt that sublime love within me as I read the same account of Judas and Jesus that I'd experienced and knew their transcendent compassion had healed me.

* * * *

Denial differs somewhat from the other four archetypes we're exploring in that it is both an archetype and an aspect of the process of recognizing, understanding and healing other patterns.

Denial is the refusal to recognize or admit the reality of a situation either about ourselves or others. And it is coloured by prejudice and judgement in that it causes us to perceive someone or something through the lens of our own beliefs rather than how they actually are.

Denial is difficult to overcome. For, depending on how entrenched it is within our psyche, evidence to prove the reality of what is being denied can literally remain unseen.

Our collective Shift of consciousness is like a wave of evolutionary energy that is flowing though our psyche. As a result, increasing numbers of people are experiencing enhanced psychic sensitivity and becoming able to perceive hitherto unseen realities. Our collective societies, however, at least in the West, and especially their authorities and media, continue to decry such experiences.

Nevertheless, for most people, their own direct experiences propel them through the denial barrier. This has certainly been true for me. So, for instance, when people ask whether I believe in UFOs, I say no. Because, like Carl Jung, who on his deathbed was asked if he 'believed' in God, replied 'No,' because he instead 'knew' God from his direct experience, I 'know' UFOs exist because I've seen them.

One sighting filled me with joy. On a glorious summer's morning in 2000, just after dawn, as I was leaving the small house that I was then living in, I happened to glance up into the clear sky. As I did so, I was amazed to see an incredibly bright and steady pointed golden light above me. I've studied astronomy from my early childhood and knew that what I was seeing was far brighter than either the brightest star, Sirius, or the brightest planet, Venus – and higher in the sky than Venus ever is.

I stood there transfixed, looking at the light, for about 30 seconds. And as I did so, I felt a gentle warmth radiate within me. The previous 12 months had been difficult and I was feeling low. But I immediately sensed the light communicating with me and offering me a benediction that raised my spirits. And as if to recognize that its aim was accomplished, it suddenly disappeared.

Indeed, it's not only the Sumerians who have held the view that extraterrestrials have been involved with human evolution and development. Many of the indigenous teachers with whom I've worked over the years, such as Credo Mutwa, the elder of elders of the Zulu nation in Africa, and the Australian aboriginal elders with whom I've stayed on their sacred lands, have maintained almost matter-of-factly that such contact has occurred throughout history.

After many years and numerous sightings, anecdotal accounts and circumstantial evidence for UFOs, the great majority of which were refuted by the local authorities, breakthroughs in the wall of denial began to occur in the 1990s. Mass sightings in Brazil, Mexico and Belgium, and in China in July 2010, forced the powers that be in those countries to acknowledge that something unknown was taking place in the skies above their nations.

Most countries have continued to rebut claims of the existence of UFOs and persisted in silencing military personnel who have attempted to disclose their experiences. Fortunately, former service personnel are now beginning to break their enforced silence. Not only have astronauts Buzz Aldrin and Edgar Mitchell, the second and sixth men respectively to walk on the Moon, recently spoken about their own UFO incidents, but investigative journalist Leslie Kean has written a 2010 book based on authoritative eyewitness reports from around the world. In *UFOs: Generals, Pilots and Government Officials Go on the Record*, with a foreword by John Podesta, US President Bill Clinton's Chief of Staff between 1998 and 2001, military officers, policemen and other experts describe, in detail and with back-up evidence, their encounters with UFOs.

Further substantiation of such events was given on 27 September 2010 when seven ex-military personnel gave a news conference in Washington, DC. Former US Air Force Captain Robert Salas and six of his military ex-colleagues described how UFOs had been seen hovering above nuclear weapons installations since 1948 and in some instances had seemed to cause nuclear missiles to deactivate.

Salas stated, 'The US Air Force is lying about the national security implications of unidentified aerial objects at nuclear bases and we can prove it'. Explaining that he personally had had such a close encounter on 16 March 1967 at Malmstrom Air Force Base in Montana, he said, 'I was on duty when an object came over and hovered directly over the site.' He went on to claim that the UFOs had remotely deactivated ten Minuteman nuclear missiles and that they had done the same at another site a week later.

In total, the ex-military personnel presented information and witness statements from over 100 former military personnel which supported their assertions of extraterrestrial intercessions at US nuclear sites as recently as 2003.

It's remarkable how hard we still collectively try to deny the reality of what is becoming more and more difficult to refute. It's as though we're all the three-year-old me that was convinced that if I closed my eyes I couldn't be seen.

Not only UFOs, but also other phenomena that have emerged and increased as our consciousness has expanded are still being denied, such as the crop circles, orbs, the incidence of synchronicities whose meaningful coincidences transcend space and time, and non-local telepathic, remote viewing and precognitive communications.

But such denial is weakening; not only because the evidence is rapidly accumulating, but also because we are collectively transcending the limitations that have held our awareness in thrall for so long.

* * * *

The last of the five archetypal patterns of behaviour that we play out on individual and collective levels is that of rejection.

This is the fear-based trauma whereby we cast out aspects of our psyche by refusing to accept them as part of ourselves. Or we reject others, diminish their humanity in order to give ourselves the excuse to discard them or treat them as scapegoats. By rejecting them, we use such escape-goats to literally escape from the consequences of our own actions.

My experiences of encountering outcasts in Ethiopia – the angel Lucifer, the vulture and the hyenas – brought home the intense pain of such rejection. For months afterwards I felt particularly sensitive to being rejected and feeling that whatever I did wasn't good enough. Fortunately, I was able to recognize my embodiment of such feelings as a learning process and was able to integrate and release the hurt. But it gave me an even deeper sense of how our rejection of others is particularly prevalent as a cause of conflict. By diminishing and dehumanizing the 'other', the outsider, the foreigner, the one who is different from us, we can justify appalling behaviour.

* * * *

Whilst the archetypal patterns that have been embodied throughout the past continue to be energized within our collective experience, their intensity is gradually being dissipated as our Shift of consciousness accelerates. As a healer, I've also noticed that people who have embodied the deepest experience and challenges of such patterns as abandonment and abuse can also, through their acknowledgement and willingness to heal, offer a great gift of healing to our collective psyche.

It is inspiring for me that previous child soldiers in Africa, the casualties of bombings and their families in Northern Ireland, ex-hostages in Chechnya and rape victims, ex-gang members and ex-drug addicts and dealers are now ambassadors for peace, reconciliation and resoulution around the world. When we see their courage, forgiveness and healing, we can also see the possibility of our own.

* * * *

We're increasingly able to attune in the unconditionally loving energies of the 8th chakra. And as research into consciousness is progressively demonstrating, as we do so, the frequency of our energies rises, our focus becomes more coherent and our healing intention becomes more powerful.

We'll now briefly turn our attention to the emerging vision of the cosmic hologram to give ourselves a broader context that will help us to understand the deeper nature of reality and how we are co-creators of the realities we experience.

CHAPTER 6
The Cosmic Hologram

'Hope sees the invisible, feels the intangible and achieves the impossible.'
ANON.

How do we understand and explain so much that doesn't fit into the mainstream worldview? Is it that more of us are going crazy these days or is there something significantly incomplete or flawed about the way that Western societies in particular have come to view themselves and the wider Cosmos?

Until the beginning of the twentieth century the scientific view of the world that had been gaining ground since the seventeenth century considered the universe to be essentially mechanical – a universal machine with absolute space and time. The beginning of the twentieth century saw the scientific revolution of quantum and relativity theories, though each only provided a partial view of the physical world, at minute and large scales respectively, and the two theories remain intrinsically incompatible. Quantum theory doesn't address the nature of space and time, and relativity doesn't express spacetime in quantum terms. Whilst scientists have searched for a unified theory for many years, as yet the quest has been unsuccessful.

Along with Ervin Laszlo and Barbara Marx Hubbard, I told the participants at the launch of the WorldShift2012 movement in London on 9.9.9:

Just as we can't understand the nature of the ocean only by looking at the waves on its surface, nor can we understand the nature of the Cosmos just by studying the physical universe. Yet mainstream science currently tries to persuade us that we can fully understand the nature of reality only by investigating the material world and reducing it to its basic components. That's like trying to analyse a Shakespeare play or a symphony by Mozart only through their letters or notes: it merely describes the mechanics of such art, without any deeper understanding, interpretation or experience of it.

If such science were able to comprehensively describe the universe then it might have reason to be authoritative. But not only are the current theories that describe the minute world of the quantum and the large-scale world of relativistic spacetime fundamentally incompatible, but over the last few years discoveries by astronomers have identified that the universe appears to be comprised of only 4 per cent of the matter and energy we are aware of and can measure, and an enormous 96 per cent of so-called dark matter and dark energy, the nature of which is as yet completely unknown.

So the mainstream science that tries to convince us that it can explain the ocean of reality can't even explain the froth on top of the waves on its surface!

What neither quantum nor relativity theory explain is a deeper realm of causality which underlies the physical world and which is beginning to be understood through the amassing of information and insights across an enormous range of scientific disciplines.

In summary, this emerging understanding contends that:

- Information is more fundamental than space, time, matter and energy.

- The universe is an integral entity, interconnected on non-local levels, and is only able to be ultimately described and understood on that wholeworld basis.

- All that we call reality is the infinity of cosmic mind expressing itself as energy and doing so through holographic processes at every scale of existence.

Leading scientists such as Leonard Susskind at Stanford University and Craig Hogan at Fermilab in the US, Anton Zeilinger at the University of Vienna in Austria and Laurent Nottale at the Paris Observatory in France are, as I describe in my book *CosMos*, co-authored with Ervin Laszlo, amongst a growing number who are beginning to consider the universe and everything within it – including us – as being expressed as a cosmic hologram.

* * * *

The WorldShift 2012 launch included a declaration that not only sounded a wake-up call about the very real state of global emergency that we are in but crucially offered hope and opportunity for the emergence of a collective breakthrough.

I also spoke about how, when we personally have an illness or dis-ease, in order to heal we don't just need to deal with the symptoms but to seek understanding and treat the underlying causes of the dis-ease.

The declaration (www.worldshift2012.com) gave a clear diagnosis that on a global level we have a communal dis-ease. Its symptoms are the economic, social and environmental issues that have brought us all to the threshold of a potential breakdown. But its deeper cause is ultimately our collective and woefully limited worldview. So if we're to heal our collective dis-ease, we need to radically change our underlying view of the world.

The mainstream scientific perspective of the world is of a fragmented, meaningless and solely materialistic universe where consciousness is only the random outcome of evolutionary forces. By collectively adopting such a sterile and limited paradigm, we've dis-membered our collective psyche. The perception of our hearts has been split from our minds, creating a rift between our inner and outer experiences of reality and separating us from each other, the Earth and the wider Cosmos. Only by expanding our worldview beyond its current and unsustainable limits and false perceptions and separations can we transform the potential of a global breakdown into a collective breakthrough.

The 'elephant in the room' that's key to our transformation and that is ignored by the current paradigm is the nature of consciousness. However, a revolutionary, comprehensive and empowering new vision of the Cosmos is emerging that is opening the way to a deeper understanding of the nature of reality itself.

* * * *

The ability of computers to analyse huge amounts of data is enabling the more profound interconnections within the universe and the supra-physical causal realm to be revealed. Many complex and apparently disparate systems of the natural world such as coastlines, the incidence of earthquakes, tributaries of rivers, weather patterns and biological ecosystems and their evolution have been investigated. And underlying their apparent diversity and complexity, simple, universal and self-similar patterns of fractal geometries are being uncovered.

But even more amazing, the same holographic patterning is being discovered in *man-made* systems such as the growth of cities, economic trends, the structure of the internet, the behaviour of financial markets and even the incidence of conflict. Even when we believe we're making choices that are independent of others, we still find that those choices become part of the collective patterns that are part of the coherent whole-world.

In *HOPE* we'll further discover how our human thoughts, feelings, choices, decisions, behaviour patterns and experiences are reflected on every scale of existence within the cosmic hologram from our individual to our collective realities.

Another fundamental aspect of the nature of reality is that non-locality – Einstein's 'spooky action at a distance' – isn't restricted to the quantum scale of existence. A huge amount of accumulated evidence shows that the immediate connection, unlimited by space and time, between apparently separate entities is also exhibited by our minds through the existence of psi effects, again showing that the Cosmos needs to be seen as a whole-world.

In *HOPE*, we'll see how, through the non-local influence of coherent intention and the power of love, we can undertake the healing of both people and places.

A third key aspect to the emerging vision of integral reality is the all-pervasive nature of cosmic *information*. The mathematics of information is exactly the same as the mathematics which describes entropy – the energetic state of order or disorder, simplicity and complexity in a system. Scientists are coming to realize that the universe can be described more fundamentally in terms of information than energy. And with information embedded at every scale of the manifest world, they are also beginning to recognize the underlying coherence and ultimately consciousness of the Cosmos.

In *HOPE* we'll continue to explore how accessing such cosmic information helps us to better understand the bigger picture of the past and present and how we may together envisage and co-create the future.

* * * *

This emerging and empowering vision which reconciles science with consciousness and universal spiritual wisdom offers us the opportunity not only to understand the Cosmos at a more profound level but also to heal our dis-membered psyche. It shows that we can no longer separate mind from matter, body from soul, and ourselves from a reality that is intrinsically connected. In this transformational vision, our existence has innate meaning and purpose.

Crucially, this revolutionary vision of the Cosmos means that we're not only the creation of cosmic mind but the ultimate co-creators of our realities. And as co-creators, our consciousness – on many different levels of perception – is far more powerful than most of us have previously thought.

* * * *

As spiritual beings undertaking a physical experience, as we expand our awareness beyond the limitations of our personality-based perception, we begin to open up to the cosmic hologram of consciousness of which we are an integral part.

Consciousness is expressed as energy, and all energy can ultimately be described in terms of frequency and wavelength. The higher the frequency, the greater the energy, and the energies of love are higher and thus ultimately more powerful than those of fear.

As we access the unconditionally loving energies of the 8th chakra and the other transpersonal chakras we'll discuss next, our frequency increases and our consciousness expands to access greater levels of holographic realities. We're able to resonate with and attune to the wisdom and insights of our higher selves and the multi-dimensional beings that guide us. And we become more coherently and consciously aligned with our purpose in incarnating at this critical time.

* * * *

As we see all around us, our fragmented and limited worldview has brought us to the edge of a global breakdown. But, at this crucial tipping point in history, this radical new vision of the ultimate oneness of reality is emerging as individually and collectively our awareness is expanding in an evolutionary Shift.

Until now, the prevalence of the mainstream scientific view of the world has meant that our personal and collective experiences of the Shift have had no broader context in which to encompass and validate our expanding awareness. But when, instead of clinging to the old paradigm that has brought us to the edge of catastrophe, we're willing to follow the increasingly compelling evidence, we begin to see with opened eyes and discover a new whole-world.

The whole-world that the emerging vision of integral reality is revealing is exquisitely co-created to enable consciousness to explore itself at many levels of awareness. And its profound and empowering insights are now crucial. Through the in-formation embodied within the whole-world, evolution unfolds throughout the universe's cosmic cycle, enabling ever greater complexity and thus consciousness to be embodied and experienced.

And whilst the limiting speed of light within spacetime ensures we experience our lives as an unfolding series of events and the playing out of choices and their implications, the reality of the non-local connection that transcends it enables the cosmic mind that *is* the whole-world to ultimately explore and evolve its own internal relationships. As the ancient mystics understood and intuitively experienced, the One is expressed through the diversity of the many.

As the Shift speeds up and as our awareness expands, we're increasingly conscious and coherent co-creators of our realities. As we begin to perceive the bigger picture of what's unfolding, it's time for us to move beyond the fears, limitations and selfishness of our ego-based selves. It's time for us to listen to the inner guru of our higher selves. It's time for us to guru – up!

If we're willing to take responsibility for our choices and ready to make those choices from love rather than fear, the emerging view of the whole-world shows that we can *really* transform our personal and collective realities.

CHAPTER 7
Re-membering Ourselves

'Hope is only the love of life.'
HENRI-FRÉDÉRIC AMIEL

After dis-membering our psyche for so long, in our collective Shift of consciousness we are literally re-membering ourselves.

As I experienced during the global pilgrimages that I wrote about in *The 13ᵗʰ Step* and subsequently, as I share in *The 8ᵗʰ Chakra*, as we begin to expand our awareness beyond the level of our personality-based sense of self, we find ourselves in an evolutionary transition where higher transpersonal levels of perception are opening up within our psyche.

Whereas the consciousness of our personality sense of self is mediated through the traditional seven major chakras, the transpersonal levels of the individuated consciousness that we call the soul are completed by the activation of a further five 'chakras'. As these are activated within us, we gain an increasingly larger perception of the cosmic hologram and the energetic unity of the Cosmos.

And as we do so, we become conscious of our reason for incarnating here and now.

Everyone, whether aware of it or not, is playing the role they've chosen to undertake in the Shift. For those whose consciousness is expanding beyond ego-based limitations, there is a growing realization that they are here not just for their own personal journey but to serve something greater, that their higher purpose is to play their unique part in facilitating the transformation of the Shift.

* * * *

As we've already discussed, the 'portal' of awareness that essentially bridges our personal self with our transpersonal self is the 8th chakra, the 'universal heart', located midway between our personal heart and throat chakras. Other teachers refer to this as the Higher or One Heart. But regardless of what, in this time of unfolding, we call it, the opening of the universal heart within us on a collective level is crucial for the completion of the Shift.

As the Shift gathers momentum and transpersonal awareness increases, my understanding and experience are resonating and concurring with those of many other teachers around the world. But there are differing perceptions of the specific levels of these transpersonal realms. So, rather than be dogmatic, especially as we are going through a transformational process, I would invite you to use your own discernment to incorporate within your understanding what feels right for you.

Whilst over the last decade I've been guided to energetically focus my awareness within the universal heart and have shared this with many others through my books, CDs, workshops, sacred journeys and healing work, I also want to emphasize that the unconditionally loving awareness of the 8th chakra is not a technique but a *way of being*.

It's a way of being that feels – and knows – an intimate and unconditionally loving connection with the whole-world and a profound sense of love, joy and gratitude for life itself.

When our ego-selves are ready to let go of fear and be open to love, the awareness of our higher selves begins to flow through us and the universal heart begins to open, like a beautiful flower in the warmth of the Sun.

* * * *

The next transpersonal chakra, the 9th or earthstar chakra, is located about a hand's length between and beneath our feet.

I first began to sense its energy when I came to live in the Avebury area of southern England. In the mid-1990s I was spending a lot of time walking in the landscape and experiencing the amazing glyphs of the crop circles. And later, as I attuned with sacred monuments and places of exquisite natural beauty around the world and with the elemental and devic realms of their guardians, the 9th chakra enabled me to ground the increasingly powerful energies I was working with and also experience a progressively more profound communication with these realms and guardians.

For the last nine years too, I've enjoyed the wonderful pleasures of gardening and learned, from the devas, season by season how to organically grow delicious fruit and vegetables.

What all my experiences have shown me and what I've come to appreciate wholeheartedly is the incredible level of cosmic support we have for undertaking the Shift. And when we begin to open ourselves to the healing of our past and the possibilities of our cosmic destiny, how simple it is. However, please note that I never said it's *easy*!

So, being in Nature whenever and wherever possible and listening to its myriad voices of wisdom energizes the earthstar chakra and enables an ever-more profound communion with Gaia and all her children.

* * * *

The 10th chakra, a hand's breadth above our heads, connects us at an archetypal level of awareness with the entirety of our Solar – or Soular – System. This is the group matrix of consciousness within which for the last five billion years or so our Sun, planets and a vast interconnected family of multi-dimensional beings have evolved – to this momentous moment.

With the perception of the 10th chakra, we're now able to communicate with all the beings of our Soular System and comprehend that the Shift of consciousness is not only for ourselves but our whole Soular family.

I've noticed in the last few years, as the 10th chakra has been energetically activated, that there has been a renewed interest in astrology, and at a more profound level than hitherto. And, as we'll see later, the influences of the archetypal logoi of our Soular System family are especially potent in this period of transformation, as we approach and break through 2012 to the manifestation of our cosmic destiny.

* * * *

The 11th chakra, approximately 18 inches above our crown, connects us with galactic awareness. I began personally to experience its activation in Hawaii in mid-2003 and then during an attunement with the Galactic Centre on 23 December of that year which I'll share more about later. But I've noticed throughout 2010 and especially since the beginning of 2011 that the connection has been progressively more powerful.

The increasing acceptance of the presence of UFOs and the technological ability to detect trans-solar planets, the most Earthlike yet being discovered in January 2011, adds to my sense that we may soon see an undisputed first contact with extraterrestrials.

* * * *

The 12th chakra, about 36 inches above our crown, resonates with universal consciousness, and together the consciousness field of the 12 chakras forms the thirteenth wholeness of our soul and the unity awareness of the whole-world of the Cosmos.

It is the activation and embodiment of such unity consciousness within us that I believe is the ultimate purpose of the Shift.

Our inner journey to such All-One-Ness is what the ancients would have described in legendary terms as the spiritual journey of the soular hero. This is the transformation of our psyche from its ego-based limitations to the realization of our innate divine presence.

And as more and more people have understood the potential and promise of this amazing opportunity, they have recognized, as I have, that such enlightenment isn't about escape but about embodying *all* that we are through our human persona and our co-creative partnership with all life.

* * * *

As we continue along our path for HOPE, we'll progressively expand our exploration to wider and wider levels of the cosmic hologram.

And as we do, with the threefold nature of our incarnation – personality, lineage and purpose – in mind, you may wish to explore for yourself an inner sense of why you chose to be born into this place and time.

Perhaps, too, as your awareness expands, you might feel called to other cultures and re-member other lives. You may also begin to connect to other realms of existence and become conscious of your guides and able to commune with other supra-physical intelligences.

And you may discover that you are here to play a pivotal role in the healing of your family, your ethnic group or nation.

So, our next step will be to take a look at how on group levels we embody similar attitudes and to begin to perceive the archetypal consciousness of societies and cultures.

CHAPTER 8
Spiral Evolution

'Learn from yesterday, live for today, hope for tomorrow.'
ALBERT EINSTEIN

As the world Shift speeds up, we are becoming more consciously resonant with and aware of embodying the energetic influences that are enmeshed within our Soular System and that have played out through the cycles of our collective realities. But because our awareness is evolving, our experiences of such cycles over time have different manifestations of the same themes but don't repeat them. So, instead of circling, the influences, and our experience of them, spiral forward, progressing with each turn.

From the beginning of history, humanity has spiralled onwards in ever more complex forms of society, beginning with small family groups and then expanding to tribes, collecting in villages, towns and cities, slowly becoming nations, empires and eventually a global community. Throughout the rise and fall of waves of expansion and contraction, there has been a gradual but inexorable spiralling rise of our collective consciousness.

In their seminal book *Spiral Dynamics*, Don Beck and Christopher Cowan modelled cultural, social and collective worldviews as such a spiral of developing stages of awareness and complexity. Their model divides our historical progression and also our current global society into a number of different levels and shows how our increasingly complex interactions have embodied different perceptions of ourselves and the wider world.

Essentially, though more multifaceted, we can model our growing up as a human family on our growing up as individuals. And, as at different phases in our own lives, the level of our collective awareness varies. Crucially, in Beck and Cowan's thesis, this occurs not only through our communal historical progress but also across our global cultures at each epoch of time, including today.

Beck and Cowan stress that the levels are dynamic rather than rigid and need to be viewed flexibly. Each can be considered as a wave of consciousness that flows then ebbs as the next level rises. Each embodies an associated worldview that is psychologically resonant with its degree of awareness, manifesting certain beliefs and aims and social and cultural structures and behaviour. Each level, beginning with the Beige of archaic awareness and spiralling to the currently emerging Turquoise of global wholism, has arisen in response to increasingly complicated interactions between people and their environments – and all are still represented within our global human community.

It came as no surprise to me that I became aware of the spiral dynamics model whilst I was writing my book *The 8th Chakra*. After working energetically for many years with the traditional concept of our personality-based energy field being modulated by seven major chakras, when in the late 1990s I began to be aware of the coming Shift of consciousness and then undertook the global healing pilgrimages that I've written about in *The 13th Step*, I began to energetically experience higher, transpersonal 'chakric' levels.

Crucially, my awareness of the 8th chakra of the universal heart was the bridge that began to connect me to a much deeper and more compassionate understanding of the Shift.

Whilst from childhood I'd experienced the ultimate oneness of All-That-Is, with the awakening of the universal heart within me, I began to feel a much more empathetic relationship with the holographic entirety of our human family and with all life on Earth.

When I first began working to help other people awaken the 8th chakra within themselves, I was often asked what colour the chakra was. I would not answer, but instead encouraged people to discover for themselves, and over a number of years I found that a great number sensed the colour of its energy as turquoise.

So later, when writing *The 8th Chakra* and synchronistically discovering the work of Beck and Cowan, I was heartened to see how they too had discerned an evolutionary spiral where the first seven levels of awareness, like the seven chakras of our personality-level consciousness, view the world from an ego-based perspective. And that they describe the emerging eighth level as being holographic in its perception of an interconnected whole-world – and assign it the colour turquoise!

As we begin to expand our awareness beyond the limitations of our ego-based selves and access the perception of the 8th and higher transpersonal chakras, the core seven chakras are still fundamental to our experience of being human and their balanced energies continue to support our overall well-being. So, too, each of the levels of the spiral dynamic model apply dynamically and holographically to the psychological development of individuals, organizations and societies and contribute to the health of the whole spiral of human evolution.

However, just as on the level of our individual chakras, where there are imbalances and traumas on the collective levels, they embody beliefs and behaviour that no longer serve but limit the manifestation of our higher evolutionary purpose.

So, understanding how beliefs, attitudes and behaviour play out on each of the spiral levels is helpful in our global understanding of the differing viewpoints of our human community. These insights can then contribute not only to how we go to the seed-points of cultural and social trauma but also to how we may best support their healing, release and resoulution.

So let's look briefly at each level of the model in turn and how they mesh into our collective experience:

- The *Beige* level is archaic and, like the focus of our own lower chakras, is dominated by the fundamental need to survive. Whilst this level is now generally tiny within our collective experience, it re-emerges and prevails in times of extreme stress such as during war or famine, such as the civil war that has been ongoing in the Darfur area of Sudan since 2003.

- The *Purple* level is the one exhibited by tribal communities of extended kinship. Its worldview is expressed through magic and ritual. At its most authentic, it is sustained by a profound awareness of the interweaving of life and its innate mystery and by cultural ties of mutual reciprocity. Whilst their traditional lifestyle is in transition, the Bedouin tribespeople of North Africa and the Middle East still experience this level.

- The *Red* level of awareness first emerged in ancient empires, being authoritarian, hierarchical and feudal. This level honours heroes and myths and both offers and requires communal evidence of respect. In general it is a stage of winners and losers – and the winners gain the spoils of war and the writing of history. In its feudal and authoritarian nature, the Taliban regime that was ousted from Afghanistan in 2001 is an example of this level.

- The *Blue* level is primarily authoritarian, conformist and loyal to what are perceived as group truths. Generally, rewards are culturally considered to accrue to those who adhere to the 'rules'. And to maintain cultural cohesion, dissidence or heresies are feared and seen as social betrayals. Singapore is an example of this level.

- The *Orange* level emphasizes individualistic advantage and is oriented to material success. It rebalances the previous levels' communal conformity by giving more weight to personal needs and rights, but often less to their associated responsibilities. The US and UK are both examples of this level.

- The *Green* level seeks to balance the rights and responsibilities of the individual with those of the community and operates from a humanistic viewpoint which considers the whole society. The importance of people in general and their feelings and social care are stressed, communal concerns are emphasized and there is a cultural consensus that all should benefit equally from opportunities. The tolerant and inclusive society of the Netherlands is a European example of this level.

Beck and Cowan consider that these first six levels from Beige to Green comprise the first tier of collective awareness and are primarily experienced as historical worldviews. The seventh and eighth levels then form a second tier of perception that is now unfolding:

- The seventh, *Yellow*, level is the first of an evolving series of levels of awareness able to adopt multiple perspectives. It is oriented to integration and takes progressively in-to-greated views of the Cosmos. Generally open to change and innovation, its holistic approach perceives the whole as greater than the sum of its parts.

- The eighth, *Turquoise*, level is now emergent in the world. It seeks to embody global wholism, spiritual interconnectivity and the purposeful nature of life by reconciling heart and mind and is aware of and beginning to directly experience the holographic nature of the whole-world.

Over the last ten years or so, Don Beck has also worked with other visionaries such as philosopher Ken Wilbur and spiritual teacher Andrew Cohen to develop spiral dynamics as an integral approach to the reconciliation of conflict and the support of global emergence. Their central thesis is that international approaches aimed at improving our human condition can only succeed if they are aligned with essential steps and stages of inner social development. Recognizing the varying stages of complexity of the leadership and general populations of different countries and cultures around the world and correlating collective efforts that align with their existing capabilities are crucial to transforming the consciousness of our global family.

In my many years of travelling around the world, I've seen for myself how important it is to put ourselves in another's place and communicate as best we can from their viewpoint. Meeting people where they're at, in the loving energy of the universal heart, is crucial to co-creating reconciliation and the resoulution of trauma and conflict. And a perspective that aims for co-creative heart, mind and purpose win-win-win solutions to issues offers in-to-greative benefits for the whole-world.

The collective awareness of Gaia and her children has evolved from the fundamental nature of the geosphere to the biological biosphere and the emerging complexity of the ecosphere to the presence of our self-aware race and over the last century the development of a burgeoning global and electronically connected technosphere. And many perceive that our Shift of consciousness extends these holographic interconnections into the self-conscious noosphere of a globally interrelated mind.

But I sense this is just the beginning!

* * * *

The spiral dynamics integral model is very useful in understanding the different worldviews that prevail at different stages of our collective awareness.

Essentially it's a reflection of the emerging vision of the holographic nature of the whole-world, where we can perceive the same scale-independent behaviour patterns playing out on personal, group, national and collective bases.

As a healer, I've worked with thousands of individuals. During my journeys and workshops around the world, I've explored with numerous participants from many countries how the cosmic hologram of our realities generates such similar experiences, themes, issues and fear-based behaviour.

In the coming chapters we'll explore the national psyches of a number of countries and regions, including the US, Russia, the Middle East, Japan, China, India and the UK. As we do, we'll be able to understand the causal seed-points and the traumas that are continuing to be exhibited within these nations and how they are affecting our wider collective psyche. And, as in our personal healing, we'll explore how we may perceive, reconcile and release the dysfunctional behaviour that limits the resoulution of our human family.

Before we go on, I'd like to emphasize that the following, whilst inspired and enlightened by the insights of numerous other people, are ultimately my own perceptions from a lifetime of 'walking between worlds' and journeying to some 70 countries around the world.

I now realize that the 'scenic route' of my own life – as for us all – has wasted no experience in enabling me to bring together the many strands that, as Carole King once sang on one of my favourite records, form a tapestry of our lives.

It has involved my training as a scientist, gaining a master's degree in physics at Oxford University, specializing in quantum physics and cosmology, and then, much later, after a corporate career, researching for a PhD in archaeology at the University of Reading studying ancient cosmologies.

Before that I qualified as a financial accountant, reaching the most senior levels of my profession and having an international business career. So I learned about finance, economics and law. And, fascinated by the many countries I visited, I also studied their history, culture and politics.

Along the way, curious about how and why the Cosmos is as it is, I delved into a plethora of topics, including complexity theory and advanced mathematics, biology, the Earth's environment and landscape energies and astrology.

And from the age of four, when my guide Thoth first appeared to me, I've had numerous mystical and revelatory experiences – which the scientist within me received validation of in myriad ways.

The understanding of national psyches is expressed as simply as I feel it can be without being simplistic. We're great at making things complex. And we sometimes use that apparent complexity as an excuse for not dealing with things. I've tried to distil the seeming complexity into its simplest form so that we can work with that understanding to heal the underlying causes of the conflicts and challenges that we need to resoulve.

****

Before we go on to do that, though, we need to place it in context and understand how the matrix of consciousness we call our Soular System influences our psyche at all levels, from the individual to the collective.

CHAPTER 9
The Bigger Picture

'Hope is a waking dream.'
ARISTOTLE

In the last few years, as the transpersonal 10th chakra, a hand's breadth or so above our heads, connecting our psyche with that of our Soular System, has begun to be activated, the sacred science of astrology has undergone a renaissance. Ever more people are realizing, as Isaac Newton and Carl Jung once did, that the interaction of the Sun, Moon and visible planets as far out as Saturn offer profound insights into the nature of our personalities. And that the telescopic discovery of the outer planets, from the eighteenth century onwards, co-creatively energized the development of our collective psyche, as Richard Tarnas, author of *Cosmos and Psyche*, has described.

Understanding the profoundly interconnected nature of the planetary bodies of our Soular System offers us a greater awareness of their influences and enables us to consciously align with their flow. Many books have been written about the fundamental nature and attributes of these archetypes, so let's rather now focus on what the planets are doing in the run-up to 2012 and beyond.

* * * *

Astrology is a cosmic language. Filled with meaning, its details can nonetheless be difficult to learn. So let's apply the 80/20, or Pareto rule, where some 80 per cent of effects arise from around 20 per cent of causes, to understanding the greatest influences that will usher us through 2012 and beyond.

On a personal level, as applied to the psychology of our astrological make-up, the 80/20 rule is reflected in the position of the Sun, Moon and the Ascendant, or rising sign, at the time and place of our birth. These essentially describe our outer mind-based identity, our inner heart-based sense of self and the path of purpose we take through life.

In addition, the position of the Moon's so-called North Node in our birth chart helps reveal our higher purpose in undertaking this incarnation. And that of Chiron, the so-called wounded healer, discovered in 1977, whose astronomical location between Saturn and Uranus bridges the personal and transpersonal, shows where our inner healing can be focused.

We'll now focus on the three outer planets, Uranus, Neptune and Pluto, which interact with us on collective levels, as it's primarily their influences that are supporting the process of the Shift. Their conjunctions, oppositions and squares, sometimes between themselves and sometimes in powerful alignments with Jupiter, the planet of expansion, and Saturn, the complementary planet of contraction, embody intense push–pull energies that are ramping up as we approach 2012 and beyond.

Uranus, the great awakener, has revolutionized our collective psyche since his discovery in 1781, between the American and French revolutions, and has energized the often unexpected changes needed to expand and uplift our communal spirit

Neptune, discovered in 1846, at a time when the foundations of global communications were being laid, dissolves the barriers we've placed around our ego-based selves and helps us to be open to the oneness of the whole-world. He teaches us how to communicate across the cosmic ether, discern the difference between illusion and reality and replace limiting barriers with more fluid and co-creative boundaries.

And Pluto, discovered in 1930 at the time of the US stock market crash, the discovery of the neutron and the incipient emergence of the extremism that would lead to the destruction of World War II and the rebuilding in its aftermath, is the planet of transformation. Named after the ancient Roman god of the underworld, he brings up from our subconscious the shadow aspects of our collective ego, breaking down what no longer serves us and helping us to heal and break through to a higher level of transcendence.

So let's look at each in turn and the effect their influence may have during these crucial next few years.

* * * *

A conjunction of Uranus and Jupiter created during their transit three nexus points from summer 2010 to early January 2011, marking the end of a 14-year cycle and the beginning of a new one. One of the aspects of this alignment that I feel may be very significant is the emergence into the mainstream of the worldview that's been percolating through the wholistic movement for some time, a paradigm based on the holographic oneness of the Cosmos as a co-creation of cosmic mind and ourselves as co-creators of our realities. This new vision, based on the raising of consciousness and personal empowerment rather than specific teachings, and understanding rather than 'belief', provides the essential whole-world context for the Shift we are undertaking.

Between 2010 and 2019 Uranus passes through the Fire sign of Aries, the first sign of the zodiac, stressing individual empowerment and heralding new beginnings marked by rebellion, liberation and grassroots movements. During his nine-year sojourn there he'll form seven challenging squares with Pluto, powerfully urging radical, challenging and perhaps completely unexpected transformation on a global scale that will affect us at every level of our personal and collective lives.

* * * *

Neptune's influence is key to the Shift, too, as it will determine how we explore our unfolding understanding of the cosmic hologram and negotiate the transformation in our perception of what we call reality.

Discovered in the sign of Aquarius, Neptune has just completed his first 'visible' full orbit of the Sun and astrologers think that this fully embodies his influence within our collective consciousness.

For the last 13 years or so Neptune has been travelling through the sign in which he was discovered and has thus been energizing the coming Age of Aquarius. Between April and August 2011 he moves into his home sign, Pisces, reflecting the transcendental nature of the enlightened human being. After briefly pulling back into Aquarius until February 2012, he will then re-enter Pisces, to remain there for the next 13 crucial years.

With him in Pisces, are we on the threshold of evolving from the technologically based communications of the technosphere to the conscious communications of the noosphere? With the increased coherence and psychic sensitivity that comes with our Shift of consciousness, will Neptune's transit herald a shift from the internet to the 'ether-net', which is interestingly what the Xerox engineers who developed one of the earliest computer-linked communication networks called their invention?

As the mutable sign of Water, Pisces also holds its highest elemental vibration. And so the presence of Neptune, named after the Roman god of the oceans, generates a powerful healing opportunity for both the emotional waters within us and the waters of Gaia.

And to ensure the maximum cosmic support for such resoulution of our collective psyche, Chiron joins Neptune in Pisces until 2019, encouraging us to have the courage to heal at the deepest levels of our psyche.

Chiron in Pisces does present the risk of compulsive behaviour which retreats into the illusory anaesthetic of addiction instead of showing a willingness to overcome the fear and challenges that will accompany our personal and collective healing. But if we're prepared to work with Chiron's energetic guidance, we can emerge from this period in-to-greated and able to fully embody our cosmic destiny.

* * * *

In late 2008 Pluto moved into Capricorn, where he'll stay until 2023. Capricorn is a cardinal Earth sign associated with physical, social and economic structures. And so Pluto's purpose during these critical years is to transform the structure of society and the fundamental ways we live on and with Gaia.

Pluto's role is to energize the transmutation of our worldview and ways of life and to destroy that which will not support the Shift. He does so by revealing what's been hidden and no longer serves us. But Pluto is an underworld archetype and if we try to cling on to the unsustainable and fear-based behaviour of the past, he will take us to the very bottom of the darkest pit to resolutely fulfil his task of transformation.

His first undertaking in Capricorn played out in the areas of financial mismanagement, government corruption and environmental degradation. And it's his influence that's already teaching us hard but necessary lessons about how to have healthier real-ationships with money.

Capricorn's involvement with power, authority and hierarchies means that Pluto's transit will also bring down what is corrupt, incompetent or unwilling to transform in government, corporations, organized religions and other forms of hierarchy.

Pluto's needful destruction of what no longer serves our higher purpose is for our greater transformation. As the outer structures of our unsustainable lives are smashed, we can emerge like a butterfly emerging from its chrysalis. And the core of what is true and sustainable can become the foundation for the way ahead.

In 2004 another plutoid, or dwarf planet, at about the same distance from the Sun as Pluto was discovered and named Orcus after a Roman god of the underworld deemed to be the punisher of broken oaths. His energetic influence is still to be fully understood, but his recent visibility adds a further enigmatic aspect to our inner healing and transformation – perhaps bringing further impetus to our re-entry into a sacred oath and communion with Gaia?

* * * *

The potent combination of the personal empowerment and rebellious nature of Uranus and the expansive energies of Jupiter in Aries, the completion of Neptune's sojourn in Aquarius and his imminent move into Pisces and the continuing presence of Pluto in Capricorn manifested, in early 2011, the beginnings of what may be a sweep of grassroots and hopefully relatively peaceful revolutions throughout the Arab world and the Middle East. Their influence is also likely to energize, directly or indirectly, social transformation much further afield.

The inner healing offered by Chiron, the revolutionary nature of Uranus, the altruistic higher purpose of Neptune and the unremittingly visible and transformative influence of Pluto are all powerfully facilitating our collective Shift in the years to come. But only *we* can manifest our destiny by discovering the courage within ourselves to heal and re-member the cosmic destiny that we chose to be here and now to fulfil.

The rebellious and revolutionary fervour and the increasingly urgent realization that things must change will be highlighted between 2012 and 2015 by an extraordinary series of seven exact square alignments between Uranus in Aries and Pluto in Capricorn, which will act as progressive crossroads and triggers for transformational change and whose influence will continue to affect world events for many years to come.

The first square alignment takes place on 24 June 2012, just after the highly significant transit by Venus of the Sun that completes at dawn on 6 June and the June solstice. So before we go on to consider the influence of the Uranus–Pluto squares, let's see how the Venus–Sun transit will add its crucial energies to what is unfolding.

Venus transits of the Sun take place in pairs eight years apart, but only every 120 years or so. The first of the current pair of transits took place on 8 June 2004 in Gemini, the sign of the heavenly twins, which is the sign of communication and the embodiment of our twin human–divine nature.

Historically, such transits in Gemini of the planet of relationship have enabled greater levels of communication to bring humanity closer together. This has been reflected this time by the eruption in global telecommunications and social networking since 2004.

The 2012 transit, though, could be even more momentous in energizing our human–divine consciousness, perhaps helping us reconcile the left and right aspects of our minds and reunite our minds with our hearts.

The dates of the other Uranus–Pluto square alignments are 19 September 2012, 20 May 2013, 1 November 2013, 21 April 2014, 15 December 2014 and 16/17 March 2015. The energy behind these triggers for transformation is generally peaceful and buoyed by hope. But frustrations will arise where the higher urge for social, political and corporate change is unmet or blocked by the powers that be, in which case there could be violence – although, as we've already seen in Tunisia, Egypt and especially Libya, this is likely to be primarily instigated by the regimes in power.

* * * *

As we re-member our personal and collective psyche, especially the divine feminine, our Soular System reflects this too. In 2006, the astronomical upgrading to a dwarf planet of Ceres, the largest body in the asteroid belt between Mars and Jupiter, named after the Roman goddess of agriculture who played a central role in the cycles of birth, life, death and rebirth, mirrored her increasing importance to astrologers and her re-empowerment within our psyche.

The trans-Neptunian bodies discovered in the far reaches of our Soular System have also been primarily named after female beings, such as Sedna, the Inuit goddess of the seas, and Eris, the Greek goddess of discord – named after her discovery caused internal strife within the astronomical community!

* * * *

For the Mayans, it's generally agreed that 11 August 3114 BCE marked the beginning of their Fifth World or Sun and of a five-millennium 'long count' calendar that is coming to an end in 2012. Its duration of 5,125 years is around one fifth of a precessional or Great Year that lasts nearly 26,000 years.

This vast time-frame reflects the wobble in the Earth's axis as we orbit the Sun, which, over time, as measured at the March equinox, means the Sun appears to rise sequentially against the backdrop of different zodiacal constellations.

For the last 2,000 years or so, the Sun has risen against the stars of Pisces at the March equinox; for the 2,000 years before that, he did so against the stars of Aries. And now, as we enter the Age of Aquarius, for the next two millennia or so, his equinoctial rising will be set against that sign of the zodiac.

Whilst astrologers continue to debate how each era is manifested in our collective psyche, my own view is that such zodiacal influences form a three-fold wave where the sway of the sign giving its name to an Age starts during that era but only reaches its fullest expression in the one following before falling away during the third.

* * * *

To get a better sense of how this triple-aspect wave of energies influences our human experience, let's take a brief look at the past three Ages: those of Taurus, Aries and Pisces respectively.

Rather than being considered cosmically cyclic, the essence of each succeeding Age forms the context for the evolutionary consciousness of humanity. We also need to note that the transition between Ages, rather like a changing ocean tide, isn't immediate. It can last hundreds of years, but within that span, as the old Age dies away, there are seed-point events, new ideas, social developments and the incarnation of individuals that embody the essential character of the Age that is emerging.

The energy wave of the Age of Taurus, which lasted from around 4000 BCE until 2000 BCE, manifested cardinal or expanding Taurean energy, a peaking of the Gemini Air energy of the preceding Age and the mutability or falling away of the Cancerian Water energy of the Age before that.

In many parts of the world, the emergence of the energies of Taurus, a fixed Earth sign, denoted the formulation and adoption of new ideas of how to relate to Gaia. The hunter-gatherer lifestyles of the previous so-called Mesolithic era gave way to the new technologies of the Neolithic, including the domestication of animals (including of course cattle), the growing of crops, the development of pottery (from the clay of the Earth) and the progressive increase of more settled ways of living. In a number of early Neolithic societies in Europe and the Middle East, the archetypal Taurean symbol of the bull and its feminine counterpart the cow were venerated.

The inspiration, communication and adoption of such radical new ideas reflected the mentality of the Gemini Air sign that peaked during this Age. And this period of transition to more fixed abodes within increasingly larger settlements reflected the falling away of the Cancerian energies where love of the traditional ways of the past and living in harmony with the land had formed the basis of Mesolithic life and shamanic beliefs for many millennia.

The feminine natures of both Taurean and Cancerian energies also continued to be balanced by the masculine energies of Gemini, enabling the new ideas of the Neolithic to be adopted peacefully and inclusively.

The next Age, that of Aries, lasted from around 2000 BCE until 0 CE. The Fire energy of Aries that emerged was forceful and aggressive. The discovery and adoption of metalworking through fire developed advanced weapons. And, as we've seen, the upheavals at the beginning of this era around 2200 BCE and at its height around 1200 BCE led to greater levels of societal stress. The consequential Arian aggression ultimately led to the competitive growth of empires, also powered by the peaking of the Taurean energies during this Age. And the Gemini energies, whilst falling away, were still influential in expanding the adoption of new ideas.

But, unlike the balance of previous eras, the Age of Aries ushered into our collective psyche energies that were strongly masculine. And by its end, its emergent assertiveness had shifted our collective psyche into the pattern that would continue to be strengthened during the subsequent Age of Pisces, within which we have played out the last 2,000 years.

The Piscean Age saw the spiritual inspiration of a multitude of world teachers being seeded within our collective consciousness. In this Age the emergent wave lasted an unusually long time. The philosophic teachings of Gautama Buddha in India, and Confucius and Lao Tzu, the author of the *Tao Te Ching*, in China in the sixth century BCE were amongst the earliest of the emergent Age. Spanning the teachings of

Master Jesus, which marked the beginning of the current era, the Piscean seeding of the Age was essentially completed by the revelations of Mohammed in the early seventh century CE.

But these spiritual seeds of the Piscean Age took root within the peaking Arian energies from the preceding era and the Taurean energies of the Age before that. So the Piscean characteristics of spirituality and altruism were played out through powerful Arian and Taurean influences that progressively transmuted the teachings of their founders into organizations. Whilst the earlier philosophies, such as Buddhism, avoided the rigid aspects of their successors, Christianity, after substantial alteration from Jesus' original teachings, became the authorized religion of the Roman Empire and the revelations of the later Mohammed were immediately enshrined in the social theocracy of Islam.

The spiritual inspiration of the Piscean Age did, however, find eventual expression in the progress of human rights, especially as the earlier influences began to wane and the discoveries of revolutionary Uranus, communal Neptune and transformational Pluto began to affect our collective psyche.

And so now the coming Age of Aquarius will sow its influences of personal empowerment and co-creativity within our psyche. The Piscean attributes of empathy and spiritual wisdom, seeded by the great teachers such as Jesus and Mary Magdalene two millennia ago, will exhibit their highest expression in our psyche so far in our evolution. And the ego-based individualistic characteristics and authoritarian structures of the Age of Pisces will finally fall away.

****

Whilst recognizing there is no unique point of entry into a new Age, nonetheless on 14 February 2009 we were offered cosmic support to this Aquarian Age re-membering by an astrological concentration that con-joined a number of planets together with the North Node (denoting higher purpose) in Aquarius and energized the possibility for transcendental breakthrough and healing. At dawn on 14 February 2009, the day dedicated to St Valentine, the patron saint of love, the Moon in Libra entered the seventh house of relationships. And Jupiter and Mars were aligned in Aquarius in the twelfth house of spiritual transformation. Forty years ago, the intuitive words of a song called 'Aquarius', from the musical *Hair*, described this cosmic pattern as the dawning of the new age in our collective awareness.

At dawn on 14 February 2009 the Cosmos actually embodied this alignment and much more to support our collective manifestation of love and peace and the dawning of the Age of Aquarius. This chart, which I called the Aquarian Dawn chart of 7.25 a.m., 14 February 2009, and which you can read more about by visiting my website (www.judecurrivan. com), revealed an incredible concentration of cosmic influences blending with the energies of Aquarius in the twelfth house of spiritual completion.

I looked back for 1,000 years and couldn't find such an alignment, except in 1962, when at the same time on the same day Jupiter and Mars were again in Aquarius in the twelfth house and the Moon in the seventh house. But then the awesome concentration of planets that energized the 2009 alignment was absent. And instead of the North Node of our higher purpose being aligned with Jupiter and Mars, it was in opposition and instead it was the South Node that aligned with them.

The South Node represents what we bring in from the past. So in 1962 the *potential* for the birth of the Age of Aquarius came through from our collective race memory, but only from 2009 have we been able to fully manifest its higher purpose. In 1962 we essentially took a collective in-breath of possibility and now, with the cosmic support of the Aquarian Dawn, we are able to take the out-breath and really make it happen.

After 40 years, another lovely synchronicity played out when one of the cast of the revival of *Hair* on New York's Broadway e-mailed me to say that they'd heard about the Aquarian Dawn and planned to sing the song in Union Square that morning.

* * * *

Both as a healer and in my own life, I know that I make things unnecessarily complicated by focusing disproportionately on my head rather than coming from the simpler wisdom of my heart. I've learned, sometimes the hard way, that my heart knows what's right, and I believe all of us do too, although we often deny or dismiss it and retreat into the often fear-based rationales of our minds.

But the Shift is offering us all the opportunity to take a collective leap into the transpersonal awareness of the universal heart. And by in-to-greating our hearts, minds and purpose in that higher level of love, we can access the insights, inspiration and co-creative empowerment to release ourselves from the limitations of the past.

To me, perhaps the greatest significance of the planetary influences of the next few years is their emphasis on our personal empowerment as a unique and yet integral aspect of our collective co-creative consciousness in undertaking transformational change.

Already, on a group level, there are revolutionary developments in organizations, technologies and societies that are extraordinary in that there are often no identifiable leaders as such, or if there are, they are facilitators of the whole. Structures are essentially transmuting from rigid and hierarchical organizations to holographically intelligent organisms.

This emergence is fundamental to our collective Shift. And not only is it in-to-greating our human psyche but we are also being empowered to expand our awareness to commune with the consciousness of Gaia through the portal of the 9th chakra.

And as the energies of the 10th chakra are activated too and we become aware of the bigger-picture astrological influences of our Soular System that are supporting the Shift, we're enabled to align with them at ever-greater levels of awareness to undertake our collective healing.

PART II
NATIONS

Indigenous elders describe the members of our human family by their colours — black, red, brown, yellow and white. And they say that just as every single person plays their unique role, so the larger ethnic and national groups also have their own special contribution to make.

We'll now widen our holographic exploration to take a look at a number of countries to consider how their past and present embody traumas and how a deeper understanding of these may offer prospects for healing and resoulution.

We'll consider the psyche of each nation as though it were an individual. Whilst obviously a nation is more complex than a single person, nonetheless the cosmic hologram plays out on this larger scale the shared experience and archetypal behaviour of a nation's people.

The origins of most nations we'll explore have accrued over a period of time, but for those whose birth — or a radical change in their history — can be defined, we'll take a look at their natal astrological charts for insights into their personality. We'll also review the seed-points in the past that have engendered the trauma that still resonates in the national character and lies at the root of the fear-based behaviour patterns that are still being played out.

Rather than review the diverse and complex symptoms of such national dis-eases in detail, as healers we'll aim to distil such symptoms to understand how they arise from the deeper wounds and dysfunctional beliefs whose characteristics continue to collectively bind and limit us.

Just as with individuals, every nation embodies such karmic patterns from the past. Here, we'll only have the space to explore a few. But this bigger-picture approach can be applied to all member groups of our human family as we seek to heal the schisms that have divided us for so long.

As for our own personal inner healing, the opportunities for reconciliation and resolution lie in acknowledging and understanding those past traumas and outworn beliefs, so as to be willing and able to release their hold and replace fear with love.

And, as for personal healing, such resoulutions are often very challenging — rarely easy! But if healing is to occur, there is no other way.

The benefits, however, of taking this collective journey of healing are literally cosmic in scope. And so finally, we'll consider how each *nation can give great gifts to our entire human family if its fears and traumas can be healed and its potential and greater destiny realized.*

CHAPTER 10

USA

'*Life without idealism is empty indeed.We just hope or starve to death.*'
PEARL S. BUCK

From an astrological viewpoint, whilst there's still debate on the subject, the birth chart for the USA originally drawn up by astrologer Ebenezer Sibly for Philadelphia at 5.10 p.m. on 4 July 1776 is deemed by many astrologers, myself included, to be the most applicable.

Since the place and date are also generally accepted by Americans as the founding of their nation, their resonance within the national psyche strengthens the claim. The traumatic attack of 11 September 2001 that some argue is equivalent to a second 'birth' of the nation also offers energetic validation of Sibly's choice of time.

We'll consider how 9/11 affects the US psyche soon, but for now we'll focus on the chart of 1776 for initial insights into the national personality.

The chart's Ascendant – which denotes the nation's future path – is in Sagittarius, emphasizing religious tradition and a strong sense of self-righteousness, deep empathy in fellowship, social idealism and a legalistic focus.

Four planets, including the Sun, representing the sense of identity, are clustered in the seventh house, symbolizing a society where contractual arrangements of all types have major significance.

The combination of the Sun and Ascendant's influences is perfectly encapsulated in the Declaration of Independence, which stresses the concept of empowering 'we, the people'.

However, with Mars in the seventh house, which also relates to conflict, both the peaceful and warlike competitiveness of the American psyche is highlighted, and this has been played out, as we'll see, in the imperialism of business as well as in political and military power.

This planetary cluster, which also includes Jupiter and Venus, also invokes Cancerian emphasis on optimism and care of the homeland, although it can equally reflect denial of reality.

Whilst the planet was not discovered until later, the subliminal influence of Pluto in the second house of materiality and money is powerful in the US birth chart. And, again as we'll see, the American relationship with both is very Plutonian, in extremely positive *and* negative ways.

So, having gained some understanding of the planetary influences surrounding the birth of this great country, let's look at its life story so far.

* * * *

In 1883 poet Emma Lazarus wrote the following, etched on the plinth at the base of the Statue of Liberty that has met the millions of immigrants reaching America over the years: 'Give me your poor. Your huddled masses yearning to breathe free. The wretched refuse of your teeming shore. Send these, the homeless tempest-tossed, to me...'

As ex-President Bill Clinton noted in 1998, 'America has constantly drawn strength and spirit from wave after wave of immigrants ... they have proved to be the most restless, the most adventurous, the most innovative, the most industrious of people'.

Those characteristics have enabled the United States, from the beginning of the nation in 1776, to embody the many positive aspects of its national personality – the diversity and multifaceted talents of its immigrant-rich community and a general belief in the 'American Dream' whereby hard work is sufficient to gain success.

The leaders who drew up the US Constitution recognized the potential power of weaving together the disparate threads of such potential, enshrining the term 'we, the people', for the first time for any nation, in its words.

But the shadow aspects of the US psyche also emanate from its collective immigrant past and from the continuing tensions of embodying the psyches of a disparate range of people. Not least, they stem from the continuing lack of full acknowledgement of two of its collegiate 'tribes': those whose ancestors were brought to America against their will as slaves and those Native Americans who were there before anyone else.

This innate stress has in my view come close to breaking the USA three times. The first was during its birth pangs in the years before and following the Declaration of Independence in 1776. The second was during the years of the Civil War of 1861 to 1865 and their bitter aftermath. The third time is now.

* * * *

At 08.46 a.m. on the clear and bright morning of September 11th 2001, the world changed when a hijacked aeroplane flew into the North Tower of the World Trade Center in New York, followed by a second jet crashing into the South Tower minutes later, a further attack at the Pentagon in Washington, DC, and another hijacked plane crashing in a Pennsylvanian field.

The emergency services telephone number in the USA is 911. And so the symbolic and energetic connections between the date and the emergency number have ensured their fear-associated resonance not only continues to resound within Americans' self-aware consciousness but also on subliminal levels within their psyche.

If we consider the USA as an individual, the inner trauma and the schisms experienced during its birth and childhood years are still to be healed. The seed-point event of 9/11/2001, during what we can think of as the USA's teenage years, and all that has subsequently been energized by its pain, threatens to destroy the *United* States of America.

On a collective level, the astrological chart for the first moment of the attack reveals a long pent-up explosion of old – very old – issues of ideological conflict whose festering and lack of just resoulution have engendered increasing intolerance and fanaticism. For the USA, Pluto's transit of the Sagittarian Ascendant of the nation's birth depicts a climactic end of national 'childhood' and a major challenge to the intuitive higher purpose of its founding.

Whilst Pluto's slow transit had actually begun a few years earlier, when the scandal of President Clinton's last year in power raised issues of moral leadership and responsibility, Pluto's position on 9/11 brought the most fundamental questions of right and wrong, truth and falsehood, good and evil into the now unavoidable light of American consciousness.

And Saturn in direct opposition to Pluto heralded a long drawn-out and enormously challenging crisis of identity to fully recognize, address and reconcile these issues – a period during which the impulse to polarize and scapegoat would be powerful and dangerous.

At the moment of 9/11 I perceived the opportunity for the USA to heal its past and step off the unsustainable road of consumerism and militarism that I felt it was on. But hearing President Bush immediately afterwards stating that it was business as usual and then seeing the Administration's instigation of bogusly justified and indeterminate wars on

Iraq and Afghanistan, I realized there would be no nexus of introspection and positive change.

The turmoil, fear and anger within America's psyche, outwardly expressed through the two wars, the boom then bust of the interwoven housing, banking and economic crisis and the worsening polarization of American society, have since created a perfect storm of dis-ease.

With greater challenges to come, including but by no means limited to the geopolitical rise of China, the sourcing and supply of resources such as oil and water, the reformation of the country's reliance on the financial sector, the unsustainability of its consumer-based culture and militaristic spending and the need to invest massively in infrastructure projects, the USA now urgently needs an open, honest and civil debate on its future direction.

On most measures that gauge quantity and quality of life, the USA is the most unequal society on the planet. And, as we'll see later, sociological studies from around the globe show that such inequality breeds enormous unhappiness. For many Americans, the American Dream has already become a nightmare, or is in danger of transforming into one.

But if Americans are able to get beyond their current anger at being betrayed by their ruling élite and their own unsustainable and fear-based affluenza of consumerism, deep healing and transmutation can still take place.

* * * *

So, to gauge the inner trauma that America continues to play out and how it may heal, let's take a look at 'who' America really is.

The immigration that has peopled the USA has come in four main waves, beginning with the colonial period of the seventeenth century, when most migrants were the dispossessed of England and France. The wave of the mid-nineteenth century was led by migrants from Germany and Ireland, along with others from northern Europe. In the early twentieth century immigrants from southern and eastern Europe predominated. And since the mid-1960s, the migrants have come from Latin America and Asia, led by arrivals from Mexico, who also make up the majority of the estimated 11 to 20 million illegal immigrants currently based in the USA.

But two other crucial threads interweave the American psyche.

The first is that of America's ancestral essence. Whilst generally hidden or peripheral, this still calls out to be heard, seeking justice for the Native Americans whose forebears first walked the land tens of millennia ago.

The second is that of the 'unwilling' immigration of slavery. Beginning in the Spanish colonies of the south in the 1560s, slavery grew dramatically before the northern victory in the Civil War in 1865 resulted in its abolition.

But before we return to consider these two fundamental threads, we'll take a look at the four main waves of immigration that form the primary strands in the tapestry of the American psyche.

****

The earliest colonists, most of whom were from Britain, included adventurers and merchants who saw opportunities for exploiting and trading the resources of the newly discovered land. Many of them, though, were poor and seeking to escape from the social and religious injustice that they and their predecessors had endured.

They were followed by seekers of religious and social freedom, including William Penn, a wealthy Quaker who purchased a large plot of American land from Charles II, the British monarch, in 1681 and founded Philadelphia, the city of brotherly love.

By the Tea Party proclamations of 1773, when boxes of tea were thrown into Boston harbour as a protest, it was the British colonists who, refusing to part with their own hard-won freedoms and resenting the unfair taxation without representation imposed by the British government, were leading the revolution that secured America's future path.

* * * *

The second wave of mainly Irish and German immigrants in the mid-nineteenth century resulted in the two largest immigrant-descended groups in the USA today.

German Americans now comprise around 51 million people, or 17 per cent of the US population. Some eight million arrivals, forming the largest immigrant group, were inspired to make the difficult ocean crossing to America by its promise of land and religious freedom. Before 1848, most were farmers pioneering the settlement of the northern and Midwest regions. Their descendants retain a strong presence there today. But after a failed revolution in Germany in that year, immigrants also flowed into the burgeoning cities of primarily the north-eastern USA.

Given their motivations for immigration, they charac-teristically not only valued individual freedoms but were self-reliant, hard working and aspirational. And perhaps if any group fully embodied the emerging American Dream, it was these hardy and upright folk.

* * * *

Until the mid-1840s, the number of people leaving Ireland for America was modest. But the Irish peasants had been forced onto tiny plots by their English landlords and were reliant on potatoes to sustain their families. When, over several years, blight caused the failure of the potato harvest, famine was widespread. The 1841 census recorded the population of Ireland as eight million people. By the end of the decade, at least one million had died as a result of the Potato Famine and another million had emigrated, almost all to America.

I gained a deep insight into the psychic wound both in Ireland and the USA when I taught a weekend workshop in Dublin in March 2010.

The Saturday morning of the workshop, Tony and I were having breakfast at our hotel when I happened to see the front page of the local newspaper. The financial crisis that had exploded around the world was still very much news. But here it was taking on a more personal flavour.

The Irish paper showed an unflattering photo of a middle-aged banker looking overfed on both food and money. I read how this particular banker had driven his financial institution to the point of bankruptcy and, having been sacked for doing so, was now suing the bank for compensation. The story and how he looked seemed both a microcosm and a caricature of the worldwide situation.

But as I gazed into the eyes of his picture, I felt a deep compassion for him. I could see how he and so many others had been caught up in the addictive need for more money and more possessions, all to try to feed a deep yearning for security, sometimes ignorant of and sometimes regardless of the harm done to anyone else.

Later that day, the workshop group energetically attuned to their ancestral past. Initially we regressed our awareness back thousands of years to the Neolithic heritage of Ireland. Around 5,000 or more years ago, a great building era saw the construction, in the Boyne Valley in the centre of the island, of wonderful monuments such as Newgrange, Knowth and Dowth. Connecting with that remote era, my workshop participants could sense the peace and harmony that had prevailed across the rich land and how the monuments, with their alignments to the Sun and Moon, linked Heaven and Earth in a cosmic balance.

We then continued on our inner journey to the awful experience of the Potato Famine. As I too energetically attuned my awareness to that calamitous time, I began to see in my inner vision a close-up of a small hamlet of tiny shabby dwellings and pathetic plots of withered potatoes. I was drawn to a young boy, maybe seven or eight years old, whose small body was ravaged by hunger. In my vision, I approached him, he looked up and our eyes met.

To my amazement, his were the eyes of the overfed banker whose face I'd seen in the morning's newspaper.

My heart lurched with sorrow as I realized how the tragic experience of that life had seared a trauma into his psyche which, a century and a half later, would drive him on a quest for the money that would ensure he never went hungry again.

That feeling of loss and grief became embodied in an abandonment pattern which has since characterized the Irish people. When vast numbers emigrated to America after the famine, their deep need to feed their inner void became a powerful motivation to amass wealth, influence and thus security.

The Irish are a warm-hearted and community-oriented people and have added those attributes to the US mix. But on a causal level, the Irish thread within the American tapestry has contributed to the consumerism that consciously or unconsciously seeks to feed emotional emptiness with outer 'stuff' – a need that can never be met in this way.

For the Irish people who remained at home and continued to suffer there for over a century of subsequent deprivation and violence, their inner need for nourishment also to some degree remained unmet. Remarkably, though, they were able to regain a deep sense of community that sustained them and helped to alleviate to some degree the still unhealed pain of history.

When in 1973 Ireland was admitted into the European Union, however, its material deprivation enabled significant amounts of funding to flow into the country. And following corporate deregulation and the reduction of taxes in the 1990s, an economic boom began to gather momentum and within a few years Ireland became the so-called Celtic tiger.

This outer explosion of development and consumerism failed to address the innate emotional wounding. For a number of years, as the boom expanded without apparent limit, the Irish were like revellers on a pleasure boat without an adequate anchor. And then came the storm of the global financial crisis that began in 2007.

As I sat in the workshop, I knew that the bust that had so precipitously ended the boom was actually a blessing in disguise. If, instead of responding with fear and anger, the Irish people could now acknowledge their inner trauma and come together in compassion and a realization of the strength of community and inner values, they could reach a point of balance between the privations and excesses of the past and experience a healing catharsis that would bring hope for the future.

The European Union and International Monetary Fund bailout that the Irish were forced to take in November 2010 to avoid national bankruptcy may be the wake-up call that enables the Irish to wean themselves off the outer attempt to resoulve their abandonment trauma. And perhaps by re-membering the well-being that they first experienced some five millennia ago, they can reach a point of inner healing and release that will also resonate within the psyche of their Irish-American cousins and thus their extended US family.

* * * *

After the German and Irish waves of immigration to the USA, the next wave came from southern and eastern Europe from around 1880 to the outbreak of World War I in 1914. This was swelled by poor farm workers primarily from southern Italy and

Sicily desperate to escape the poverty of their homeland and encouraged by their government to go to America.

Over the generations, their emphasis on family – and good food, church and fraternal societies – has enriched American society, although the organized crime that reached out its tentacles from their homeland has also had a covert and detrimental influence.

Unlike many of their earlier US compatriots, the Italian incomers brought with them a continuing connection with their families back in the 'homeland'. As such, their psyche wasn't as traumatized by the archetypal pattern of loss and abandonment as that of previous immigrants and this helped to mitigate the pattern in the overall national character.

* * * *

The fourth wave of immigrants, from the mid-1960s onwards, hailed mainly from Central and Latin America, notably Mexico, and the countries of southern Asia, including Vietnam. They too generally maintained ties with their extended families back 'home'.

For the Vietnamese, their country's associations with America during the Vietnam War made it a yearned-for destination. The Vietnamese immigrants arrived soon after the end of the war, with many having fled persecution from the communists in their homeland. They settled mainly on the west coast, where their strong communities are now a well-grounded feature. Their assimilation into the USA has, I feel, in some way helped heal the pain of the Vietnam War.

The relationship between the USA and the continuing flow of immigrants from Central and Latin America, principally illegal incomers from Mexico, is far more problematic, especially in the southern states.

The reason so many Mexicans are prepared to undergo the dangers of trying to cross into the USA is the impoverishment of their own country. And there is a level of cultural schizophrenia within America with regard to the millions of illegal Mexican immigrants it harbours. Though the authorities have now made it more difficult to cross the border, once the immigrants have arrived, many employers will hire them regardless.

Views are also split between those who perceive illegal immigrants as a drain on social welfare and those who feel that the work they undertake in the agricultural, service and construction industries offers a net benefit to the US economy.

This lack of clear and consensual policy is but one example of many within the currently troubled psyche of America.

* * * *

When I was in my late teens, I read a book that shocked me to the core. *Bury My Heart at Wounded Knee* by Dee Brown was the harrowing story of how the Native Americans who had roamed free across America for millennia had been appallingly treated by the European incomers who had taken their lands. Specifically it related the events of the Battle of Little Bighorn in 1876 and the shocking massacre of Sioux prisoners at Wounded Knee, South Dakota, by US soldiers.

When, many years later, I had the opportunity to visit a number of reservations and work alongside Native American elders, I appreciated both their deep understanding of the land and of Nature. For some, their compassion and wisdom had brought them to a place of inner healing. But for many, their hurt and anger, not only about the genocide of the past but also about the lack of reparation in the present, were palpable.

So I was heartened when in 2008, symbolically in a valley near the Little Bighorn River, Hartford and Mary Black Eagle sponsored the 'adoption' of Barack Obama, then a presidential candidate, into the Crow tribe, naming him 'One Who Helps People Throughout the Land'.

Often, restorative justice isn't solely about compensation. In such a litigious society as America, people are loath to acknowledge guilt. But often what victims of crime – such as the crime perpetuated against its Native American members by the USA – really want, often more than money or any other form of compensation, is a heartfelt apology.

And so I was even more heartened when in late 2009 President Obama was the first president to sign an apology on behalf of the government for its historic treatment of Native Americans. As he added, 'No statement can undo the damage that was done. But it is only by heeding the lessons of our history that we can move forward.'

In December 2010 he also signed the Claims Resolution Act into law. This compensates tribal communities for some of the past discrimination towards them and also sets up a scholarship fund to improve access to higher education for young Native Americans.

Much is still needed to heal the schisms between America and its earliest inhabitants, but I believe that the Obama Administration has taken important first steps. And a forum of annual Tribal Gatherings has been set up to enable open discussion, debate and hopefully resoulution of the issues that remain.

* * * *

The other great stain, not only on America's past but also on our collective history, is slavery. This is still tragically endemic in the abuse of modern-day people trafficking.

On 4 November 2008, I joined my friend Michele as she voted in the presidential elections. The polling station was close to her home in New Jersey and as we drove there we came across an elderly lady hobbling down the street. We stopped and gave her a lift and heard her story. She told us that though she was barely able to walk and unable to afford a cab, she was still determined to make her voice heard by voting for Obama. She had heard his rallying cry of 'Yes, we can' and 'Change we can believe in.'

We arrived at the polling station and she made her painful way into the booth. When she came out, she was beaming. And as we drove her home, so were we.

Later that evening, as Obama gained enough votes for victory, I joined countless others both in the USA and around the world in praying that the hope and change that he had campaigned on would be possible.

And as I looked at America's first black president on that night of acclaim, I could clearly sense the benign presence of Abraham Lincoln standing behind him.

* * * *

The waves of immigration into America have been motivated overwhelmingly by a yearning for freedom. And America's freedoms have indeed been a light for the entire world.

But by strongly emphasizing the rights of the individual, it has tended to neglect the compensating responsibilities to communal society. The inherent tensions between freedom and control, rights and responsibilities, individual and community have resulted in national stress that is approaching the point of breakdown.

So, in order to understand how the American psyche might resoulve its issues, let's briefly consider the State of the Union today and then look at the astrological and other influences that may play out in the coming years.

The two main political parties, the Republicans and the Democrats, line up along an ideological spectrum that essentially spans from the haves to the have-nots within the USA. Both parties uphold the image of the American Dream based on the assumption that anyone prepared to work hard enough will achieve their aims. That American Dream, however, has been progressively defined by material wealth. Money – and who has it and who doesn't – is, in my view, the greatest polarizing force in the USA, both politically and socially, and this inequality is, I believe, the most dangerous threat to the Union. According to the US Census Bureau, the gap between rich and poor has never been as great as it is now.

And it is now, perhaps more than ever before, that corporations and billionaires with extreme political views are able to covertly seed and breed dissent and further their very specific agendas.

In January 2010 the US Supreme Court, with its stated conservative bias, voted to allow unlimited corporate funding for political campaigns. This ruling, in many people's view, and indeed my own, is potentially catastrophic for democracy, as it has opened the floodgates to virtually unregulated political access and funding by corporations and large-scale pressure groups, for electoral campaigns at every level, from town to national.

Regardless of left- or right-wing views, the ability of such hidden controllers to buy and sell elections as never before is a move that all Americans should regard as a fundamental attack on their democratic rights.

The recently formed Tea Party, for example, whose name harks back to the revolutionary fervour of the late eighteenth century, is usually seen as being a leaderless and unplanned grassroots movement of citizens that arose spontaneously. However, as Jane Mayer of the *New Yorker* magazine clearly showed in her August 2010 report, it was founded and is funded by élite interests.

Three billionaires are primarily responsible for funding the movement and manipulating its ongoing expansion: Rupert Murdoch, the well-known Australian businessman, and David and Charles Koch, brothers who between them own 84 per cent of the second-largest private company in the USA and run a huge oil, coal, chemical and logging empire.

The 2010 documentary *(Astro) Turf Wars* by Australian film-maker Taki Oldham exposes the corporate and élite interests that lie not only behind the Tea Party but also the US healthcare debate and the opposition to climate change legislation. As the documentary puts it,

> *Most of these groups define themselves as 'free market think tanks', but their ploy is to dress up crony capitalism with free enterprise and free enterprise with personal freedom. So whilst the great numbers of Tea Party members are activists for freedom, they have little awareness that they are opening the door for self-interested corporations and corporate players to trample that freedom underfoot...*

Moreover, despite the enormous amount of information available online, the bias of both politicians and media has generally been inadequate to the task of offering the American people a truthful and clear understanding of the social reality of their country.

Throughout America, there has also been a progressive underinvestment in infrastructure over the last number of years, with serious consequences for economy and society. The US Society of Civil Engineers recently estimated that the situation is so bad that more than $1.2 trillion is needed to repair and upgrade transportation, wastewater and energy utility systems and school and other federal buildings.

And yet, with a military budget of some $700 billion per year and with indirect costs related to defence spending boosting the annual total to around $1 trillion, the USA accounts for almost half the annual military spend of the entire world. In his 1961 farewell speech, President Eisenhower warned of the dangers of the burgeoning military-industrial complex and its unwarranted influence, but since his day it has continued to grow inexorably.

The military and its related industries need wars and conflict to justify their existence. And these activities also contribute significantly to how economic activity is currently measured. Indeed, during a conversation between President Bush and the then President Kirchner of Argentina in January 2004, Bush contended, 'The best way to revitalize the economy is war.'

With such motivation, it's unsurprising that currently the USA is by far the biggest exporter of wars and war paraphernalia across the globe.

* * * *

The disparate origins of the people who collectively make up the American psyche make it more diverse than any other society on Earth. Whilst historically the USA was seen as a melting pot where such origins were subsumed within the greater whole, fundamental tension has been present from the beginning.

The USA faces an enormous task of rebalancing if it is to heal itself and fulfil its leadership role in the years to come. The challenges include weaning itself away from rampant consumerism, reducing governmental waste and undertaking a radical programme of federal reformation, reining in a still almost unfettered financial system, instigating a Green New Deal of innovation and infrastructure investment, and reducing and refocusing its military operations on peace-making and humanitarian efforts, both domestically and abroad.

The diversity within America was once one of its greatest strengths, but in recent years it has fragmented into polarized bitterness. It's now the time for the USA to become the *United* States once more and for its people to work together for the greater good of both the nation and the wider world.

* * * *

On 8 January 2011 on a sunny Saturday afternoon in Tucson, Arizona, Congresswoman Gabrielle Giffords was meeting her constituents when a gunman approached her, shot her in the head and went on to shoot a total of 16 people, of whom six died. One of them was a nine-year-old girl called Christina Taylor Green.

When I heard of the tragedy, I immediately recognized the dire mental state of the perpetrator, but also felt energetically there was something much more here than an unhinged loner seeking revenge for some perceived slight.

Some take the view that such murders are the sole responsibility of the killer. But I don't believe that. We are all fundamentally interconnected and such actions ultimately arise from the state of our collective psyche. So they call us to look within, at our own capacity for fear and anger, and to consider how we see ourselves and treat each other.

At the memorial service for Christina and the others who had died or been injured, President Obama sought to begin a healing process, saying,

> But what we can't do is use this tragedy as one more occasion to turn on one another… Rather than pointing fingers or assigning blame, let us use this occasion to expand our moral imaginations, to listen to each other more carefully, to sharpen our instincts for empathy, and remind ourselves of all the ways our hopes and dreams are bound together.

It may be that the symbolic nature of Christina's birth and passing is the seed-point for a national resoulution. For she was born on 9/11. And then at nine years old, she perished on the eighth day of the first month of the eleventh year of the millennium – another numerologically resonant 9/11.

Even her name, Christ-ina, subliminally resonates within our deep need for resoulution.

She was born on a dark day whose awful events offered the USA the choice of seeking a more profound peace in the world or going to war – and the choice was made for war. Perhaps her passing will result in the choice for reconciliation and healing.

Indeed, her mother, Roxanna, speaking on ABC's *Good Morning, America*, said, 'She didn't really look at 9/11 as so much a tragedy like the rest of us did. She looked at it as an opportunity for change, for hope… She always wanted peace.'

* * * *

As the most diverse and the most unequal society on Earth, the USA is a microcosm of our collective issues and opportunities. And as the only extant superpower, its international role – for good or for ill – is crucial to the future of the entire world.

From the nation's birth, Pluto's transformational influence has offered cosmic support to America's realizing its full potential for good, and it continues to do so, albeit through a time of massive challenge. Powerful forces for potential national reconciliation were seeded by the events in Tucson which occurred as Uranus, the great awakener, moved into the empowered sign of Aries. In April 2011, when Neptune moves into the altruistic sign of Pisces, the nation, and indeed our global collective, has the opportunity to ally the highest purpose embodied in the Arian energies with radical and benevolent communal change.

If America can release itself from the fear of loss that has played out particularly strongly since 9/11 and that can be traced back to the archetypal traumas of its ancestral past, it has an unprecedented opportunity to cure its affluenza, balance its society between 'me' and 'we' and use its vast resources to convert the conflict of war into the co-operation of peace.

If the immense strengths of this great country – its idealism, principles of democracy, innovation and dynamic energy – can be regenerated within its psyche in a newly mature way, it can provide a beacon of light to the world and truly embody the American dream.

As President Obama said when elected, 'We can do it!'
Together, yes, they can.

CHAPTER 11
Russia and Poland

'Without hope, life is meaning less and less.'
ANON.

Unlike the USA, Russia has no history as a democracy. Before the revolution of 1917, it was ruled by a long line of monarchist tsars and then by the absolute rule of the Communist Party. After the revolutionary leader Vladimir Lenin's death in 1924, Joseph Stalin came to power and ruled Russia and the expanding Soviet Bloc with an iron fist until his death in 1953. In the 1920s he transformed what was primarily an agricultural economy by launching a rapid programme of industrialization, which led to massive disruption and widespread famine in the early 1930s. In the late 1930s he unleashed two years of what became known as the Great Terror, a pervasive campaign operated through the vastly increased network of secret police to purge everyone seen as not totally loyal to the communist regime. Spiritual beliefs were also the subject of an unremitting terror campaign, for communist ideology viewed religion as 'the opiate of the people.' During the two years before the outbreak of World War II, Soviet archives suggest that nearly three-quarters of a million people were executed.

In 1939 Stalin sided with Hitler's Nazis in World War II until Germany violated the agreement by invading the Soviet

Union in 1941, whereupon he switched sides and fought with the Allies at enormous cost in terms of the deaths of Soviet citizens in German-occupied territories.

Before, during and after the war, Stalin also exiled enormous numbers of diverse victims and ethnic peoples to Siberia and Central Asia. In the horrendous conditions of the gulag work camps, vast numbers perished of hunger and disease. Official Soviet estimates record that from 1929 to 1953 over 14 million people passed through the camps and up to a further 8 million were deported to remote areas.

Overall, recent historians estimate that the various campaigns of intimidation, deportation and famine of the Soviet era claimed at least 15 million lives and perhaps many more.

Yet despite all the horrors Stalin unleashed on the Russian people, in a 2006 poll more than a third of Russians stated that they would vote for him if he were still alive. And in a 2007 poll, over half of young Russians maintained that he had done more good than bad. Nearly half refused to accept he was a cruel tyrant.

By the time of his death in 1953, the communist system had benefitted its people in terms of universal access to education and social and health welfare, but unceasing propaganda, complete control and increasing physical well-being had all contributed to a Russia that was increasingly homogenous and patriotic domestically, and closed and paranoid in its international relations.

****

By the time Mikhail Gorbachev came to power in 1988, the state's economy was stagnant. Gorbachev instituted the transformational reforms of *perestroika*, which means 'restructuring', aiming to reduce the inefficiencies and corruption that were rife within the system, and *glasnost*, meaning 'openness', to liberalize the media and politics.

In foreign relations, he initiated a new relationship of non-intervention in the affairs of the Eastern Bloc countries, enabling the fall of the Berlin Wall in 1989, and he and American President Ronald Reagan reached out to each other, effectively ending the Cold War and beginning the process of nuclear arms reduction.

The astrology of that moment when the Soviet Union fell was particularly powerful. Transformational Pluto transiting its natal Sun in the intense sign of Scorpio energized the complete 'death' or collapse of the political structure that had been embodied since the revolutionary storming of the Winter Palace in St Petersburg on 7 November 1917. And the clustering of Uranus, Neptune and Saturn in Capricorn, the sign of structure and authority, strongly influenced the break-up from within.

Gorbachev was awarded the Nobel Peace Prize in 1990 for his reforms, but with more openness, the true scale of the communist mismanagement and parlous state of the Soviet economy were laid bare, and the ending of the Communist Party's supremacy was inevitable. Poignantly for an atheistic regime, Gorbachev resigned on Christmas Day 1990 and the Soviet Union itself collapsed the following year, with many former member states choosing independence.

Boris Yeltsin, the new Russian leader, was left with managing the aftermath and trying to pilot Russia into a new and unknown era.

He almost immediately began the transition to a market-based economy by cutting state subsidies to loss-making industries and farming, removing price controls, including those that had artificially held down the cost of bread and other staples, and allowing the Russian currency, the ruble, to be freely converted.

It was during this turbulent time that I visited Russia.

Since my teenage years, I'd read Russian literature and history and followed as many of the Soviet regime's activities as had been published in the West. I perceived a long-term archetypal pattern of abuse that had pervaded the country's psyche since its feudal history and greatly worsened during the Stalinist era.

Sadly, what I saw during my visit and what has continued to play out within Russia since then are two aspects of that fear-based pattern of trauma.

The first is that an abused person takes on the belief that the abuse is justified and either chooses to succumb to it for longer or even psychologically misses its certainties once it stops. Gorbachev stopped the abuse that the Russians had endured for so long, but for many in Russian society, these had been the only circumstances with which they were familiar and so his reforms were an unknown and frightening development. Instead of seizing the chance to reform, in many instances the previously authoritarian forces of the Kremlin merely undertook the leadership of progressively corrupt activities that perpetuated abuse in different forms.

The fear-based yearning for the leadership of a 'strong man' in preference to democratic freedom also paved the way for Vladimir Putin and the continuing abuse of power and people that has recrystallized the pattern within the Russian psyche.

* * * *

During that early visit I discovered the Soviet-era beige drabness was unrelieved, and with the country still reeling, food was very expensive and I saw the misery of people reduced to bringing their belongings onto the street and laying them out on cloths to sell what they could to raise money.

A number of men were walking purposefully between the tiny stalls that were dotted around trading the basics of life and I noticed they all seemed to be wearing shiny shellsuits. I subsequently discovered the suits marked them out as the incipient Russian mafia, often ex-KGB and secret police operatives who in the new era had morphed into gangsters who were intimidating the stall-holders into paying them 'protection' money.

And behind the scenes Yeltsin and his cohorts were ensuring there were opportunities for their circle and other favourites to seize former state-owned properties, utilities and organizations, leading to the rise of business oligarchs making vast fortunes.

Market economists in the West believed that the overturning of the old centrally administered and inefficient system would open up the Russian economy and raise the living standards of its people. But throughout the 1990s, amid the turmoil of radical change, conditions actually deteriorated and a series of crises, both financial and social, were only narrowly averted.

* * * *

On the last day of the twentieth century, Yeltsin unexpectedly resigned and his deputy Vladimir Putin stepped in as acting president. His subsequent eight-year double term as president brought a new era of prosperity to Russia, but was allied with a resurgent authoritarianism within Russian society. Strong economic management, significant policy reforms and high prices for oil and energy exports enabled Russia's economy to surge forward. More recently, with Putin now prime minister, continued high prices for Russia's natural resources and the political and social stability enabled by the relative increase in prosperity have encouraged major investments and business development.

Despite his successes and his consequential popularity with the Russian people, Putin has been criticized for his abusive record on internal human rights and press freedoms, for cronyism and bullying, for developing a cult of personality with his many photo opportunities in heroic poses and latterly for stoking up right-wing nationalism. In its 2008 Report, Human Rights Watch described how during the run-up to elections in late 2007/early 2008 Putin's administration had carried out brutal abductions, torture and illegal detentions. And according to opposition leaders and other commentators, the level of institutionalized corruption, the abuse of power, has been on the increase too.

Putin's support for ultra right-wing groups as a form of managed nationalism also became dangerously close to becoming unmanageable during 2010, when the violence of football hooligans and skinhead gangs resulted in the worst ethnic riots in Russia since the fall of the Soviet Union. More recently, too, such gangs have become the core for an administration-backed movement aimed at controlling the streets and preventing the rise of pro-democratic political groups.

Beatings and killings of human-rights activists are increasing and the wave of militant nationalism that Putin has manipulated in the past may be about to unleash a tsunami of violence within Russia.

*　*　*　*

Russians are a proud people and highly patriotic. Whilst they have a general distrust of authority, they also have a prevailing unwillingness to confront it, although now the ultra-nationalist factions seem to be gearing up to do so. Generally, Russians are swayed by propaganda and prefer leaders who are deemed to embody archetypal Russian attributes and to be strong in the defence of perceived Russian interests.

Ex-KGB Putin exemplifies this, being openly insistent on Russia 'roaring back to the table of world power.' Russia's vast natural resources and the fact that climate change is potentially opening up huge swathes of resource-rich territory in the Arctic have enabled him to be belligerent towards other countries.

But Russia's psyche has been damaged and its maturity stunted by the Soviet era and the loss of self-esteem caused by the fall of its erstwhile empire. So Putin's abusive personification of patriotic bully boy reflects Russia's trauma.

In 2009, with the apparently more reasonable and progressive Medvedev as Russia's president and Obama recently inaugurated as the US president, there was the chance of resetting the relationship between the two countries. Both men were open to this and a series of meetings strengthened their personal rapport and led to a commitment to mutually reduce the levels of nuclear arms and proliferation.

The ongoing Presidential Commission also set up by Obama and Medvedev announced in June 2010 that its first year's work had substantially expanded bilateral cultural, educational exchanges and innovation partnerships and was focusing on developing trade and investment opportunities, including a joint initiative to promote energy efficiency and clean energy technologies. And in December 2010 the European Union added its support to that of the USA for Russia's entry into the World Trade Organization in 2011.

As Russia integrates further, there needs to be an ongoing dialogue that understands and deals diplomatically with its psychological need for acknowledgement and works towards a peaceful restoration of its self-esteem.

And in return Russia needs to overcome its abusive trauma and its associated tendency for bullying and its distrust of and prejudice against foreigners and ethnic minorities and appreciate the benefits of a more inclusive and collegiate worldview.

****

As one of the world's two energy superpowers (the other being Saudi Arabia), this abusive archetype is particularly dangerous.

In addition to enormous oil and mineral resources, Russia has the largest known natural gas reserves on Earth. And climate change in the Arctic is likely to open up the availability of still greater mineral and energy resources. Although tempered by international pressure, there have already been examples of

Russia politically bullying states it disagrees with by withholding supplies or raising prices on its exports of oil and gas.

Whilst the gas, primarily made up of methane, has been extracted so far from conventional deposits, far greater amounts are in the form of so-called clathrates, vast deposits of methane-rich icy sludge. Held in either seabed or permafrost deposits not only in Russia but around the world, the gas is held stable due to a combination of high pressure and/or low temperatures. However, in 2008 in the Siberian Arctic, millions of tons of methane were found to be being released as the Arctic permafrost thawed; in some areas at a hundred times the normal level.

Methane is a powerful greenhouse gas, much more so than carbon dioxide. In sufficient and rapid volumes, its release into the atmosphere could trigger, as US climatologist James Hansen has warned, feedback loops that could lead to runaway processes of global warming and atmospheric oxygen depletion.

Such a situation has been posited to have caused catastrophic change in the past. And so serious is the possibility of this risk that in 2008 the US Department of Energy and Geological Survey identified potential clathrate destabilization in the Arctic as one of the four most serious scenarios for abrupt climate change.

The Siberian Arctic was also the area where dissidents of the Soviet era were exiled to survive or die in the notorious gulags. And so it is here in this huge and desolate region that the energetic imprint of Russia's archetypal abuse pattern holds sway, especially in its remote north-eastern part.

Currently most of the gas extraction has been from western Siberia. But Russia aims to strategically develop in the coming years its north-eastern resources to supply China's burgeoning needs.

The extraction of oil and gas has already caused enormous environmental abuse to Gaia. Further development could not only worsen this depredation but also increase the opportunity for Russia to potentially further abuse those who rely on it for their energy needs.

And as co-creative evolutionary partners, unless Russia heals its inner trauma, will the fear, anger and resentment that it engenders be mirrored in the explosive release of methane clathrates that would in their most extreme outpouring, as it appears has happened before, could be the cause of mass extinction of life on Earth?

* * * *

One of the troubled relationships – a further example of its abusive archetype – that Russia has had since World War II is with Poland.

During the war Stalin's secret police massacred some 22,000 officers and men of the Polish army and other Polish nationals in the forest of Katyn. It was an atrocity that the Soviet authorities refused to admit to for nearly half a century. Only in 1989 did the truth begin to come out when, with the new policy of openness initiated by President Gorbachev, Russian scholars revealed that Stalin had ordered the killings.

In 1990 Gorbachev allowed a Polish delegation to visit the Katyn memorial and Russia formally admitted responsibility and expressed 'profound regret' for the murders.

Even then, the relationship between the two countries was far from healed. But in 2010 another tragic event was to open the door for a deeper reconciliation.

For the first time ever, Prime Minister Putin invited his Polish counterpart, Donald Tusk, to join him at a Katyn Memorial Day ceremony in early April to mark the seventieth anniversary of the massacre. Before the visit, again for the first time and probably due to Putin's influence, the 2007 film *Katyn* was aired on Russian state television and brought the reality about those awful events to the Russian populace, a large proportion of which had been unaware of the truth.

Only three days later, on 10 April 2010, an aircraft heading for a separate ceremony to commemorate Katyn carrying 89 dignitaries, including Polish President Lech Kaczynski, his wife, other politicians and high-ranking military officers, crashed in Smolensk in western Russia, killing everyone on board.

* * * *

Like the plane crash a few months before in Ethiopia, I felt the Polish crash in Russia was hugely symbolic. Again, through inexplicable pilot error the plane crashed in a storm and caught fire as it clipped a 33-foot high tree – embodying the elemental Water and Fire of sacrifice once more.

Putin commiserated with the Polish people over the tragedy, and his sympathy was warmly received. It appeared that the first crucial steps towards a deep healing between the two countries had been taken.

Synchronistically, only days after the crash, I was in Philadelphia for a workshop hosted by my friend Susan Duval and had the opportunity to visit the US national Polish Memorial and the church of the Black Madonna there. Enveloped by the loving energies of the Madonna, I prayed for the healing of the events of Katyn and the sacrifice of the crash.

And although I wasn't to understand fully for a further six weeks why and how its elemental theme was playing out, as we'll see, it subsequently became clear during my own healing journey to Auschwitz.

* * * *

The healing of the abusive enmity between Russia and Poland offers a powerful example of how such reconciliation can become a key turning point in the psyche of nations. And whilst still early days, if its promise of rapprochement continues to be fulfilled, it can offer a role model for the forgiveness and release of other deeply felt traumas between and within countries.

CHAPTER 12
Old to New Covenant

'Never deprive someone of hope — it may be all they have.'
ANON.

In May 1940, the first transport of prisoners arrived at Auschwitz. So began the extermination that would eventually kill more people than the entire US and British losses of World War II. Not only vast numbers of Jewish people perished there, but also gypsies, homosexuals, the disabled, Poles, and Protestant and Catholic clergy. Auschwitz has thus become recognized around the world as the symbol of the death camps of the Nazi regime.

At the end of May 2010 a group representing the Path for HOPE journeyed to Poland. Our aim was to visit Auschwitz and its nearby death camp Birkenau in an attempt to understand the causes of the horrific events that had taken place there and heal the trauma. Not only were the victims traumatized, but the perpetrators were brutalized, and the witnesses left helpless or shamed by their experiences. Our intention was to be in service to all who had been through or associated in whatever capacity with the horror of Auschwitz and had experienced such camps and genocidal events throughout Europe.

As our pilgrimage unfolded, we found ourselves journeying back many millennia into the past. And we came to realize that the trauma was re-energized rather than excised when in 1948 the modern state of Israel arose from the sacrificial ashes of the Holocaust.

* * * *

In *The 13th Step* I describe the journey to Israel that we undertook in 2006, focused on healing the rift between the peoples of the three faiths of Judaism, Christianity and Islam.

The initial schism had begun with Abraham, revered as the patriarch of all three religions. As I wrote then,

> *We were here on a quest to understand the nature of the spiritual direction received by Abraham and the identity of the being that came to be known to the Hebrew people as YHWH, Jehovah, and to the followers of Islam as Allah.*
>
> *It is the essence of the guidance of YHWH that, as narrated in the Bible to Abraham and the bloodline of the patriarchs that followed him, continued to Moses and on to David, Solomon and the biblical prophets. In a very tangible form, it is embodied in the Jewish people and their perceived covenant with the land once known as Canaan and now as Israel.*
>
> *In service to healing the seemingly intransigent rift between the three faiths descended from Abraham and sowing the seeds of a yearned-for peace, we were here to ask the fundamental questions, 'Who is YHWH? And what does he want?'*

Biblical scholars place the time of Abraham as around 4,000 years ago. The deity appearing to him and referred to by the Bible as the Lord, El or, when later he appeared to Moses, as YHWH, is now generally considered as being synonymous with El Shaddai, the high god of the Canaanites. Indeed, the Bible refers to YHWH, or Yahweh, in ways that strongly suggest he was perceived as being a god amongst gods – but more powerful and able to prevail over the other deities.

The Covenant that Abraham and his descendants entered into was that by worshipping only Yahweh, who describes himself in the Bible as 'a jealous god,' the Hebrews would become his chosen people and the land of Canaan would be theirs. And so the Covenant is fundamentally about land – land promised by Yahweh. And in return there would be a 'sacrifice' to pay.

To the ancients, a sacrifice was not as narrowly defined as it is today and was often depicted instead as a gift to be given. From the beginning, when Yahweh instructed Abraham to sacrifice his younger son Isaac – or, in the Islamic tradition, his firstborn son Ishmael – the 'price' offered by all who enter the Judaic Covenant has been sacrifice, which in Latin literally means 'sacred gift'.

And this deal is re-entered into by every generation, irrespective of whether someone is born Jewish or converts to Judaism. So, the recurring notion of sacrifice within Jewish history and experience isn't just an aspect of that history, but remains its essential core.

The 'sacrificial' deaths of the indigenous Canaanites energized the Covenant and led to the establishment of ancient Israel.

In the centuries to come, on the altars of the First and Second Temples in Jerusalem, blood offerings sublimated the human sacrificial Covenant through the vast numbers of animals who perished there. But the fall of the First Temple in 586 BCE and the temporary exile of the Hebrews to Babylon and the eventual destruction of the Second Temple in 70 CE ended the sacrifice by proxy. The sacrificial price enacted by the Covenant once again became embodied by the Jewish people themselves, leading ultimately and tragically to the gates of Auschwitz and the other sacrificial altars of the Holocaust.

The nature of the Covenant is thus not redeemed through sacrifice, but for four millennia has been continually regenerated by it in each generation. So the tragedy of the Holocaust energized the Covenant, as did the founding of the modern state of Israel. And the sacrifices of both Israelis and Palestinians have continued to reinvigorate and thus perpetuate its energetic pattern.

Midway between the time of Abraham and today, the coming of Jesus offered the possibility of redeeming the Covenant of sacrifice through the fire of his Spirit and the Water of his unconditional love. But, having attuned to his Passion, I feel that whilst on the cross in mortal agony, his words 'Father, Father, why have you deserted me?' re-energized rather than released the old Covenant.

And whilst his example of divine love was seeded within our collective psyche, I sense that only now, after two more millennia, are we poised to emulate that love through re-membering and awakening the universal heart within us.

****

During our 2006 journey to Israel, I became ever more aware of the vital significance of what Judaic tradition calls the Shekinah, the divine feminine aspect of the presence of God. And as my understanding deepened, I began to perceive her crucial role in discovering answers to our fundamental questions 'Who is Yahweh? And what does he want?'

The presence of the Shekinah within the Holy of Holies of the Temple of Jerusalem was seen as essential to maintain its sanctity and that of Israel as a whole. But during the Jewish uprising of 66 CE against the Romans, according to mystical tradition the Shekinah left the Temple. Four years later, the Romans finally captured Jerusalem and utterly demolished the

Temple. Following further revolts, Jewish history claims that they eventually dispersed the Jewish people – a diaspora that lasted almost 2,000 years until the establishment of the modern state of Israel in 1948.

The diaspora mandated that to retain their sense of identity and their hoped-for reconciliation with the land of Israel, each Jewish person should continue to engage with the universal presence of the Shekinah. Specifically, she is invited each Sabbath to the inner heart of every Jewish family, wherever they may be.

But in 1948, the absence of the Jerusalem Temple meant that the Shekinah was not invited to return there, and so the presence of the divine feminine remained exiled from the heart of Israel.

Throughout our journey to Israel I'd attuned to the biblical Yahweh and come to realize that in contrast to the universality of the divine feminine, the primordial nature of his consciousness was territorial – profoundly rooted in the land covenanted to the Israelites.

But, standing on the Temple Mount of Jerusalem, I began to become aware of the yearning of a higher transcendent essence of Yahweh. I now understood that he was finally seeking release from the pattern of conflict and sacrifice, a resoulution that could only be made possible by the return of the Shekinah.

With her reconciling grace, I sensed Yahweh was ready not to re-establish the ancient Temple with its blood offerings and patriarchal authority, but a metaphysical temple denoting the birth of a new and transcendent Jerusalem. And not to continue the Old Covenant based on sacrifice but to enter into a New Covenant of Peace.

So our journey culminated at the Golden Gate of Jerusalem at dawn on 19 October 2006, when we invited the presence of the Shekinah to return to the Holy of Holies on the Temple Mount of Jerusalem.

As the Sun rose and an almost ethereal light flooded onto the Gate, I profoundly felt her return and sensed the opening of a portal of possibility – the manifestation of a holy city, not of one faith or faction but of the heritage and hope of all humanity.

But whilst Yahweh had indeed received what he wanted, it took longer for me to perceive that his consciousness was still too wounded to energetically consummate the sacred reunion. It took a further three and a half years before, at the gates to Auschwitz, it was revealed to me who Yahweh *really* was and how he could be healed.

****

Almost exactly 70 years before our visit, on 20 May 1940, the first concentration camp prisoners, 30 criminal offenders, had arrived at Auschwitz. Three weeks later, on 14 June, the first mass transportation brought 728 Polish political prisoners.

The European ghettos were emptied as Jewish men, women and children were packed into the appalling death trains that ran to the camps. Soon 2,000 people a day were being exterminated. In all, the slaughter killed more than a million Jews in the Auschwitz-Birkenau complex alone, as well as many non-Jews who were deemed unacceptable to the Nazi regime.

And Auschwitz was only one, albeit the most infamous, of many death camps. The twentieth century saw the brutal and ruthless extermination of millions of people in Europe, not only in the Nazi death camps, but in the Armenian massacre, the Russian gulags, the ethnic cleansing of Bosnia and more.

As we travelled the last few miles to Auschwitz, those two essential questions about Yahweh returned with an urgent force and suddenly I was immersed in a vision that brought clarity to both.

Many years before, when I'd first begun to communicate with the devic beings of Gaia, they had told me that as elemental beings in parallel with biological life, they too evolved. They taught me that each of them began their evolutionary path embodying the elemental essence of either Earth, Air, Water or Fire. Then there was a natural urge within their evolutionary process, as with our own spiritual journey, to ultimately become whole. And so they evolved by gradually incorporating additional elemental attributes until they embodied all four elements and advanced to the state of angelic consciousness.

As we neared the gates of Auschwitz, my vision was of Yahweh, many millennia ago, as an immature devic being who at that time had evolved to embody the archetypal elements of Earth and Air. The Earth aspect of his consciousness constrained him on a territorial basis – in the land that came to be known as Canaan – and the Air aspect of his being drew him to the high places of that land. Eventually, to fulfil his evolutionary urge, he would need to incorporate the elements of Water and Fire into his consciousness.

I don't know, and perhaps it doesn't matter, whose consciousness called to whom, but before the time of Abraham, the ancient Canaanites and the being we know as Yahweh made contact. The Canaanites began to construct altars in the high places and make sacrifices to the deity they called El Shaddai, the storm god, who, with perhaps a subconscious urge to evolve energetically, fed on the elemental aspects of the sacrifices, the Water – blood – of the victims and the Fire in which their bodies were consumed.

Rather like an adolescent human becoming addicted to junk food, Yahweh/El Shaddai gorged on the lower vibrational energies released by the sacrifices. Apparently nourished but ultimately left unsatisfied, he mistook the 'food' of sacrificial energy for food for his evolutionary path.

With the coming of Abraham, Yahweh offered the Covenant that has been enshrined in the Judaic tradition and embodied within the Judaic and our collective psyche for the last 4,000 years. Throughout, he has been seeking to become whole in

151

the only way he has come to know: through the Water/blood and Fire of sacrifice – a path that would lead to Auschwitz ... and beyond.

* * * *

Just before our trip, it had seemed that we might not be able to visit Auschwitz after all, when unprecedented major flooding caused it to close for the first time ever.

The nearby Sola river, into whose waters the ashes of many of those who had perished had been thrown, had washed into the camp. Even the name of the river was resonant with the soul-level healing of our intention. And I felt the Water and Fire symbolism of this unique event and sensed it beginning a deep cleansing process when I also read that Auschwitz had reopened on 20 May, the seventieth anniversary of the arrival of its first victims.

Still integrating my vision of Yahweh and the Covenant, I joined my friends and fellow pilgrims as we walked through Auschwitz's infamous gate, whose arch proclaims *Arbeit Macht Frei* – 'Work sets one free.'

In virtual silence, only speaking occasionally in hushed voices, individually and as a group we stopped a number of times as we followed our guide around the camp. In the spartan buildings that had been the dormitories for those prisoners whose age and fitness had offered them a brief but harsh reprieve from death, we were surrounded by their photographs and the almost unbearably poignant relics of their passing.

In front of an urn holding the ashes of myriad unknown victims, we stood together and in the universal heart offered unconditional love to all those who had experienced life and death here. Leaving a single white rose in commemoration, we moved on to room after room filled with heartbreaking exhibits of baby clothes, shoes and heaps of spectacles. An entire side of one large room was heaped with women's hair, long tresses shaved from the heads of those who were killed. And yet these remains were only a fraction of the intimately personal plunder that had been stolen from the victims of this death camp on an industrial scale.

It is virtually impossible for me to express in writing the impact of Auschwitz. Perhaps only being in the midst of the heartbreaking details of these lost lives can really bring home the reality of what went on – not only here but in many other death camps and sites of genocide.

In attuning in the universal heart, we unconditionally offered compassion for everyone caught up in such experiences: victims, perpetrators and witnesses, all needing forgiveness and release for healing to happen.

Finally, as we stood only feet away from some of the ovens that had cremated the remains of thousands of people, I understand that to complete the healing Yahweh too would need to be included.

As the full realization hit me, we came together and again in the universal heart opened ourselves to the unconditional love of Spirit, understanding that this was the divine essence of Water and Fire that needed to flow through Yahweh for him to realize the wholeness of his angelic transcendental self.

As a shift of energy surged through us and I remembered that we were here on the Jewish Sabbath, I wholeheartedly thanked the Shekinah, whose guidance had enabled us to undertake our healing work.

* * * *

The following day we visited the monastery of Jasna Góra, the third largest Christian pilgrimage shrine in Europe, which contains one of the world's greatest spiritual icons, the painting of the Black Madonna.

During our journey, as we'd continued to attune with the Shekinah, we had come to perceive a primordial aspect of the divine feminine – a fundamental aspect that has been denied and marginalized. Her presence, whether as the talmudic Lilith, the biblical Mary Magdalene or as Asherah, Yahweh's purported consort expressed for instance on an eighth century ceramic inscription found in the Sinai desert, is symbolically enshrined in the image of the Black Madonna and was now also calling to be fully acknowledged and reconciled within our collective psyche.

As we, with hundreds of other pilgrims, viewed her image, we attuned again in the universal heart and, at the altar of the church, sensed the presence of Yahweh, now complete, and here to finally reunite with his divine feminine consort in all her glorious aspects.

Finally, our journey took us to the powerful energy vortex of Wawel Hill at the heart of Krakow to complete our service of healing. From this nexus point of the energies of Gaia, we again invited the healed essence of Yahweh and of Shekinah to fully come together. And as we did, the third, child, aspect of the divine trinity whose creative essence is manifested by the sacred reunion of masculine and feminine within us all arose within the unconditional love in the universal heart of our combined intention and radiated outwards to Jerusalem and around the world.

****

The completion of our healing work in Poland coincided with the attack by the Israeli navy on an aid flotilla heading for Gaza. Given the work we had undertaken to reconcile the highest essence of Water and Fire in Yahweh's nature, did the firing on the *Mavi Marmara* ship and the death of nine flotilla activists mark the final act of sacrifice and the turning point towards a new Covenant of Peace?

We hoped and prayed so.

But inwardly I wondered, whilst taking the saga onto its next chapter and hopefully towards a final resoulution of the toxic situation in the Middle East, whether things would become worse before the much-needed breakthrough.

CHAPTER 13
Atonement to At-One-Ment

'When the world says, "Give up," hope whispers, "Try again."'
ANON.

The healing work we'd been in service to in Poland had revealed that the millennia-long pattern of sacrifice at the core of the Old Covenant was not and never had been necessary. It is now time to release it from our communal consciousness and enter into a New Covenant – of Peace.

As the Old Covenant of sacrifice for land is re-energized in every Jewish generation and thus throughout our collective psyche, it remains for the living to complete the repudiation of the ancient Covenant that I feel Yahweh himself now no longer sustains.

Each year, dating back to the time of Moses, Yom Kippur, the Jewish Day of Atonement, has marked the absolution of sins and the beginning of a new year. I feel this is an energetically perfect moment to revoke the Old Covenant and, through the power of unconditional love, confirm a New Covenant and the transformation of atonement to at-one-ment.

The tortured recent history of Israel has, however, made the possibility of peace seem further away than ever. So let's begin by reviewing that history to see how the unsustainable patterns of fear-based behaviour have played out to further discern how they may be resoulved.

* * * *

In the late nineteenth century in Europe a political movement arose to further the aim of establishing a Jewish homeland, the re-creation of the biblical Zion, in the country that was then called Palestine, and Jewish migrants began to settle there.

During World War I, the British government issued a formal declaration stating that Britain viewed such a proposal favourably. But, to protect both Jews and the Arab inhabitants of Palestine, it also stated: 'It being clearly understood that nothing shall be done which may prejudice the civil and religious rights of existing non-Jewish communities in Palestine, or the rights and political status enjoyed by Jews in any other country.'

Whilst Jews then helped the British to conquer Palestine, the Arabs resisted until, in 1922, the League of Nations, the forerunner of the United Nations, gave Britain a mandate over the then predominantly Arab and Muslim nation on similar terms to its earlier declaration.

Between the two world wars a massive influx of Jewish people into Palestine, many escaping discrimination, especially the rise of Nazi Germany in the 1930s, caused an Arab revolt. But regardless, by the end of World War II, Jews comprised a third of the total population of Palestine.

After 1945, as more and more Jews sought to emigrate to Palestine, Britain and the Jewish community were in armed conflict. And in 1947 Britain withdrew, stating that it was unable to mediate a solution that was acceptable to both Arabs and Jews.

In November the newly created United Nations sought to partition Palestine, create a two-state solution and designate Jerusalem an international city administered by the UN.

Whilst the Jewish community accepted the plan, the Arabs rejected it. After initial armed skirmishes, the Jews gained the upper hand, and some quarter of a million Palestinian Arabs who had lived on the land for many generations fled. And on 14

May 1948, the Jews unilaterally proclaimed the independent state of Israel.

* * * *

Whilst some astrologers time the birth of the modern state of Israel to its Unilateral Declaration of Independence on the afternoon of 14 May 1948 and locate it where that declaration took place, in Tel Aviv, I consider a more energetically appropriate chart to be based on when the declaration came into effect – at sunset on the same day, which occurred at 7.27 p.m. – and located in the country's hugely symbolic capital city of Jerusalem.

This birth chart is especially individualistic, as the Sun, Moon and the inner planets, Mercury, Venus and Mars, which affect us on personal levels, are powerfully aspected.

The Sun in Taurus denotes reliability, but also a strong need for security and the tendency to be stubborn. The Moon in Leo embodies an emotional need for praise and attention, which under stress can become arrogance. Mercury in Gemini reveals a love of information and discussion, Venus in Cancer an emphasis on strong emotional bonds with the family and perceived 'tribe,' and Mars in Leo confidence, dynamism and creativity, but again with the possibility of arrogance.

Jupiter in Sagittarius emphasizes Israel's fundamental philosophical and religious aspects, whilst Saturn in Leo energizes working for recognition, power and success.

Uranus in Gemini reflects Israel's ability for original thinking and innovation, whilst Neptune in Libra embodies concerns with social justice, but sometimes confusion over what designates appropriate relationships.

And Pluto in Leo denotes leadership able to use power, but in polarized ways that are both positive and negative.

But it is Chiron's position in Scorpio in the twelfth house that reveals in the chart the intensity of Israel's pre-birth pain and its ongoing emotional suffering from deep wounds and sometimes almost overwhelming anguish. And the position of the North Node in the chart shows Israel's higher purpose of transcending its tendency to lash out at others due to the trauma of its past.

The archetypal pattern of rejection which generations of Jewish people have embodied adds to the intensity of this extraordinary chart.

And, as in the case of an individual, such past pain can either continue to be played out, to the detriment of both Israel and those, especially the Palestinians, who in turn the Israelis have rejected, or it can be healed.

* * * *

After the state of Israel was proclaimed, there was another year of fighting, during which the Arabs of Egypt, Syria, Lebanon and Iraq went to the aid of the Palestinians and nearly a further three-quarters of a million Palestinians left the country. Then a ceasefire and temporary borders were declared.

Over the following years, positions hardened on both Arab and Israeli sides and in 1967 skirmishes erupted into a full pre-emptive strike by Israel which led to it occupying the West Bank, Gaza, the Sinai Peninsula and the Golan Heights and expanding its territory into East Jerusalem.

In 1977, when Menachim Begin was appointed Prime Minister of Israel, there was a new attempt at reaching a peaceful settlement. Egyptian President Anwar Sadat was the first Arab head of state to speak before the Knesset, the Israeli parliament, and to recognize Israel as a state. And, brokered by the USA, the Camp David Accords and a peace treaty where Israel agreed to enter negotiations for Palestinian autonomy in the West Bank and Gaza and to withdraw from Sinai boded well. But the assassination of Sadat by a nationalist Arab in 1981 and Begin's encouragement of Jewish settlements in the West Bank and Gaza halted the peace process.

In 1993, when Yitzhak Rabin became prime minister on a campaigning promise to promote compromise, Israel and the Palestinians signed the Oslo Accords, whereby the Palestinians were allowed to partially self-govern in return for a pledge to end terrorism and recognize Israel's right to exist.

But over the following years, Arab support for the Accords was undermined by the expansion of Israeli settlements, the imposition of increasing numbers of checkpoints and the worsening of economic and social conditions. Israeli support also waned as the people were attacked by increasing numbers of suicide bombers frustrated and radicalized by the lack of progress and hope. In 1995 Rabin was assassinated by an ultra right-wing Jew.

The last 15 years have witnessed retrenchment on both sides. The Israelis unilaterally withdrew from Gaza in 2005. But with right-wing political will strengthened by a massive influx of ultra-conservative Russian Jews and the support of the political right wing in the USA, they have massively expanded settlements on disputed territory, built an enormous defensive wall that crosses and separates Palestinian land and more recently enacted discriminatory policies against their own Israeli-Arab citizens.

In Palestine, the rise of the Hamas Islamist faction within Palestinian politics has increased the level of violent rocket attacks from Gaza into southern Israel and led to the official Palestinian acknowledgement of Israel's right to exist being repudiated by their faction. Hamas gaining power in Gaza in 2007 led to an ongoing Israeli blockade and, despite an ostensible ceasefire, to a massively asymmetric attack by the Israeli military, beginning in late December 2008. Operation Cast Lead lasted for three weeks and, with nowhere to flee, according to UN estimates some 1,400 Palestinians were killed, a figure which included hundreds of women and children.

The continual and ultimately pointless tit-for-tat ebb and flow of mutual violence continues to scar the psyche of both peoples. A controversial UN report on Cast Lead in 2009, headed by Justice Richard Goldstone, concluded that war crimes and possibly crimes against humanity had been perpetuated by both sides, although in April 2011 he acknowledged that the Israelis hadn't intentionally targeted civilians.

It wasn't in his brief, but his conclusion could have applied in principle to the last 60 years of the history of the Holy Land.

* * * *

By the time of our visit to Poland in May 2010, a fragile ceasefire was holding between the Israelis and the Palestinians. But as we left Poland after our healing work at Auschwitz, the shocking news of the lethal Israeli attack on the *Mavi Marmara* was unfolding.

Before we go on to see what effects the sacrifice of the activists has had on the peace process, let's consider the fundamental question of whom the land really belongs to.

The issues between Israel and Palestine since 1948 look complicated and are often described as being so. But actually I don't believe the situation is complex.

Whilst difficult to resoulve, the basic issues are simple: the determination of borders and the assurance of security, the right of return for Palestinian refugees and the status of Jerusalem. These all revolve around whose land it really is. The Israelis say the land is theirs by right of their ancient Jewish lineage. The Palestinians argue that they've been on the land since time immemorial. So who's right? And will a clearer understanding of the heritage of both help the cause of peace?

* * * *

Perhaps this truer perspective may be found in a recent book by Israeli historian Shlomo Sand, based at Tel Aviv University. His *The Invention of the Jewish People* goes back to the turmoil of 2,000 years ago when the Roman Empire forcibly suppressed the Jewish people, destroyed the Jerusalem Temple and, according to Jewish history, exiled the people from their land. Sand researched the evidence for this communal exile.

What he found was that elsewhere throughout their huge empire, the Romans had neither shown the inclination nor had the means to deport whole populations. And to Sand's amazement, he could discover no evidence that they uniquely exiled the Jews exists.

According to Sand and others such as writer Arthur Koestler, the depiction of the Jews as a wandering nation of exiles is essentially a national mythology that was developed some time in the nineteenth century by intellectuals of Jewish origin in Europe, primarily in response to the emergence of ethnically based nationalism and continuing anti-semitism, especially in Russia. Influenced by the growing folk character of the then increasing German nationalism, a similar folk history was effectively invented, Sand maintains, for the emerging Zionist Jewish agenda.

So if that was the case, where does Sand consider the Jewish people derive from?

In late antiquity conversion to Judaism was widespread. So for Sand, while his views are controversial, most of the ancestors of the world's current Jews are primarily converts of the various peoples around the Mediterranean and neighbouring areas, including the Ashkenazi Jews of eastern Europe, who are primarily descended from the Khazar folk of far eastern Europe who converted to Judaism in the eighth century CE.

If Sand's extensive research and conclusions are correct, as having reviewed it I believe they predominantly are, then who are the descendants of the biblical kingdom of Judah that became the state of Israel?

In an interview with the Israeli newspaper *Haaretz* in 2008, Sand answered that question when he stated:

No population remains pure over a period of thousands
of years. But the chances that the Palestinians

are descendants of the ancient Judaic people are
much greater than the chances that you or I are its
descendants. The first Zionists, up to the Arab Revolt
(1936–9), knew that there had been no exiling and that
Palestinians were descended from the inhabitants of the
land. They knew that farmers don't leave until they are
expelled. Even Yitzhak Ben-Zvi, the second President of
the State of Israel, wrote in 1929 that, 'the vast majority
of the peasant farmers do not have their origins in the
Arab conquerors, but rather, before then, in the Jewish
farmers who were numerous and a majority in the
building of the land.'

He added that since the great expansion of Jewish immigrants to Israel following World War II and the perceived need to build a nation, such truths had been progressively suppressed. Even raising the possibility had brought forth accusations of anti-Semitism.

Sand reiterates the view of historians of the nineteenth and early twentieth centuries that the most important addition to the current world Jewish population was due to the conversion of the entire kingdom of Khazaria, which in the eighth century, caught between Christian and Muslim empires to their west and east, chose to remain neutral by converting *en masse* to Judaism. Ultimately, after the downfall of Khazaria, the Jewish converts headed west and finally met up with Slavic Jews who'd been pushed eastwards. Together they formed the basis of the Ashkenazi Jewish communities of eastern Europe and indeed the great majority of Jews who perished in the Holocaust.

When Sand was asked why he believed the issue of the Khazars was so frightening, he replied, 'It is clear that the fear is of an undermining of the historic right to the land. The revelation that the Jews are not from Judea would ostensibly knock the legitimacy for our being here out from under us.'

While I don't subscribe at all to the delegitimacy of modern Israel and regard it as the historical home of the Jewish culture, I do believe that knowing the truth of the origins of its current population is an important part of the healing of this troubled land.

* * * *

But ironically it wasn't so much the Jewish people who began what's now emerging to be the myth of the Jewish exile but the early Christians, beginning with Saint Paul.

Paul grew up in the town of Tarsus in what's now south-central Turkey. As an adult, in the early years after the death of Jesus, following his declaration of a revelation of Jesus on the road to Damascus, he converted to Christianity.

But Paul's vision of Christianity was very unlike the Judaic Christianity that had continued through Jesus' family and disciples in the years following his death. And it was Paul, with his willingness to convert non-Jews whose cultures resonated more with his own vision, who in the coming years gained the upper hand and created the basis of what would become Catholic Christianity.

There are a number of crucial aspects to Paul's teachings that overtook the early Judaic-Christian faith and reformatted it to comply with his views.

First, growing up in Tarsus, Paul would have been surrounded by the followers of the cult of Attis, a religion whose god died under a tree each year at the March equinox and whose resurrection three days later was celebrated with a meal of bread and wine.

A number of biblical scholars have questioned the chronology of the Passion of Jesus as depicted in the gospels, which are deemed to have been written later than Paul's early writings and which therefore may have incorporated his view of Jesus' Passion as reflecting that of Attis.

The gospels tell of Jesus' entry into Jerusalem accompanied by shouts of 'Hosanna!' and the laying of palm fronds. Both are associated with the harvest festival of the Jewish Feast of Tabernacles, a festival that marks the Jewish New Year and follows the Day of Atonement – timing that would have made perfect sense for a Jewish teacher such as Jesus and his message of redemption and celebration of the coming of a new era.

However, the Day of Atonement and Feast of Tabernacles take place in the autumn, when palm fronds grow their leaves, not in spring, where Pauline Christianity has the Passion, a time which instead marks the death and resurrection of Attis.

Paul also essentially created the communion ritual of the bread and wine being transfigured into the body and blood of Jesus and emphasized the sacrificial nature of Jesus' mission, all again resonating with the cult of Attis he'd grown up with and now accreted onto the story and mission of Jesus.

Crucially, too, it was Paul who in his first letter to the Thessalonian congregation, deemed to be the oldest known Christian document, also raised the spectre of the Jewish people being responsible for Jesus' murder. This would, in the centuries to come, drive increasing levels of anti-Semitism and the casting out of the Jews throughout the Christian world.

On a separate point, it was also Paul who effectively peripheralized women in the emerging Church.

Intriguingly, there may be an underlying personal reason behind Paul's anti-Jewishness and misogyny, fragmented echoes of which have survived in the scarce accounts of the contemporary Ebionites, Jewish-Christians who may well have had the actual family of Jesus at their core.

Many scholars consider the leader of the Ebionites to have been James the Just, the brother of Jesus, rather than the apostle Peter. Rejecting Paul as abandoning true Christianity for his own version, they were subsequently condemned as heretics and persecuted by both Paul's and Peter's followers.

The early Church leader Epiphanius of Salamis relates, in his book *Against Heresies*, that some Ebionites viewed Paul as a gentile who had initially converted to Judaism in order to marry the daughter of a high priest of Israel. When she rejected him he abandoned the religion 'in a rage' and went on to convert to the version of Christianity ostensibly revealed to him by Jesus in a vision.

It may appear to be merely 2,000-year-old gossip. But when I read it, a shiver ran up my spine. Not only did it help to explain Paul's accretion of the cult of Attis into his version of Christianity, but was his rejection by a Jewish woman the seed-point that, thanks to Paul's intensely driven personality, created the wave of rejection of Jews and women that has flowed through Christianity and tainted the western worldview ever since? And that in turn gave rise to the myth of the Jews being communally exiled for their crime of deicide – a collective exile that, as Sand maintains, never occurred.

* * * *

As with personal healing, moving beyond denial and accepting the truth is a crucial first step in the healing process for nations. Sand's view is that the Israelis need to acknowledge the truth of their heritage and in the light of that to include all their people in an egalitarian and truly democratic state. And he recognizes that a two-state solution for Israelis and Palestinians is now the only viable way forward.

Also, as for any process of reconciliation, being willing to accept the other and hear their voice with openness, honesty and compassion is key to any resoulution.

The status quo in both Israel and Palestine is unsustainable and, I believe, close to some kind of breakdown or breakthrough. Having been there myself and stayed in both Jewish areas and on the West Bank, I have seen on a day-to-day basis how the current situation ultimately serves no one.

Israel's current right-wing government is embedding itself in conservatism. The view that anyone critical of Israeli policy is anti-Semitic is still stifling the open debate that needs to take place. Both Israelis and Palestinians are also in denial and ignorant of each other's recent traumatic history. Israeli schools and media generally don't educate their people about the *Naqba*, the Catastrophe, the disastrous day, as seen from the Palestinian perspective, when Israel became a state in 1948 and the vast majority of their people lost their homes and livelihoods. And Palestinian schools and media don't explain the horrific genocidal events of the Holocaust that caused the Jewish people to yearn for a state of their own.

Whilst the fear-based behaviour of many continues to obstruct the way forward, there are other voices within both communities that are beginning to speak more loudly for peace. For them to prevail, the main barriers to peace must be addressed, and viable, just and sustainable solutions agreed and implemented.

In March 2009 I led a small group on a journey throughout Israel and the West Bank and then Jordan. During our visit to the Mount of Beatitudes, where tradition maintains that Jesus gave the Sermon on the Mount, we spoke his words together as we overlooked the Sea of Galilee. In the bright sunlight, as I gazed over the calm waters beneath us, his benediction 'Blessed be the peacemakers, for they will be called the children of God' felt especially poignant.

It's surely now time for the peacemakers rather than the warmongers to be heard.

* * * *

I don't know how long it will take for the trauma embedded in the Jewish and Palestinian brotherly psyche to run its course, but ultimately if there is to be a sustainable peace, the terms –

most of which have been agreed in principle – will essentially need to be as follows:

- The Palestinian faction Hamas acknowledges Israel's right to exist and renounces all violence.

- There is a sustainable reconciliation between the Hamas and Fatah factions of the Palestinian leadership to enable the appointment of a single unity government able to speak and negotiate for all Palestinians.

- A Palestinian state is formally set up in both the West Bank and Gaza and significant international investment provided to develop its infrastructure and economy.

- The border between Israel and Palestine is that established by the 1967 war, with land swaps and possibly financial compensation for the realities on the ground of Israeli settlements built beyond that border.

- Israel stops settlement construction, withdraws from all settlements that even their own legal system considers illegal and pays for the relocation of their people to within the 1967 border.

- Israel withdraws fully from the West Bank and Gaza and completely lifts the blockade of Gaza.

- To ensure Israeli security, a UN force is based in both the West Bank and in Gaza. After a prescribed period, the Israelis dismantle the Barrier Wall and return any separated land to Palestinian control.

- Instead of the infeasibility of allowing a right of return to Palestinian refugees, a comprehensive compensation package is agreed and funded by the international community.

- The 1947 suggestion by the UN that the Old City of Jerusalem becomes an internationally administered city of peace is implemented. Its administration includes representatives of the three faiths of Judaism, Christianity and Islam for whom the city is holy.

- All prisoners held by both sides are either tried for their alleged crimes in an international court or released.

- A bilateral peace and reconciliation committee is set up to encourage cross-border education, co-operation and trade.

Compared to the geopolitical complexities that have needed to be resolved following other major conflicts, these generally agreed solutions are actually relatively straightforward.

What they do fundamentally require, though, is the authentic intention and will for peace from both sides. At the time of writing, whilst it appears to me that at least the Palestinian Authority leaders President Mahmoud Abbas and Prime Minister Salam Fayyad are genuinely willing to make the compromises necessary, neither the Hamas leaders in Gaza nor I feel the Israeli leadership are yet ready to lead their respective people down the real path to peace.

In March 2009 I visited the Temple Mount in Jerusalem once more and as the group I was leading attuned to the possibility of peace we heard an inner voice that foresaw that 'Resolution will come when the men of war become the men of peace.'

Given that Binyamin Netanyahu is prime minister of Israel at this crucial moment and that he describes himself as a soldier first and a politician second, what does this portend for the possibility of peace?

And yet, despite the current uneasy hiatus, the cosmic influences of the Shift are flowing onwards. Whilst hope seems far away, as I've seen many times in apparently intractable situations, the darkest hour really is before the dawn of a new day.

* * * *

At Auschwitz I first sensed that the annual Day of Atonement was the energetic nexus of the Jewish year that resonated most powerfully with the possibility of peace. And a few months later, the 2010 Day of Atonement was to take place on 18 September.

That year the dates of the Jewish New Year leading up to the Day of Atonement and the completion of Ramadan, the holy month of Islam concluding with the Festival of Eid, wonderfully coincided.

The last ten days of Islamic Ramadan and the first ten days of the Jewish New Year are especially significant. Both traditions view these times as offering opportunities to engage with the divine at a deeper level, to gain forgiveness for past transgressions and to resolve that the coming year will be better than the last.

For Muslims, it is these ten days that mark the revelation of the Quran to the Prophet Mohammed. And the Night of Destiny (during which, four years earlier we had held vigil and recalled the divine feminine presence of the Shekinah through the Golden Gate of Jerusalem) takes place on the seventh of the ten days, when their tradition says that the gates of heaven are open to prayers and resolutions.

For Jews, Rosh Hashanah, the new year festival, ushers in ten days of repentance and intentions for the coming year leading up to the Day of Atonement when the past is released and the future covenant is sealed.

In 2010, after a hiatus of nearly two years, the timeline of new peace talks unfolded in energetic resonance with the harmony of the Jewish and Islamic festivals. Talks resumed on 1 and 2 September in Washington, Rosh Hashanah and Eid took place on 9 and 10 September, and then further talks were held on 14 September in Egypt and 15 September in Jerusalem before the Day of Atonement on 18 September.

In Jewish tradition the Day of Atonement is shortly followed by a seven-day period of rejoicing. In 2010 this began on 23 September, the autumn equinox – a moment of balance, of equal day and night, a tipping point in the cosmic cycle of the year.

During the negotiations the astrological influences were powerful, with Pluto, the planet of transformation, going direct on 14 September, and Venus, the planet of real-ationship, going retrograde and thus expressing her energies on an inner level from 8 October to 18 November in the intense waters of Scorpio.

To have a sense of Netanyahu's views and the possibilities for his decisions during the negotiation process, I looked into his life, especially the crucial years during the previous Venus retrograde cycles of November 2002 and November 1994.

By late 1993 the Oslo Peace Accords had been brokered in Norway. Throughout 1994 Netanyahu led militant opposition to the Accords, effectively blocking their acceptance within Israel. But in an interview with Neill Lochery, a reporter with the *Middle East Quarterly*, on 8 November of that year, Dan Meridor, a close political colleague of Netanyahu, told the journal that some of his colleagues were privately reconciled to at least some of the Accords' requirements and predicted that Netanyahu would change his position if a majority of Israelis were in favour.

In November 2002, after having been prime minister from 1996 to 1999 and then spending a period away from politics, Netanyahu re-entered the Israeli government as foreign minister. He was already, as was obvious from an interview he gave to Caroline Glick of the *Jerusalem Post* on 7 November 2002, seeing himself as a leadership candidate once again. And in that interview, again despite his public stance, he stated that as prime minister, he would 'work for solutions.'

So both prior Venus retrogrades in Scorpio were, it seems, points when Netanyahu was at least contemplating how to follow the path towards peace. But his innate conservatism would only lead him to respond to what he perceived as a majority view in Israel rather than attempt to change hearts and minds.

During the initially promising beginning of the September 2010 talks when Pluto moved direct, it seemed Netanyahu was willing to be a real partner for peace. But finally there was a retreat not only of Netanyahu but also of the coalition Israeli government into the more right-wing majority position of intransigence.

Whilst the outcome appeared to be yet another disappointment, the wheels of destiny continue to turn.

Whether the ultimate outcome is further conflict or a longed-for peace depends on the willingness of both Israelis and Palestinians to see the bigger picture and resoulve the old pattern of tit-for-tat sacrifice that serves neither.

* * * *

Energetically, the sacrificial covenant that continues to play out in the current generations of Israelis and Palestinians has two predominant energetic nexus points.

The first is the Well of Souls, the natural cavern beneath the Dome of the Rock on the Temple Mount in Jerusalem where traditionally Abraham prepared to sacrifice his son, who in the Jewish tradition is his younger boy, Isaac, but in the Muslim tradition is his elder, Ishmael.

The second is at a place called Sechem in the Bible, which is now the modern-day town of Nablus in the West Bank. Here the Bible states that Abraham built an altar to Yahweh and confirmed the Covenant. Following the return from Egypt led by Moses, Sechem was the first capital of Israel. And here, led by Joshua, the Israelites reconfirmed their oath of Covenant. When the city was later destroyed in internal conflict, the victors sacrificed the inhabitants by burning the temple into which they'd fled.

Jewish law maintains that for a Covenant to be revoked, those who originally agreed to it must be present. So both within the Well of Souls and at Sechem the spirits of those who entered into the Covenant can be energetically called to stand alongside the living to witness and finally release the sacrificial pattern that has limited our collective psyche for so long.

I hope and pray that the Day of Atonement that begins at sunset on 7 October 2011 ushers in such a release.

* * * *

Lasting peace in the Middle East, however, requires a resoulution of old conflicts on a wider regional basis.

Israel's return of the Golan Heights to Syria is looking increasingly necessary as the first step. In September 2010, for the first time that I was aware of, the Israeli army itself stated its support for such a development.

But as yet the Israeli government has refused to open negotiations.

* * * *

Throughout the region, too, states are increasingly worried by Iran and its nuclear aspirations.

Iran and its trenchant political leaders do need to be taken very seriously. Sometimes the sheer scale of the country is unappreciated. Its landmass is equal to that of Iraq and Afghanistan combined, and its population is 74 million. Its huge cadre of Revolutionary Guards now forms a vast military and industrial and commercial organization. And since it became an Islamic republic in 1979, it has refused to accept the existence of Israel and actively supported its proxies Hezbollah and Hamas in their attempts to overthrow the Israeli regime.

Ironically, the existential threat that the Israelis believe Iran currently poses to them is directly opposite to the countries' historical real-ationship.

In the seventh century BCE, the Iranians, or Persians as they were then known, embraced the new religion of Zoroastrianism, whose followers believe in a dualistic universe of good and evil and see history as an epic conflict between these forces with a final battle at the end of time to decide which will ultimately rule.

Around a century later, the Persian king, Cyrus the Great, believed that Persia would bring about the triumph of good in the final battle by conquering all peoples and creating an empire in which it would prevail. Maintaining that he was prompted by Yahweh to restore the Temple in Jerusalem, which had been destroyed by the Babylonian King Nebuchadnezzar some years before, he ordered the Jews to be freed from their exile in Babylon. And to show his support further, he returned the sacred vessels which had been taken from the Temple and gave the released Jews a large amount of money to buy building materials.

Zoroastrianism remains within the Iranian psyche despite the later conversion of the nation to Islam and there is still an underlying tendency in Iranians to perceive the world in profoundly polarized terms of light and shadow, right and wrong, good and evil.

Historically, that trait has caused the Iranians, as Herodotus, the ancient Greek known as the 'father of history', wrote, to 'value the truth above all things'. So loving of the truth were they that to tell a lie was a capital offence. However, with the introduction of the Islamic Shia tradition of *taqiyah*, where it is permissible to mislead adversaries – in bald terms, to lie – in hostile environments to serve the 'higher' truth and ensure one's survival, their ancient trait has become distorted and this makes it difficult for countries whose cultures differ from Iran's current Islamic ideology to find common ground with them.

The Islamic Revolution of 1979 was a key rebirthing moment in the long history of Iran. When the astrological chart for 1 April, the moment when its leader Ayatollah Khomeini announced the new Islamic Republican structure, is drawn up, it is telling in the insights it offers into the evolving psyche of the country.

The Sun in Aries stresses how Iran's perception of its identity is taken personally by its people. And with both Mars and Uranus in Leo it yearns for a leadership role that is associated with its Islamic revolutionary fervour

The placement of Pluto in Gemini in the tenth house also energizes in a transformational and intense way how it has imposed its strict Islamic philosophy throughout its own society. But when taken together with the Leo energies of Mars and Uranus it also reveals its ongoing intention to do so beyond its own borders – an ambition that is sadly served by the current inability to achieve peace between Israel and Palestine.

Respect and pride, however, continue to be very important to the Iranian psyche. And whilst the theocrats of Iran reject the modern capitalist world, in some way they yet feel that their legitimacy cannot be ensured without the acceptance of that world.

****

For peace to be achieved, resoulution of regional tensions is needed. However, I continue to stress that the crisis in the Middle East is *not* complex – that has just been a perennial excuse for not sorting it out. Whilst it *is* difficult, the path to peace is clear.

We've seen the potency of Israel's birth chart. But, just as for individuals, it's often those nations who have suffered the most who can be the catalysts for not only their own healing but also the healing of others.

One key contributor to Israel's current paranoia is the influx of Russian Jews following the end of the Soviet era. The largest number now live in Israel not Russia and some 16 per cent of Israelis speak Russian. Bringing their traumatic experience of abusive anti-Semitism and a deep-felt Russian trait of fearing the 'other', they are the most right-wing sector of Israeli society and government and vehemently opposed to a two-state solution.

If Israel can transcend its current fear-based paranoia and denial and not only recognize the pain held within its psyche but also how that pain has caused it to lash out and reject opportunities for real peace, it can transform its own future and that of its brother and sister Palestinians and truly become a seed-point of our collective healing.

* * * *

I do believe something significant did change at the time of our healing work in Poland and the attack on the *Mavi Marmara*. For previously hidden prejudiced views, racist attitudes, extreme biases and selfish and dishonest positions have undeniably begun to come out into the open since that time.

This may make the outlook seem darker. But beneath the surface, a backlash of decency is building up. And on the cold and miserable Saturday night of 22 January 2011, at least 10,000 Israelis showed up in Tel Aviv to march for democracy, social justice and peace with the Palestinians.

That night Bradley Burston, the senior editor of the Israeli newspaper *Haaretz*, 'saw something crucial, shattering, game-changing happening.' And he was overcome by a sudden sense of hope.

CHAPTER 14
The Power of One

'He who has health has hope;
and he who has hope has everything.'
Arabian proverb

Twenty-six-year-old Tunisian Mohamed Bouazizi was a fruit and vegetable seller and the sole income-earner in his extended family of eight people.

On 17 December 2010, local police confiscated his allegedly unlicensed cart and all its produce. This had happened before, but this time when Mohamed tried to pay the fine – the equivalent of a day's wage – he was reportedly assaulted and insulted. And when he subsequently tried to complain to local officials at their headquarters, they refused to see him.

In an act of desperation and hopelessness, Mohamed returned to the authorities' headquarters and, dousing his body in inflammable liquid, set fire to himself.

Public outrage, already simmering due to rising prices, high levels of unemployment and lack of basic freedoms, broke out in peaceful protests in support of Mohamed and then continued to grow despite authoritarian reaction.

Unrest escalated sharply in what has been described as the first WikiLeaks revolution as Tunisia was further shocked by the release of previously secret information revealing the depths of governmental corruption.

On 4 January 2011, Mohamed passed away as a result of his terrible burns.

On the 14 January, after 23 years of despotic rule, President Zine El Abindine Ben Ali was deposed and fled the country. And an interim government began the process of reformation that is still unfolding.

Mohamed Bouazizi's self-sacrifice – again symbolically by Fire – in an act of desperate hopelessness has dramatically lit the fire of hope for others.

* * * *

Seeing the events erupting in Tunisia emboldened the people of Egypt, who had been living under the authoritarian and brutal regime of President Hosni Mubarak for the last 30 years. Beginning on 25 January, a popular uprising that grew to include millions of people from all walks of life engaged in peaceful but adamant protest that demanded the end of his regime.

The symbolic heart of the peaceful revolution was Tahrir Square in the centre of Cairo where many thousands of protesters gathered. After vicious assaults by Mubarak loyalists, the army refused to fire on its own citizens and sided with the people against Mubarak, who eventually stood down on 11 February.

Despite widespread efforts by both the Tunisian and Egyptian regimes to shut down internet communications, many of the protests were organized via social networking sites.

After a gap of three years, I had been in Egypt in early November 2010 with a European and American group and again in early January 2011 with a group from Japan.

For months before the two visits I'd been feeling strongly that these would be the last during which I would lead a group to the wonderful country that is often referred to as a Temple of the Cosmos for its ancient insights into our true spiritual nature.

I've been guided by Thoth, the ancient Egyptian wisdom-bringer, since I was four years old. And for very many years I've worked energetically with and been mentored by the great archetypal beings, or *Neterw*, who are the deities of the ancient Egyptians and whose presence still pervades the monuments and temples of this sacred land.

Over many years, the guidance of a pantheon of *Neterw* has been key to my understanding of the 8th chakra of the universal heart, our collective Shift of consciousness and our cosmic destiny. This pantheon is comprised of *Osiris*, guide of initiatory intention, inner tuition and integration, *Isis*, embodying the essence of nurturing, unconditional love, *Horus*, whose far-sighted and clear inner and outer vision and energies were believed to flow through the high-adept pharaohs, *Hathor* and *Sekhmet*, who combine spiritual purpose with creative abundance, *Nepthys*, the sister of Isis, who embodies inner reflection and gnosis, *Anubis*, who offers exploratory openness and dedication, and *Maat*, the cosmic principle of harmony and balance, who is at the heart of the ancient teachings of ancient Egypt.

Arriving in Egypt for the November visit, I was shocked and saddened to realize that the hard-line regime of Hosni Mubarak was now causing unprecedented difficulties for both Egyptians and visitors. My friends and hosts at Guardian Travel made wonderful efforts to alleviate its effects, but despite this, for the first time in some 15 years of undertaking spiritual journeys here, we were prevented from meditating in the temples, however quietly and unobtrusively. And even though we had paid an enormous sum for the privilege of private access to the Great Pyramid – a highlight of every trip – we were disturbed in a way I'd never encountered before by pyramid guards clearly under orders to ensure we didn't stay a moment longer than necessary. Corruption was even more rampant than before and I could feel a stronger level of frustrated anger amongst the people than I'd ever experienced.

Trying to deal as best I could with the outer difficulties present throughout the journey, I felt a deep sense of unease and challenge that was also uncharacteristically present within the group. I had a powerful sense of foreboding that something was building, but at the time, and with Mubarak's apparent invincibility, could put no name to my concern.

Later, at home, I attuned within to heal and release my own frustration and anger at what had transpired and realized that to some degree our group had reflected the deeper emotions stirring through Egypt's psyche.

In early January I left for Egypt for the second time in two months and for the first time to lead a Japanese group. I don't speak Japanese, and as this was the working language of the trip, we were travelling with a local guide who spoke fluent Japanese. Bearing in mind the challenges of the previous journey, I knew this trip could be extremely difficult. But instead it was miraculous.

On our first full day, as though embodying a benediction for our journey, I stood with my Japanese group in the sacred King's Chamber of the Great Pyramid as we attuned for reconciliation and transformation. Unbeknown to me at the time, it was the eve of Mohamed Bouazizi's passing, which was to light the hope of the Egyptian revolution in the coming weeks.

Thirteen years before, I'd been with a small group in Egypt only a week or so after the infamous massacre of tourists by gunfire at the Temple of Hatshepsut at Deir El Bahiri near Luxor. Many died that day, of whom ten were Japanese. And at the time Mubarak's regime had used the killings to crack down even harder on the Egyptian people and extend the state of emergency that had already been in place for many years.

After undertaking previous healing work here, I'd come to sense that the trauma could only be finally released by a Japanese person. On the day we visited the site, we brought with us a single red rose to commemorate the deaths. I intuitively asked one of the women in the group to attune to where those who had died that day, whose spirits I felt remained here, wished the rose to be placed. In a profoundly moving and simple way, she did so. And afterwards, as she cried gently for those who had passed, she shared her experience with the group. She told us that until I'd asked her to place the rose, she'd had no real idea why she'd felt called to be on the trip.

There is a profound belief amongst many Japanese people that for their spirits to be released on passing they must return to their homeland first. By attuning to the spirits of her compatriots who had perished here this woman gained a powerful sense that she had come to take them home.

I felt that healing the trauma of the temple massacre, an ostensible excuse for the regime's ongoing brutality, meant that its fear-based hold on the Egyptian people could now be released.

After that, our experiences of the other temples we visited were remarkably different from earlier and also from my previous journey. The guards and stewards at the temples not only welcomed our meditations but also joined in, and remarkably, on our last visit to Hathor's Temple at Denderah, even applauded us afterwards!

Something had shifted!

And just a few weeks later, on 11 February 2011, Mubarak was gone.

****

As I write, protests are continuing in other countries throughout North Africa such as Libya and Algeria, and in the Middle East from Bahrain and Jordan to Syria and Yemen.

Throughout the Arab world, there are pervasive common issues of high prices, high unemployment and despotic, authoritarian and corrupt governments, most of whom have been in power for many decades. The difference now is the ability of technology to enable people to organize and the presence of predominantly young populations who are transcending their fears of their erstwhile rulers and are willing to die if necessary for the right to be free and to have their voices heard.

Around 60 per cent of the population in the region is under 30 years of age. And a recent survey of Middle Eastern youth, carried out before its eruption, showed that the number one wish of young people was to live in a free society.

During the global journeys between 2001 and 2006 that I describe in my book *The 13th Step*, I discovered, both through my own inner journey and the outer pilgrimages I made, that there is a rebirth within our collective psyche of the impulse of the leaders the ancients called solar – or soular – heroes. In myth and legend these were ordinary folk who felt a deep calling to serve something beyond themselves and, through the challenges and inner growth of their tasks and journeys, discovered their extraordinary capabilities.

We're all potential solar/soular heroes able to meld the ordinary and extraordinary, the human and the divine within. We've seen that powerful and long-term Uranian, Neptunian and Plutonian astrological forces are supporting the power of one – the emergence of a multitude of soular heroes in every society and walk of life. And, as the people, and especially the young, of the Arab world are discovering for themselves, when we transcend the fears that have bound us and dedicate ourselves to the service of something greater than our own personal needs, we can be inspired and empowered to literally change the whole-world.

The country that is perhaps most fearful of what is emerging in the region is Israel. And the government of Prime Minister Netanyahu is unfortunately using this moment to energize an even greater level of national fear than hitherto and attempting to hold onto the unsustainable status quo and actively avoid making any real attempt at peace.

Despite Israeli fears, I also feel that the Iranian regime, far from being strengthened by the ongoing wave of revolutionary change in the Middle East, is actually being weakened. For, after its corrupt elections in 2009 and brutal suppression of subsequent protests, it is finding its own divisions and economic incompetence are proving a threat. Its current sabre-rattling is, I believe, merely an attempt to cover that weakness. And Arab youth who are rebelling against authoritarian regimes are in my view hardly likely to adopt the Islamist repression of Iran.

As Roger Cohen, a Jewish columnist for the *New York Times*, declared on 28 February, 'It isn't a time of uncertainty, but a period of hope – and we need to seize it.'

* * * *

In a number of countries of the region, attempts by their people to peacefully seize the moment for change have been met by violent suppression. In Libya, this has been particularly brutal. Its leader Colonel Gaddafi, announcing in effect that he *was* Libya and that as he had created the country he could now destroy it, imported foreign mercenaries to join his army to attempt, at any cost to human life, to annihilate the uprising.

What is tragically playing out here on a national level is conflict between the emergence of a new empowerment and the attempt by the old paradigm to keep command. In effect Gaddafi and other dictators who are clinging to power are reflecting our ego-based attachment to control and trying desperately to avoid change. Whilst those who are shaking off their fear and struggling for freedom are part of a collective yearning that is rippling through our psyche.

Given the bloodshed and loss of life, though, I've been asked why I'm so hopeful about the events that have been unleashed. In answer, whilst whole-heartedly grieving the turmoil and violence, I maintain that they embody the processes of death and re-birth that represent the transformational Shift of our collective consciousness.

Poet Khaled Mattawa, who comes from the Libyan city of Benghazi, I feel has given voice to this in the most inspirational way I have yet heard, in his poem 'Now That We Have Tasted Hope.'

Now that we have tasted hope
Now that we have come out of hiding,
Why would we live again in the tombs we'd made out of our
souls?

And the sundered bodies that we've reassembled with prayers
and consolations,
What would their torn parts be other than flesh?

Now that we have tasted hope
And dressed each other's wounds with the legends of our
oneness
Would we not prefer to close our mouths forever shut on the wine
That swilled inside them?

Having dreamed the same dream,
Having found the water that gushed behind a thousand mirages,
Why would we hide from the sun again
Or fear the night sky after we've reached the ends of darkness,
Live in death again after all the life our dead have given us?

Listen to me Zow'ya, Beida, Ajdabya, Tobruk, Nalut, Derna,
Musrata, Benghazi, Zintan,
Listen to me houses, alleys, courtyards, and streets that throng my
veins,
Some day soon

In your freed light and in the shade of your proud trees,
Your excavated heroes will return to their thrones in your martyrs'
squares,
Lovers will hold each other's hands.

I need not look far to imagine the nerves dying rejecting the life
that blood sends them.
I need not look deep into my past to seek a thousand hopeless
vistas.
But now that I have tasted hope
I have fallen into the embrace of my own rugged innocence.

How long were my ancient days?
I no longer care to count.
How high were the mountains in my ocean's fathoms?
I no longer care to measure.
How bitter was the bread of bitterness?
I no longer care to recall.

Now that we have tasted hope,
Now that we have lived on this hard-earned crust,
We would sooner die than seek any other taste to life,
Any other way of being human.

CHAPTER 15
China and Tibet

'We must suffer finite disappointment,
but we must never lose infinite hope.'
DR MARTIN LUTHER KING JR

China is an ancient country with a great pride in its history and culture. Unified from warring factions in 221 BCE, it was given its name by Q'in, the first emperor of the nation. More than 2,000 years later, his enormous burial mound near Xian, with its attendant army of life-sized terracotta warriors, is now a World Heritage Site.

The long history of China since Qin has seen alternating waves of unity and conflict. After many dynasties of rulers, the last emperor was dethroned in 1912 and spent his later years as a gardener for the state. Since then a series of internal and external conflicts, primarily involvement in World War II and, in the 1960s, the so-called Cultural Revolution led by Mao Zedong, have been hugely traumatic.

Since 1989 and the horror of Tiananmen Square, where the military killed people demonstrating for democratic rights, the communist regime has continued to maintain ultimate control. Nonetheless, its leaders have successfully pursued a strategy of economic growth and despite a number of serious international flashpoints during the 1990s and increasing levels of domestic corruption, standards of living have continued to improve significantly.

From 2002, under President Hu Jintao and Prime Minister Wen Jiabao, the stated aim has been to develop a scientific basis for a harmonious society, reflecting the principles of Confucian philosophy which have recently been regaining ground. However, whilst the economy has continued to expand, social issues, environmental degradation and an increasing need for resources are growing challenges. And human rights have remained a cause for international concern.

But with its centralized decision-making, the country's response to the large-scale disasters such as the Sichuan province earthquake and severe flooding in southern China in 2008 has been inspiring and effective.

In 2012/13, in line with the consensual politics of China, new leaders will be appointed for a ten-year term. And unlike in the West, the leaders are already lined up: Xi Jinping to take over from President Hu and Li Keqiang to take over from Prime Minister Wen.

Xi also oversaw the 2008 China Olympics. From an impoverished background, with a reputation for achieving conciliation and fighting corruption, this largely enigmatic man will soon lead over 1.3 billion of the world's people. While generally affable, he lashed out in 2009 at 'a few foreigners, with full bellies, who have nothing better to do than try to point fingers at our country... China does not export revolution, hunger or poverty; nor does China cause you any headaches. What else do you want?'

* * * *

What many in the West want is resoulution of China's disputed claims over Tibet. These began with the Mongol emperors of the thirteenth century CE and continued more consistently from the eighteenth century. In 1904 a trading agreement imposed by

Britain required Tibet to pay a substantial indemnity to ensure compliance. Two years later, following a treaty between Britain and China, the latter took over the indemnity, thereby claiming suzerainty over Tibet. Until 1950, China's other priorities meant that Tibet was pretty much left alone. But then the Chinese army invaded and in 1951 Tibetan representatives entered negotiations that formalized China's sovereignty.

For the next eight years, despite the presence of troops, the Chinese allowed traditional Tibetan culture to continue to function. However, they did initiate what their government continues to view as a process of liberation. They put an end to slavery and the Tibetan system of unpaid labour and reduced unemployment and beggary. They got rid of a number of taxes, began major construction and infrastructure projects and broke the Buddhist monasteries' hold on education by establishing non-religious schools.

But following progressively more disruptive land reform, Tibetan opposition steadily grew until in 1956, backed by American CIA training and funding, as acknowledged in 1998 by the Dalai Lama organization, an armed uprising began.

At that time the majority of the people did not support the uprising, but by 1959 further crackdowns by the Chinese resulted in full-scale resistance. Brutally put down by the Chinese, this led to the fourteenth Dalai Lama fleeing into exile in India.

In the 1960s the cultural vandalism unleashed by China's Cultural Revolution spread throughout China and Tibet, with the revolution's fanatical Red Guards deliberately seeking to destroy the cultural heritage of both.

So, from Tibet's perspective, the period from 1950 has been one of cultural genocide, whereas from China's, it has been one of liberating Tibet from its feudal past.

In 2006, from his exile in India, the Dalai Lama insisted, 'Tibet wants autonomy, not independence,' but this is a statement the Chinese refuse to believe.

* * * *

In August 2008, I returned to China, seven years after the second of the 13 pilgrimages of *The 13ᵗʰ Step*. Just before that earlier visit, China had been awarded the Olympic Games. This later trip was timed to experience a solar eclipse in southern China, but it so happened that it took place just before the opening ceremony of the Games.

With the world's attention focused on China, the people of Tibet had seized the opportunity to highlight their plight. In March a number of protests had turned violent. China had imposed a strict clampdown and also, without warning, banned all foreigners from entering Tibet. We had planned on visiting, so had to rearrange our itinerary and a number of people who'd specifically wanted to visit Tibet dropped out. Those who remained took the view that 'we'll be wherever we are meant to be.'

Having let go of expectations and being willing to go with the flow of whatever the Cosmos had in store for us, I wasn't surprised when, with only a couple of weeks to go, the ban was suddenly lifted and we were given renewed permission to visit Tibet.

* * * *

The early days of the journey took us to Beijing. In Tiananmen Square where, nearly 20 years before, Chinese tanks had tragically fired on their own citizens, our small group formed an attunement circle standing under a giant photo of Mao Zedong.

During my previous visit, the attitude of the numerous guards around the well-known sites had made it impossible to come together in such an open way. But as we did so now, I felt no intimidation. Remarkably, we were left in peace to attune, our prayers calling for unconditional love to flow through us in the universal heart and heal the schisms of the past.

As I stood there, remembering those who had died in this very place for democratic and human rights and knowing we were about to travel on to Tibet, I prayed that such freedoms would be empowered here and throughout China and Tibet.

When afterwards I looked around, all I could see was people smiling – a sign, I hoped, that our prayers had been heard and would one day be answered.

* * * *

Throughout our stay, the Chinese people we met seemed delighted to be hosting the imminent Olympics and genuinely welcoming of visitors. We experienced a China emerging onto the world stage with pride in its history and culture and a greater openness than I'd experienced on my previous visit. As we wandered around the huge park in the centre of Beijing, we saw people of all ages enjoying themselves – making music, dancing, singing or just basking in the warm sunshine.

I was especially moved to see the older people who had survived the horrors of the Cultural Revolution and its aftermath in the 1960s and '70s. Now they were laughing and taking great pleasure in their various outdoor activities. Many were physically robust, but it was heart-warming to see those who were physically fragile being lovingly helped along by younger members of their families.

Most of my fellow travellers, who were visiting China for the first time, acknowledged that they'd come with a view of the country as totalitarian and harsh. But instead, to their surprise, we were encountering friendly, open and generous people.

* * * *

After a few days, we flew on to Lhasa, the capital of Tibet, and, after the pre-Olympic euphoria of Beijing, a very different environment. Still only a few months after the crackdown on demonstrations, the city was awash with troops and the normally ubiquitous monks were notable by their absence. Some had gone into hiding, others were understandably keeping a very low profile and many had been thrown into jail.

As we began to walk around the city, on the steps of one of the monasteries we came across an old lady, the first of many pilgrims we saw prostrating themselves in prayer. As we watched in silence, honouring her devotion, she knelt then lay full length before rising and beginning the cycle once more. She continued this arduous dedication for some time before she became aware of our presence. When she did, she leaped to her feet and came over to me. Indicating a nearby seat, she gestured to me to sit. This wonderful old lady who was without care for her own comfort but full of concern for mine moved me immensely. As tears filled my eyes, I thanked her, but motioned that we were about to move on.

As we continued to make our way through the city and I saw more and more pilgrims doing the same rituals over and over again, while I felt enormous respect for their beliefs, something began to nag at me.

Later, visiting the vast Potala Palace that looms high above the city, we discovered more about the history of Buddhism in Tibet. To my surprise, it had arrived here fairly late, in the seventh century CE and in unusual circumstances.

As far back as prehistory, the spiritual tradition of Tibet had been based on the shamanic beliefs known as Bon that viewed all nature as animate and the beautiful but harsh environment as being filled with spirits, both good and evil. Rituals involved seeking the blessing of the benevolent spirits and propitiating or seeking protection from those deemed evil.

When Songtsän Gampo came to the throne in the early seventh century, his warlike nature caused him to attack his more peaceful neighbours, Nepal to the south and China to the east. In attempting to placate him, each king sent him a princess to marry. The brides were both Buddhist and eventually converted their warrior husband, and by his subsequent edict the whole of Tibet, to Buddhism.

So, I now understood that Tibetan Buddhism overlaid the much more ancient shamanic Bon tradition. And that began to make sense of the prayers and rituals we'd been seeing.

I realized that the old lady's repetitive pleas and those of the numerous pilgrims visiting shrines and temples were practices that reflected this accretion of traditions. I sensed that the prayers were more shamanic than Buddhist in their entreaties. And I felt uncomfortably as though they had become compulsive, driven by the fear that only through the turning of the prayer wheels, the continual prostrations and the many other rites could they be heard.

I was saddened and shocked to sense that as the Chinese have expanded their presence in Tibet, the Tibetans have retreated into the perceived sanctuary of their tradition – which is rather a prison, as the time and effort involved actually make the lives of the people even more difficult and diminishes their meagre resources still further.

I now appreciated even more the Dalai Lama's view that he didn't want Tibet to pull away from China but to take advantage of the technical innovations and infrastructure investment that the Chinese could bring.

China has already spent enormous sums on building projects in Tibet, albeit in many instances to enable the extraction and removal of natural resources. The Chinese people we spoke to felt disappointed that the Tibetans didn't consider themselves part of China and bemused that what they believed to be beneficial progress had been rebuffed.

From their side, the Tibetans deeply resent the cultural and social oppression that has come with the Chinese ingress.

As we continued our journey, we could all see that China and Tibet could offer each other so much if they would only open their hearts to each other's viewpoints.

And we hoped that such mutual and compassionate awareness would come soon.

* * * *

Whilst I was inwardly mulling over the opportunities for both China and Tibet if they could overcome their deep differences, we visited Sera monastery just north of Lhasa, one of the few that were open to foreigners following the crackdown.

After visiting the various buildings within the monastery compound, we took a rest on the steps of a shrine and chatted over our experiences. As we were doing so, we noticed a Tibetan family close by. One of the children, a young boy perhaps four years old with beautiful apple cheeks, smiled at us. Realizing we were speaking English, he piped up, 'Hello!'

'Hello,' I responded.

This little one beamed and then, in perfect English, said, 'My name is Tensing. Welcome to Tibet.'

I grinned as I told him my name.

And then, with a pure simplicity that melted my heart, he looked at me and, with purity shining out from his beautiful lustrous dark-brown eyes, simply said, 'I love you.'

As I gulped away tears and beamed back at him, I told my new friend, 'I love you too!'

Later, as we waved goodbye to Tensing and his family, I hoped fervently that one day soon he would know a Tibet where Chinese and Tibetans were reconciled and that he could enjoy a life that embodied the best of both cultures.

* * * *

After a fascinating onward journey that included a 36-hour train ride from Lhasa across the Tibetan Plateau and down through the fertile loess farmlands of north-west China, we eventually came to the city of Xian, which I'd visited before, in 2002.

After visiting the huge pyramidal mound that houses Emperor Q'in's as yet unexcavated tomb and the amazing display of his now world-famous full-size Terracotta Army, we travelled on to Mount Huashan, the highest of China's five Taoist sacred mountains, to witness one of the most incredible sights in nature, a total solar eclipse.

For many years I've shared my understanding that to find and embody inner balance and wholeness we need to in-to-great the three aspects of the divine feminine, masculine and child within ourselves on both personal and collective levels. The trinity can also be experienced on a cosmic scale by the integration of the Sun (masculine) Moon (feminine) and Earth (child). Their most exquisite alignment takes place during an eclipse.

The eclipse we'd come all this way to see took place late in the afternoon. We made our way to the lookout point on one of the five peaks of the mountain, ready to witness the eclipse taking place above one of its other peaks beyond an intervening valley. We made sure we arrived in good time, only to be surprised that so few people were there.

Eventually the time for the eclipse drew near. It had been a lovely afternoon with a clear blue sky and we were becoming excited when guess what? Just above the peak where the eclipse was due, a single small cloud that had been hovering for a while covered the Sun just as the Moon's disc began to move across it.

I couldn't believe it! In an otherwise clear sky, the eclipse for which we'd come so far was about to happen out of sight. Taking a deep breath, I resigned myself to accepting that obviously we were only going to experience the eclipse on an inner energetic level. Closing my eyes, I centred myself in the universal heart of the 8th chakra and inwardly envisaged the magnificent coming together of Sun and Moon and Earth in this transcendent alignment.

A few moments later, though not yet feeling fully attuned with the energies, I inwardly heard a powerful clairaudient message to open my eyes.

As I did, I almost couldn't believe what I saw.

At the last moment, the path of the eclipse had carried the Sun and Moon beneath the small cloud and at the point of totality, as the Moon completely covered the Sun, the two literally stood poised on the apex of the peak across from us.

In that instant, a cosmic miracle happened. The divine feminine essence of the Moon communed with the divine masculine energy of the Sun and co-created anew the divine child of the Earth. We watched spellbound throughout the minutes of totality. And then, as the energies reached their crescendo, the combined Sun-Moon slid majestically behind the peak. Moments later, now hidden from our view, as they silently parted to go their separate ways until their next communion, the sky behind the mountain crest before us exploded into golden light.

We were awed into grateful stillness by what we'd just witnessed. And I was reminded yet again of the profound perfection and purpose of all things.

* * * *

Such harmony lies at the core of the Chinese psyche. The ancient perception of the oneness of all creation, its eternal cycles and the yin and yang of cosmic feminine and masculine principles that interweave throughout it, has pervaded the culture for millennia. The aim is not to fight either Nature or destiny but to flow and be flexible and pragmatic with regard to both. Nothing is to be rushed, whether negotiations, a good meal or the attainment of long-term strategies.

The perception that energy, or *ch'i*, is all-pervasive is integral to the Chinese traditions of medicine and the technique of acupuncture. On a geomantic level, too, the perspective of *feng shui,* which translates as 'wind and water', recognizes the archetypal and elemental nature of the world.

In perceiving the wholistic reality of experience, the Chinese emphasize the collective good more than the individual. And the group *guanxi,* or network of connections, commitments and obligations that people develop and maintain through their lives, links personal and group endeavours and buffers the uncertainties and dangers of existence, which, as the *I Ching,* the Book of Changes, explains, are ever-present in the inevitable change that life engenders.

In recent years, the Chinese leadership has encouraged the principles of Confucianism, the philosophical and ethical system based on the teachings of the sixth and fifth century BCE philosopher Confucius.

Confucianism maintains that moral virtue can be perfected through both personal and collective endeavour. The principles of honesty, modesty, loyalty, altruism, forgiveness and respect are all valued and to be aspired to. And the Confucian version of the Golden Rule, the 'Ethics of Reciprocity', reflects its universality by stating 'Do not do unto others what you would not have them do unto you.'

The teachings state, as does the American Declaration of Independence, that essentially everyone is created equal. To the Chinese, it is people's conditioning and choices that make the difference. As Confucius said, 'By nature men are similar; by practice men are wide apart.'

Loyalty is central to the Confucian philosophy, both to the living, especially the elders, and to the ancestors. The bonds of *guanxi* extend from the family to friends and work colleagues and to the entirety of the nation.

In the last few decades, the expansion of Chinese power and influence has brought it to the centre of the world stage. For future harmony, the wider world needs to understand the Chinese psyche. And the Chinese need not only to reciprocate with a deeper understanding of others, but to actively extend loyalty and friendship in the greater global network of *guanxi* of which they are now participants and partners.

* * * *

One of the most important aspects of China's burgeoning growth is its exploding need for an inflow of natural resources and an outflow of consumer markets to sustain its manufacturing output. Africa, home to around a third of the world's mineral resources and an enormous prospective market for goods, is potentially the perfect partner for China in the twenty-first century.

Whilst China needs the iron ore of Gabon, the oil of Nigeria and Sudan, the copper of Zambia and latterly the diamonds of Zimbabwe, Africa needs new and better transport systems, telecommunications and social infrastructures.

The relationship is still relatively new, but is being carried on in a very different way from the relationship between Africa and the West, which was formerly based on colonialism and is now primarily focused on the provision of aid.

Despite the good intentions of many of the donors, foreign aid is being seen progressively as problematic. Zambian Dambisa Moyo, a London-based economist, in her book *Dead Aid: Why Aid Is Not Working and How There Is a Better Way for Africa*, sees such involvement as having been a curse that has crippled and corrupted Africa, and that the new and evolving relationship with China has the potential to offer a way out of the mess the West has made.

In contrast to aid, China has emphasized trade and commercial investment and has moved rapidly to implement deals. Crucially, it has also refused to become involved in African governmental policies and its 'no strings' investments have been made without requiring reforms. With its lack of colonial history, its track record of pulling its own people out of poverty and its developing reputation as a reliable trading partner, it is being viewed by many African commentators as a good friend.

But is China's hands-off approach to local governance the right one, not only for itself and its African partners, but for the wider global community?

Three highly disturbing examples of where such an approach is concerning are in the Democratic Republic of Congo, Sudan and Zimbabwe.

The DR Congo has only recently emerged from three decades of horrifying civil war. In 2008 it agreed a 25-year deal to swap its enormous copper and cobalt production for a multi-billion development investment in rail and road links, hospitals and schools. Whilst potentially beneficial, there are growing concerns that it may end up like its neighbour Zambia, who in 1998 did a smaller ore-for-development deal which went sour and where there has been criticism of harsh and sometimes dangerous Chinese work practices and the lack of training and development of local people.

Sudan is currently the number one recipient of Chinese investment in Africa, due to its vast oil reserves. Two-thirds of its oil is sold to China. But Chinese thirst for oil has enabled the Khartoum regime to buy weapons for its military and militia allies who have been supporting the deadly conflict in the Darfur region and putting down opponents in the south of the country, which in January 2011 voted in a referendum for independence.

In Zimbabwe, a top-secret deal between long-term President Robert Mugabe and China swapping Zimbabwean diamonds for weapons seems to be aimed at keeping Mugabe's murderous Zanu-PF regime in power, as was reported by the UK press in September 2010. The industrial quality stones are being flown directly from an airstrip at the Chiadzwa mine to China in return for weapons. And this so-called blood diamond trade with China may well fund a bloodbath in the next presidential elections in 2011 as Mugabe and his faction seek to hold onto power at all costs.

But it is land and agriculture deals that are likely to become the most contentious in the expanding relationships between China and its African partners.

In 2006, China hosted a large-scale China–Africa summit in Beijing during which it promised to set up 10 agricultural centres demonstrating Chinese farming methods. It also acknowledged in 2009 that as it is faced with increasing pressure from its growing population on food security, buying and renting land abroad to secure its domestic food supply is a priority.

Throughout history, land has been synonymous with a nation's sense of identity. And, as we've seen in the Middle East, disputes over land and its resources are profoundly emotional and contentious. So China's policy could lead to conflict.

If, however, China exhibits a progressive strategy of empowering local farmers in Africa, helping them to improve their techniques and paying fair prices for their produce, the relationship can become an immensely positive win-win. For the indirect social benefits of such an enlightened approach go far beyond the ones that directly impact the bottom-line profitability.

* * * *

Just over two years after our prayers in Tiananmen Square for human rights and peace, our small wave of intention flowed with those of many others around the world and on 10 December 2010, Liu Xiaobo, a Chinese human-rights activist, was awarded the 2010 Nobel Peace Prize.

An academic, Liu had been teaching abroad, but in 1989 had returned to China to participate in the fledgling democracy movement. In early June he had tried, with only partial success, to prevent a violent clash between the government and students who were protesting. In 2008 he co-wrote the Charter 8 Manifesto that, on the sixtieth anniversary of the United Nations Declaration of Human Rights, called for such justice to prevail in China. For his defiance, on Christmas Day 2009, he was sentenced to 11 years in prison for 'inciting subversion of state power.'

At the 2010 award ceremony, the Nobel Committee congratulated China on achieving rapid growth over the last 30 years and raising hundreds of millions of people out of grinding poverty. And yet, as chairman Thorbjørn Jagland said,

China's new status entails increased responsibility. China must be prepared for criticism and regard it as positive – as an opportunity for improvement. This must be the case wherever there is great power... Many will ask whether China's weakness – for all the strength the country is currently showing – is not manifested in the need to imprison a man for 11 years merely for expressing his opinions on how his country should be governed... Liu has exercised his civil rights. He has done nothing wrong. He must therefore be released!

Jagland's final words were a hope that Liu's views would eventually be accepted by and strengthen his home nation. I hope so too.

****

One development that may suggest a recognition within China of its need to reform politically and socially whilst differentiating itself from western democracy and Marxist-style communism is the revival in the teachings of the ancient sage Confucius as the state ideology. Following the award of the Nobel Peace Prize to Liu, China announced the inauguration of a Confucius

Peace Prize. And in January 2011 a statue of Confucius was ceremonially erected in Tiananmen Square, the political centre of China.

The Chinese leadership profoundly fears the uncertainty and popular will and self-interest enshrined in democratic processes. And with China's lack of historical experience of communal freedoms, such a system as has been seen in Iraq for example could indeed be highly problematic for good governance and the continuity of this broadly based ethnic state.

Whilst so-called Political Confucianism advocates social responsibility and harmony, it could also be used to justify passivity, misplaced loyalty and the continuing dominance of the ruling Communist Party. At its most benevolent, however, it could promote ethics and social responsibility, mitigate the fear of an aggressive China abroad and defend Chinese culture against degradation at home.

Only time will tell, but the next generation of Chinese leaders, instead of being engineers, like the current leadership, are trained in developing and managing large urban areas and commercial interests. And with the self-empowering and altruistic planetary influences supporting transformational change in the coming years, if China can overcome its aversion to criticism – even when constructive – and recognize it has global responsibilities, it has the opportunity to play a benevolent and wise leadership role in the world.

CHAPTER 16
India, Pakistan and Afghanistan

'Courage is like love. It must have
hope for its nourishment.'
Napoleon I

In the early fourth millennium BCE, at around the time that the Egyptian and Mesopotamian civilizations were surging forward, in the north-west of the Indian subcontinent a civilization developed in the vast basin of the Indus river. Named after Harappa, the first of its cities to be discovered and excavated, its geographic extent surpassed Mesopotamia and Egypt combined.

It thrived until around 2000 BCE, when it went into a calamitous decline and its people seem to have left suddenly as refugees in small groups that gradually spread out across the subcontinent. Thanks to recent archaeological and satellite-based research, it's now recognized that it was the loss of the life-sustaining waters of the Indus river and its many tributaries that caused the collapse. This civilization was perhaps the last major casualty of the long-term drought that, as we've seen, began around 2200 BCE, lasted around 300 years and also destroyed or severely diminished societies across an enormous area from the Aegean through Mesopotamia and the Middle East to Egypt.

Recent archaeological studies are also proposing that the ancient Indian Vedic era, which provided epic texts such as the *Rig Veda*, whose hymns, verses and prose describe philosophy, ritual and sacred science, was synonymous with that of the Harappans. And that, as archaeologist Dr N. S. Rajaram has said, 'the mature Harappan civilization was the last glow of the Vedic age.'

Dating the Vedic texts has been a challenge. Whilst for example the *Bhagavad Gita*, recognized as one of the most important spiritual texts of all time, is traditionally dated at around 3000 BCE, some scholars have insisted on a later dating and many deem a specific dating irrelevant in any event, as its teachings of the oneness of the Cosmos and its breadth of spiritual insight are essentially timeless.

Abraham Seidenberg, an American mathematician and historian of science, has shown that the Vedic ritual mathematical texts known as the *sulb sutras*, which are the oldest extant, are on the same basis as those of ancient Egypt and Old Babylonia, and therefore part of geometric knowledge which tracks back to the earliest times of Sumer.

So, if the Vedic age ended with the demise of the Harappans, when did it begin?

The *Rig Veda* describes the now dry Saraswati river of northern India as the 'greatest of rivers', which flowed from 'the mountain to the sea'. An Indo-French group has now shown, through satellite imagery, that this stopped being the case long before 3000 BCE, which dates the text to at least that far back.

Some experts of Vedic astrology, however, contend that it goes back as far as 7000 BCE or even earlier. Due to the texts' portrayal of a period of environmental abundance, some scholars want to push back the dating of at least the oral tradition that may have been the precursor to the texts to as early as 8000 BCE, a date for which there is evidence of lush conditions.

And as yet contentious underwater discoveries of submerged city-like structures and artefacts by the National Institute of Ocean Technology since 2000 in the Gulf of Khambhat off the coast of Gujarat further south may in due course add further evidence of a much earlier time-frame for the Vedic era.

Whilst much more evidence is needed to support this emerging understanding, to me it strongly suggests the same origins of knowledge for the Vedic peoples as for the Sumerians.

* * * *

Around 2000 BCE, as we've seen, the Harappan epoch that benefitted from the wisdom of the Vedic Age came to an end. However, its people migrated elsewhere within the enormous subcontinent, as cultural continuity, albeit much diminished from the Golden, Silver and Bronze eras depicted in the epics, evolved into the underlying philosophy of Hinduism and its associated life paths such as yoga.

Such spiritual teachings were augmented by those of Siddhartha Gautama and Vardhamana Mahavira, who both taught in India during the fifth and sixth centuries BCE and who respectively founded the spiritual path of Buddhism and developed the pacifist philosophy known as Jainism.

In the third century BCE the great emperor Ashoka, who ruled almost the entirety of India for some 40 years and whose name means 'painless, without sorrow,' played a crucial role in helping to make Buddhism a world religion. After an early life of violence and conquest, he converted to Buddhism and throughout his long reign put into practice the Buddhist principles of tolerance, non-violence, compassion and righteousness. He is considered an exemplary ruler.

Throughout his enormous kingdom he raised stone pillars and had engraved on massive boulders the moral edicts of his reign. A copy of one of these now stands in the grounds of the national museum in Delhi. When Tony and I visited, despite it being a replica, I found this beautifully engraved huge rock commemorating one of the most enlightened rulers in history profoundly moving. It seemed to be a symbolic sentinel keeping an enduring watch over the nearby building, within which, to our astonishment, relics of the Buddha himself were encased in an exquisite golden altar. And over 2,000 years later, the emperor's emblem, the Ashoka Chakra, the spinning wheel of 24 spokes that is the Buddhist symbol of *dharma* or virtue, is now memorialized at the centre of the national flag of the Republic of India.

So, India has a profoundly ancient tradition of spirituality which still pervades the country today and is a great strength in the lives of its diverse peoples.

* * * *

Another deeply ingrained aspect of Indian life is the hereditary social stratification and restrictions known as the caste system. So powerful and all-encompassing is its reach that even in the democracy that India has had since 1947, the adage is that people don't cast their vote, but vote their caste.

The caste system persists despite the country's constitution, which explicitly prohibits discrimination against the lowest castes of Indian society, such as the *Dalits*, or oppressed, and a number of castes termed 'Other Backward Classes.' There continues to be massive and demeaning segregation, especially in rural areas.

In contrast to the international business organizations founded in India, whose need to compete on a global scale means they are leading the way to modernization and meritocracy, India's progress in general is being significantly held back by its out-of-date economic policies, together with the continuation of the hereditary limitations on lower-caste Indians and the privileges accorded to upper-class castes. With a system deeply flawed by the acceptance of 'jobs for life' or roles acquired because of caste rather than merit, it seems that massive corruption and a woeful lack of effectiveness within politics, local businesses and society are the norm.

Whilst Tony and I were travelling throughout India's northern province of Rajasthan in February 2011, we daily encountered the segregation of caste and the corruption that directly or indirectly arises from it. But our travels took us to a beautiful place called Pushkar, which I'd felt called to before our trip, and which, when we arrived, we realized played a significant energetic role in the foundation and perpetuation of caste.

****

According to Hindu tradition, Brahma, the Hindu creator god, killed a demon who was causing havoc by striking him with his weapon – a lotus flower. I know it's not what you or I would have used! Anyway, three lotus petals then fell at three places to create three lakes, the largest being that at Pushkar.

Deciding to undertake a Fire sacrifice at the lake, Brahma called on his wife Savitri, after whom the ancient Sarasvati river is named, to perform the ritual with him. So here again we see the Fire and Water associations of this energetic seed-point.

Unfortunately Savitri was late for the ceremony, in some versions of the legend due to waiting for her fellow goddesses. Angered by her absence, Brahma asked his fellow god Indra to find a suitable girl as a consort. The only one available was a lowly milkmaid of the Gurjar caste, one that is still officially one of the 'Other Backward Classes,' so she needed to be sanctified, and renamed Gayatri, before being deemed acceptable.

When Savitri finally arrived to take her rightful place, there was Gayatri already seated next to Brahma. Furious, she cursed

Brahma, and in the version of the tradition that we became aware of on our arrival in Pushkar, she also cursed Gayatri for usurping her role.

Since that time, Hindu scriptures describe Brahma's temple at Pushkar as the only place where he has been worshipped throughout the world, and although his temple, which is believed to date back some 2,000 years in its original form, has now been joined by a few others, it remains the most important.

Savitri then moved to the high hilltop to the south-west of the lake and her essence there was honoured by the construction of a temple within which her image is still worshipped. The presence of her rival Gayatri is also enshrined in a temple on a lower hilltop across the lake.

Pilgrims to Pushkar are invited to climb the two hills to honour first Savitri and then Gayatri and to pay homage to Brahma at his temple. So that's what we did.

The roof terrace of our guest house gave a wonderful view of both temples and hilltops. And so, on the morning of our climb, I attuned to Savitri to see whether I could discern any guidance as to what, if anything, we should energetically undertake there.

Almost immediately I had a very strong sense of Savitri's presence and that she was allowing me to feel her very personal emotions at the time of the Fire ritual.

I sensed that she'd prepared herself with great care but had been unaware of the importance to Brahma of the exact timing of the ceremony. It was as though on a very human level she'd been a bride who, traditionally late, had arrived at the altar only to discover that in her absence the groom had chosen someone else and gone ahead with the wedding.

Her disappointment, though, was far more than personal umbrage. In recognizing that Brahma had placed greater importance on his perceived need for a feminine presence –

any feminine presence – than on honouring her specifically, she embodied the rage of all women so treated then and since. In the version of the legend that we were told, in her rage she lashed out at both Brahma and Gayatri, whose pain at the injustice was also powerful.

Continuing to attune to Savitri and then Gayatri, who seemed to hold a combined sense of injustice and sorrow, I had the sense that not only had Savitri cursed Brahma but also the Gurjar caste of Gayatri and that this ancient curse was still being energized far beyond the waters of Pushkar Lake and being played out through the rigidities and exclusions of the caste system.

That morning, as I sat quietly contemplating how Tony and I might be in service to the healing of this schism, I understood that we needed to climb first to Savitri's temple and energetically accompany her as a bride once more to Brahma. Then, in the resoulution of their communion, we had to redeem and release the curse by going on to Gayatri's temple and finally to the sacred *ghats*, the steps that led down to the waters of the sacred lake.

We spent that day doing as Savitri had guided. We undertook the strenuous climb to her temple and then, with the sense of her being with us, we went on to the temple of Brahma. Afterwards we climbed to Gayatri's small temple and finally, with the Sun low in the sky, arrived at the *ghats*. Here, we prayed for the release of the curse that had enfolded Gayatri and her caste, and with it the energetic seed-point of the entire caste system.

We prayed first at the Brahma *ghat*, the traditional site of the Fire ritual. Then we moved onto the Gandhi *ghat*, named after the Mahatma, the pacifist leader of India's Independence Movement who struggled on behalf of freedom for India's lower castes and inspired civil rights movements worldwide, and whose ashes were scattered there.

As we did so, we visualized the release of the curse flowing through the waters of the lake and rippling far beyond to heal past injustices and to free the psyche not only of India but of all nations and peoples.

And as the Sun lowered towards sunset, I attuned to Savitri, Gayatri and Brahma and felt our work here was complete.

* * * *

The following morning, as we prepared to journey on, I managed to access the internet and read how, at 6 p.m. local time the previous evening, after weeks of peaceful protests by demonstrators, Egypt's people's-led revolution had finally toppled President Mubarak after 30 years.

Tears flowed down my face as I thought of our Egyptian friends. And also when I realized that Mubarak's resignation had been announced at almost exactly the time of our prayers at the *ghat* where the ashes of Gandhi, the great hero of the peaceful struggle for freedom and civil rights everywhere, had been scattered. Thank you, Mahatma!

* * * *

At the stroke of midnight between 14 and 15 August 1947, parts of India's northern provinces were sundered on the basis of religion from the rest of the country, and a new nation, Pakistan, was created.

Whilst the British, who'd ruled India since 1858 and were about to withdraw, enabling independence, had favoured keeping the country united, negotiations between the Hindu Congress and the Islamic League had broken down.

The resultant Partition began with appalling violence and disruption to millions of lives, as Muslim refugees moved into Pakistan and Hindus into what remained of India, and created feelings of mutual suspicion and hostility that have continued to plague the relationship between the two countries ever since.

Whilst initially Pakistan was formed as two geographically separated enclaves, West and East Pakistan, conflict between the two resulted in East Pakistan, with India's aid, seceding from the West, and a third country, Bangladesh, being formed in December 1971. This only served to deepen Pakistan's psychological trauma and paranoia.

For our purpose here we'll focus on what is now Pakistan and its relationship with India, as it is this schism which continues to cause concern and whose healing would have far-reaching effects. We'll explore how the two modern countries are like twins separated at birth. By looking at the moment of birth and separation and locating their respective energetic centres at Pakistan's capital Islamabad and India's at New Delhi, we can look at the astrological charts of these 'Midnight's Children' of Partition to see what insights we can gain into their national psyches.

And we'll also see how the geomantic hotspot that underlies Pakistan energetically contributes to the rifted nature of the nation's psyche.

* * * *

Given the same timing, despite their energetic 'birthplaces' being some distance apart, the natal charts of India and Pakistan, as I've mentioned, are similar to those of twins.

In both charts, but especially India's, the elements of Fire and Water are strong, signifying both creativity and conflict and a tendency to follow emotional urges. The presence of Fixed signs in both charts also emphasizes an underlying predisposition for rigidity and stubbornness.

The Sun in Leo in the fourth house for both denotes the paramount importance of nation and family and both personal and collective roles and status.

The Moon in Cancer in the third house shows an emotional need by both countries to be recognized and appreciated by each other and the wider world. This need being communicated and met is vital to both countries' well-being, as shown by the

Ascendant in Gemini, the sign of ideas and communication, for both charts.

The presence of the 'wounded healer' Chiron in the intensely emotional sign of Scorpio in the sixth house, again for both, reflects their deep pain, the pre-birth trauma of Partition and the countries' shared cosmic destiny to seek the healing of their schism.

And their shared North Node in Taurus in the twelfth house reveals that their higher purpose is to overcome their distrust of change and intransigence and see themselves as part of a greater whole.

But it's Saturn, the planet of discipline and perseverance, and Pluto, the planet of transformation, conjunct in the leadership sign of Leo but with subtle and significant house differences between the two countries that most clearly reveal the deep mutual trauma and the enormous benefit of its potential resoulution.

The Saturn–Pluto conjunction emphasizes pride and authority and an ambitious focus on attaining power and recognition. The transformational opportunities of the combined influence arise from the prospect of transcending selfish ends and working for the collective good.

For India, both planets are in the third house, denoting communication and transportation, whereas for Pakistan, they reside in the fourth house, indicating circumstances and events relating to the environment and material interests.

For India, the house position of Saturn infers the country's need to build up skills in communication on both domestic and international levels, including listening to other viewpoints, and also relates to the need for effective transportation infrastructure. Pluto's house position shows an astrologically classic power struggle with a sibling, reflecting India's fundamental issues with Pakistan, including their competitive development and brinkmanship as nuclear weapons rivals.

If Pakistan were an individual, its Saturn house position would reveal a lack of home support leading to an insecure emotional footing. And Pluto's placement would indicate a home environment which could be described as volcanic, with early traumas seething beneath the surface.

* * * *

So let's look at the current situation of both countries and how each may be helped, physically and energetically, to heal their traumas. We'll begin with India.

In my own view and that of many other commentators, India's development continues to be undermined by the continuance of the caste system, which perpetuates hereditary entitlement and inherent corruption at the expense of meritocratic advancement. The political expediency of affirmative action that purports to advance the poor but lacks the female emancipation and universal education truly needed to benefit them only exacerbates the inefficiency and corruption endemic in the system.

India's great strength lies in its spiritual traditions and its multi-layered diversity of peoples and lifestyles. But again, experiencing the daily adherence of devotees and pilgrims at its numerous temples, Tony and I were struck not only by their genuine piety but in many instances by the monetary nature of their worship and their prayers for greater status and material wealth. This mirrors India's entire society, which, reflecting its astrological placements of Sun and Moon, is based on perceived status, both embodied within the all-pervasive caste system and in the way in which increasingly wealthy citizens flaunt their money, despite the presence of enormous poverty around them.

The astrological emphasis on developing communications and transportation is clearly seen in India today. Whilst the former are thriving in terms of quantity – from the proliferation of mobile phones to the hubbub of multiple media channels – the quality of the society's ability to discuss its fundamental issues and explore possible resoulutions is questionable.

And in terms of transportation and the 'communication' of energy, the infrastructure of the country remains inadequate to its burgeoning needs and has been hijacked by vested interests and corruption.

Even though at the moment there seems to be no social or political will to address the fundamental issue of caste, the larger astrological influences of empowerment and reform that are unfolding around the world in 2011 will, in ways not yet apparent, also affect India, the world's largest democracy.

And when they do, I hope that this incredibly vibrant nation with its ancient and profound tradition of spirituality can resoulve its internal issues and take its place as a guiding light to the whole of our human family in the years to come.

* * * *

Before we go on to consider Pakistan, we also need to take a look at the role that Pakistan's neighbour Afghanistan is playing in the region.

Afghanistan is located at the strategically important junction of the Middle East and South and Central Asia. It lies east of Iran and north of the Harappan civilization in an area that was home to some of the earliest farming communities in the world. For millennia it has seen military incursions and conquest, as well as meddling in its affairs by various powers, including Britain, Russia, the USA, Saudi Arabia, Iran and Pakistan.

Since the late 1970s, the country has experienced a continuous state of conflict, including occupation by Soviet forces in 1979. After ten years during which the USA, with Saudi help, armed and funded Islamic fighters, including Osama bin Laden's al-Qaeda, the Soviets were finally expelled. After a fragile peace followed by a further period of fighting, the

Islamic Taliban took over in 1996, with the substantial help of Pakistan, Saudi Arabia and al-Qaeda militants.

Only two days before the terrorist attack of 9/11, the Afghan leader Ahmad Shah Massoud, who had beseeched the international community to provide humanitarian help for his people, made it clear that without Pakistan's support the Taliban and al-Qaeda would be defeated and warned that a large-scale attack on the USA was imminent, was assassinated.

Following the attacks and the Taliban refusal to hand over Osama bin Laden and disband al-Qaeda bases in Afghanistan, US and British forces supported Afghan forces in a civil war that resulted in the fall of the Taliban regime and a new government led by Hamid Karzai.

Since 2002, with international support, Afghanistan is slowly being rebuilt, but in the shadow of a continuing insurgency by Taliban forces. Widespread illiteracy, power struggles and political and social corruption continue to blight this poverty-stricken country that nonetheless has a currently estimated one to three trillion dollars' worth of untapped mineral resources.

In the aftermath of 9/11, al-Qaeda jihadists retreated to the tribal areas of western Pakistan. And in that regard, whilst the issues within Afghanistan are substantial, they may still be a distraction from the far more serious ones involving Pakistan. For the latter's permeable borders, large-scale popular support for fundamentalist Islam, virtually unassailable tribal heartlands, dangerously unstable political and social structures and nuclear arsenal have led to it being called the most dangerous country in the world.

***

So let's now look at Pakistan, and how India and the rest of the international community can help this nation of 180 million people, the second most populous Islamic country in the world, heal the traumas of its psyche.

215

India's struggles to deal with the threat of its sibling are ongoing. When India tested five nuclear weapons in May 1998 at an underground site near the Pakistan border, within days Pakistan had exploded six – symbolically one more than its rival – on its side of the border. And the country now has the largest growing nuclear arsenal in the world.

Pakistan's psyche, especially the traumatic 'home environment' denoted by its natal Saturn–Pluto conjunction, powerfully reflects the geomantic reality, where a seismically unstable triple junction of tectonic plates literally lies beneath the city of Islamabad where the natal chart is centred.

Such geomagnetic trauma, allied to the ongoing risks from the Indus Valley river system that cataclysmically flooded in 2010, adds to the Fire and Water aspects in Pakistan's chart, exacerbating the mental and emotional issues within its psyche since Partition.

Despite a secular constitution that envisaged Pakistan as a modern and moderate secular state, since the 1950s its leadership has been characterized by an unstable and imbalanced military–civilian relationship and its civil society by ongoing tensions between moderates and extremists, leading to it being the home of more terrorist organizations than any other country in the world.

And as if its domestic issues and real-ationship with India weren't bad enough, the ongoing foreign attempts to control Pakistan's policies have further destabilized the country and undermined the development of civil institutions, resulting in appalling governance adding to the economic and social woes suffered by its people.

Yet despite over 60 years of trauma, the psyche of Pakistan, I feel, still yearns to fulfil the destiny set out by its founder, Mohammed Jinnah, and become a modern, moderate and democratic nation. To enable it to do that, the international community first needs to understand its trauma, which is rather like that of an abused child whose unstable home life causes it to lash out in anger and despair.

The USA, which provides enormous amounts of aid to Pakistan, should I believe focus it far more on humanitarian and social causes than on the military and should be supporting rather than undermining democratic institutions, encouraging good governance and helping Pakistan and its alienated and long-suffering people normalize their relationships with India and Afghanistan and the wider world.

Like an abused child that grows into a monstrous adult, Pakistan is an enormous danger to the world unless it can be rehabilitated and brought fully into the international community of nations.

* * * *

Our human journey began on the Rift Valley of Africa, at a triple junction of tectonic plates in the Afar region of Ethiopia that profoundly links our destiny with that of Gaia. As we approach 2012 and the rifted energies of our collective psyche have the opportunity of rebirth, on another triple junction in Pakistan we now have a collective choice to make, for we can't ignore this dangerous trauma within our human family.

Healing the schism between India and Pakistan is healing the relationship between two brothers. India, the senior sibling, has a hugely important role. Whilst acknowledging the challenges, if it can find the willingness to spiritually embrace its younger brother, it can give Pakistan the acknowledgement and respect it craves. Then, through honest and generous support and the progressive opening of transport, business and social links, allied with international efforts, especially by the USA and China, it can be instrumental in defusing the tensions within Pakistan.

By envisaging within the universal heart the healing of the two countries' schism, each of us can add our intention and unconditional love to its resoulution. And from the geomantic nexus that underlies Pakistan, this will resonate around the world, healing our people and the Earth herself.

CHAPTER 17

Japan

'Expect to have hope rekindled. Expect your prayers to be answered in wondrous ways. The dry seasons in life do not last. The Spring rains will come again.'
SARAH BAN BREATHNACH

The ancient culture of Japan and the psyche of its people are very different from those of the West. Over a period of eight years or so from 1989 to 1996, I was very fortunate to visit Japan about a dozen times in my corporate roles, helping to set up and strategically manage businesses there. And after an interval of some years, since October 2008 I've been there a further nine times.

The history of Japan goes back an astonishing 16,000 years to the Jomon period, from which we have evidence of an extraordinarily simple but profoundly sophisticated society that harvested the abundance of the environment and lived in harmony with it for some 14 millennia until the encroachment of newcomers from mainland China and Korea some 2,000 years ago.

Living in wonderful wooden stilt houses, some of which have been recreated in the excavated village of Sannai-Maruyama in Aomori, northern Honshu, the Jomon combined hunting and gathering from the natural richness around them with the deliberate cultivation and harvesting of particular resources such as chestnut trees, which they used in myriad ways to provide house-building and domestic products and even food.

It's the Jomon from whom we have the as yet earliest evidence of pottery in the world. And their understanding of Nature and the energies pervading the landscape and Cosmos goes back, it seems, to the vastly ancient time that also saw the construction of the Gobleckli Tepe temple in E'din.

Rather than building temples, the Jomon revered the natural landscape, especially mountains. They somehow moved massive rocks, such as those clustered on the sides of Mount Towara in the Mayogatai Forest, to modify, harmonize and enhance the energies of sacred sites, and raised dolmens and constructed stone circles such as the double circle at Oyu in Akita prefecture in northern Honshu, aligned with the seasons of the year and especially the solstices.

From the Oyu circles, the amazing pyramidal mound of Mount Kuromata can be seen rising above the surrounding plain. Having climbed its 262 feet and attuned to its energies, which now seem to be slumbering, awaiting Japan's deeper appreciation of its ancient heritage, I wasn't surprised to learn that the local people have long considered it to be a 'pyramid built by an ancient people' and that the interior of the mound was discovered in the 1990s to comprise a series of seven terraces, showing that the Jomon had at least modified its shape.

The so-called Yayoi people began to arrive from mainland China and the Korean peninsula around 400 BCE, bringing with them new technologies of weaving, rice farming and metal-working. Whilst archaeologists maintain that they supplanted the Jomon, there are relatively few signs of conflict but rather an overall integration of the two cultures. And written records of the third century CE relate that by that time, the Japanese community was a unification of some 30 tribes led by a shaman queen named Himiko.

* * * *

In late 2008 I returned to Japan in a very different capacity from my earlier visits when my book *CosMos*, co-authored with Dr Ervin Laszlo, was published in Japanese.

Thanks to a wonderful synchronicity, I'd been approached some months before by my now friend Hideki Miura, who was seeking to become my representative in Asia. Our agreement was timed perfectly to enable me to travel to Japan at the same time as Ervin.

One of the first things we did after arriving in Japan was to journey to the southern island of Kyushu and visit Yoshinogari Historical Park, the most famous archaeological site of the Yayoi period, and the site of a large Yayoi settlement that was inhabited for several hundred years from around 400 BCE.

In the Northern Inner Enclosure, there is a special place where successive early leaders of Yoshinogari were buried. This spot was later revered as the resting-place of their spirits. A small group of us attuned there, energetically connecting Heaven and Earth and asking for their blessing. As we did so, a raven flew from the back of the burial mound, and just as Hideki and I opened our eyes after our attunement, an enormous and very beautiful black and white butterfly flew by us. Only the two of us saw this wonderful sign, as the others of our small group still had their eyes shut. And I knew that the ancestors were blessing us.

* * * *

Since then, Hideki-san and I have visited many sacred sites with my Japanese co-author and friend Shinichi Nakaya, a renowned expert in Japanese spirituality. We've explored further back into the ancient times of the Jomon and, like Shinichi-san, I've come to understand that the traditional animist Shinto beliefs of the Japanese had their deepest roots in the age-old understanding of the Jomon.

I discovered such an integration of profoundly ancient wisdom enhanced by later inspiration when we visited the most energetically powerful site I have yet encountered in Japan. In February 2010, Hideki-san, Shinichi-san, a film crew and I visited the Haruna shrine in central Honshu to experience its energies, which are traditionally considered to embody the primordial energies of Fire and Water.

We journeyed on a bitterly cold day into the mountainous area of Gunma prefecture, where the shrine is located at the foot of Mount Haruna. The freezing mist that surrounded us significantly limited our visibility. And so, instead of viewing the outwardly majestic surroundings of the shrine, I felt invited to go within and connect with the shrine's hidden treasure trove of wisdom.

Standing at the entrance, beneath the traditional *torii* gate that denotes the threshold between the mundane world and the sacred precincts of a shrine, I let go of any expectations and opened myself unconditionally to what would unfold.

Climbing up the path at a steady pace with Shinichi-san, I felt my awareness slowing down as though preparing to meet a consciousness that thought, felt and moved at a different pace from that of human beings.

As we went further into the shrine, I also began to discern faces in the rocks around us witnessing and, I sensed, welcoming our presence.

Eventually we crossed the further threshold of a bridge over a mountain stream. As we came to the other side, I suddenly came face to face with the guardian rock of this sacred site. From the edge of the path he loomed over us and I felt his powerful presence scan me as though to decide whether I was worthy of going any further.

The face of the guardian was that of a primeval dragon.

Feeling that he supported our continuing journey, I thanked him and carried on up the ascending pathway until we reached the base of a steep flight of steps that rose up to a further elaborate gateway.

Climbing the steps, I felt something momentous was coming, but had no idea what it would be! Walking into the gateway, I noticed that sculpted within it were two interconnecting dragons. Immediately I passed on through, an enormous energetic shiver flowed through me.

As I looked up to my left, my gaze was captured by a huge rock with a deep fissure running vertically alongside it. The masculine energies coursing through the rock and the feminine energies sinuously streaming down the fissure came together exactly where I was now standing.

The Chinese tradition of *feng shui* refers to such telluric energy currents as *lung mei*, the paths of the dragon, and these energies felt primal and draconic – and, I sensed, elementally embodied the archetypal energies of Fire and Water.

Despite the severe cold, the powerful energies revived me. Walking on into the inner sanctuary of the shrine, I saw a gigantic rock rising up behind the beautiful building before me. As I looked more closely, it revealed itself to be shaped like a human being. Shinichi-san informed me it was known as *Misugata-iwa*.

Walking around the building to view the rock more easily, I could feel beneath my feet the powerful flow of the dragon energies interweaving with each other and flowing towards it. Looking at *Misugata-iwa*, in my inner vision I could see the two currents of energy then spiralling up and down in a great vortex within the body of the rock. And at the centre of their spirals, rising vertically like a *shin-no-mihashira*, the sacred pillar erected at the centre of Shinto shrines, there pulsed a clear beam of energy.

I suddenly realized that *Misugata-iwa* was, on a grand scale, replicating the three main energy meridians of the human body, the *ida*, *pingala* and *shushumna*. Embodying the cosmic/divine feminine, masculine and child energies within us, these spiral up through our spine and to the crown of our head, just as I was seeing in the clear beam of energy pulsing within *Misugata-iwa*. With this incredible revelation, I became aware of the huge significance of this shrine and knew that this freezing February day was just the beginning of working with its energies.

But by now I was feeling physically unwell, without as yet understanding why. I felt very uncomfortable, as though unable to digest a large meal – but I hadn't eaten!

Trying to put aside my increasing discomfort, before leaving we decided to continue on the beautiful Lake Haruna. Whilst thanks to the persistent mist we were unable to view the peak of Mount Haruna-fuji behind it, I could feel its presence. But again, my inability to see the mountain ensured that my focus remained on the lake.

Earlier, when I'd first felt the dragon energies swirling through the rocks, I'd wondered where they had originated. But now, as I gazed onto the frozen surface of the lake, I knew.

Rising up from deep within the magma of the living Earth, through the volcanic bedrock within which the caldera lake had formed, the telluric dragon of Fire communes with the Water dragon and together they begin their landscape dance that culminates at *Misugata-iwa*.

There a third telluric dragon joins them, embodying the elemental essence of Earth. And high in the mountains, the elemental dragon of Air flows around them.

So, here I was encountering a four-fold elemental embodiment of some of the most powerful telluric energies I'd yet experienced anywhere in the world. I was not only witnessing their energies in my inner vision but feeling them flowing potently through me. So enormously strong and archetypal were they that I realized this was the source of my severe physical discomfort.

Only many days afterwards was I finally able to fully integrate the archetypal presence of the elemental dragons within me and learn how to channel their intense energies by focusing on their flow through me and down through the 9th chakra beneath my feet. I am enormously grateful to them and their guardianship during whatever will be the next steps of my journey in discovering and sharing the deeper mysteries of the Jomon. With the sunken ruins that have been discovered at Yonaguni off the southern coast of Japan, there may even be the possibility of tracing their heritage back to the legendary land of Lemuria.

* * * *

Following the Yayoi period, the next millennium saw the gradual growth of the Japanese state, with military clans and the intensification of internal conflict as each clan jockeyed for power.

By the so-called Edo period of the fifteenth century, a federation of clans had come to rule and instigated some significant changes. The warrior *samurai* class was raised above other sections of society and commoners were subdivided into groups of five people, all held accountable for the actions of each individual. To prevent local leaders from rebelling, the state required them to maintain large residences in the capital city Edo, undertake costly processions, contribute to the cost of religious buildings and roads and gain permission before making any repairs to their castles. And with the relative peace, the arts thrived.

In the seventeenth century, fearful of military conquest, the Japanese began an era of seclusion. Only in 1853, when Commodore Mathew Perry of the US Navy sailed into Yokohama Bay with four warships that became known to the Japanese as *kurofune*, the black ships, did they agree to his 'request' to open up trade with the West.

The treaties that were signed were unequal, however, having been forced onto the Japanese through military-backed diplomacy. And so began a difficult real-ationship between Japan and the United States, and between Japan and the West generally, that continues to be challenging today.

* * * *

The signing of the enforced treaties was viewed within Japan as a cause of humiliation and shame, and a period known as the Meiji Restoration followed, aimed at integrating the best of Japanese tradition with western technological advances.

Such was the revolutionary focus and effort that in only a few decades the nation had transformed from a feudal state into a modern power. But, due to its earlier sense of humiliation, within Japan the prevailing belief was that the country had to compete successfully with the West on both technological and military levels to achieve equality. The utter focus on these goals dictated every aspect of life and thrust to the edges of society the ancient beliefs that had sustained the people from Jomon times.

The increasing militarism finally erupted in wars with China and Russia which left Japan as the dominant power in the Far East by the early twentieth century.

After fighting on the side of Britain and the USA in World War I, the country became increasingly militarized and in the run-up to the outbreak of World War II, the Japanese committed atrocities in China and southern Asia.

Tensions with America were also mounting and when the USA tried to rein in Japan's imperial expansion by an embargo on the oil and iron on which their military depended, instead of retreating, on 7 December 1941 the Japanese navy unleashed a surprise attack on the US base at Pearl Harbor in Hawaii.

The USA retaliated with a full commitment to go to war against Japan and its allies, escalating the existing conflict in Europe into a war that engulfed the entire globe and culminated, almost four years later, in the dropping of atomic bombs on Hiroshima and Nagasaki.

Symbolically, when Japan signed a declaration of surrender on the deck of the USS *Missouri* in Tokyo harbour, a flag that had flown on Commodore Perry's ship when he had sailed into the same bay a century before was flying.

* * * *

The war had been politically, socially and economically a disaster for Japan and afterwards the country was placed under the international control of the US-led Allies. As well summarized in *Shutting Out the Sun* by Michael Zeilinger of the Institute of East Asian Studies, UC, Berkeley, the pre-war focus on militarism was now replaced by a national urge to rectify the nation's perceived failings and an intense focus on attaining superiority in global trade. The country grew wealthy by mastering the mysteries of the shop floor. It pioneered lean production systems and just-in-time manufacturing, and appropriated the methods of total quality control. It also knew how to export uniform, high-quality goods at low prices to mass markets.

To achieve its aim, as Zeilinger goes on to state,

> ... seldom had a society so evenly meshed the disparate interests of business, government and political élites. Its people accepted limits on their personal liberty in service of this higher calling, as if newly conscripted soldiers. Time after time, the nation responded adroitly to gradual, foreseeable change. Indeed, by 1990, this small island nation had vanquished its former conquerors, producing more economic output per person than the USA and paying higher wages.

It was an incredible achievement, but came at a huge cost to the Japanese psyche and its dislocation from its Jomon roots became almost complete.

Focused on its monolithic goal and accustomed to hierarchical and rigid controls, when the emerging computer and communications age revolutionized global business and the trading environment became far more flexible and open, Japan found that the strengths that had enabled it to become a world leader now became weaknesses. At the beginning of the 1990s it entered the so-called 'Lost Decade' of progressive decline.

An inability to significantly reform in the years since, despite the election of a more progressive ruling coalition in 2009, resulted in stress gaining an increasingly unsustainable hold over the Japanese psyche.

****

The Japanese culture is very strong and its people take great pride in its continuity and inherent values. Its predominant characteristics are the cohesion of family and group ties, respect for authority and the elderly, and the importance of stoicism and not losing face. Since the Meiji Restoration, the positive aspects of these traditional strengths have suffered and their dysfunctional aspects been exaggerated. A point has now been reached, as witnessed during my visits and by the many Japanese with whom I've spoken and undertaken healing work, where this is both deeply unhealthy and barely sustainable.

The archetypal pattern embodied within the Japanese psyche is reflected clearly in the policy of seclusion that was in force from the seventeenth century onwards. When outside influences have been forced on the Japanese, they have only been accepted after being morphed into a specifically Japanese mould. And even today the country's imports and foreign-owned investments are proportionately the lowest of any developed nation.

Recently, events have revealed the deep trauma beneath the façade of an apparently serene nation.

One example, reported by the BBC in September 2010, was the discovery by police, on a hot July day, of the mummified corpse of Mr Sogen Kato still lying in the bed where he had died 30 years before.

The Japanese people are renowned for their longevity and at 111 years old, Mr Kato was believed to be Japan's oldest man. But his 81-year-old daughter had hidden his death and claimed more than 9 million yen, some £65,000, in pension payments.

Following the macabre discovery, officials found more and more cases of 'missing' pensioners. The country went into collective shock when the Justice Ministry, after a nationwide search, reported more than 230,000 missing centenarians.

A number of reasons were put forward to explain the enormous number, primarily the poor record-keeping of the family register of births and deaths. But even when the resident register, which is deemed to be far more accurate, significantly reduced the figure, hundreds of people over the age of 100 were still unable to be located.

For Japan, a country that prides itself on its veneration for its elderly, the scandal was deeply troubling, as it indicated a breakdown within families and throughout wider society.

Whilst historically, married women bore the brunt of family care, now, with an economic need for more married women to work and an ageing population, the National Institute of Population and Social Security estimates that a third of Japanese over the age of 65 live alone. Whilst there are public care homes, these are institutionalized, and many people prefer to live on their own. Many also die alone – either of natural causes or by suicide, a modern and unwelcome development which has been increasing and is described by the term *kodokushi*, or 'lonely death'.

On the other end of the age scale, due to the economic and social freedoms that still traditionally end on marriage, fewer young women are marrying and the birth rate continues to topple.

Another symptom of Japan's social malaise and deep-seated pattern of rejection is the phenomenon of more than a million (primarily) men in their teens and twenties, known as *hikikomori*, withdrawing from society and shutting themselves away in their rooms.

****

As *Hua-yen*, one of the traditional spiritual teachings of Japan, maintains, and as leading-edge science is coming to recognize, 'All things freely interpenetrate each other.' Japanese society has long sought to embody such interdependence. With the social real-ationships, especially between parent and child, known as *amae*, the network of obligations summarized as *giri* and the group consciousness of *shudan-ishiki*, the entire collective is focused on the harmonization of such dependencies.

But the national intensity of focus since the Meiji Restoration, first on military might and then on corporate success, has taken these traits to a pathological extreme where dissenting views and individual initiative have been rejected and suffocated through bullying, peer pressure, derision and exclusion.

I believe that the *hikikomori* phenomenon of young men withdrawing from the world is a deep sign of this malaise. And whilst the young women of Japan are generally reacting in a different way, increasing numbers are rejecting and withdrawing from the traditional roles forced on them by a homogenous society. The stifling nature of that society is slowly suffocating the life out of the Japanese psyche and the sadness and sense of resignation of many people echoes the feeling of *aware*, a softly despairing sorrow with which a number of Japanese folk stories end.

Some Japanese commentators have maintained that Japan is fundamentally a feminine psyche, although the patriarchal system that has been in place for many centuries has obscured this deeper truth. Here the Sun is a goddess, Amaterasu, and the Moon a god, Tsukuyomi-no-Mikoto, her brother, and it seems that the people of the Jomon era realized and respected the complementarity between men and women.

For healing to occur, as many of my workshop participants have informed me privately, Japan needs to find a way of first becoming open and honest about its past and its current issues. Secondly, society needs to resoulve its pattern of rejection and include individual voices in a national discussion for change. And thirdly the Japanese people need to re-member and return to the core of their society, the spirit of the *Dô*. Rather like the Chinese Tao or Way, this cosmic harmony can guide them once again both in terms of how to treat themselves and others within our global human family and how to make the connection with nature and the wider Cosmos that was fundamental to the well-being of their Jomon ancestors and their ability to live in harmony with their world for longer than virtually any other people on Earth.

The Japanese have a word, *teire*, that on a mundane level means 'to repair'. But in a deeper sense it means 'to put one's soul into caring for something'. The Japanese now need to put their own souls into repairing and caring for the soul of the nation.

Another aspect of the Japanese psyche, the patience and determination of *gambari*, can be allied to overcoming the ice-soulation of rejection and to a reinvigorated integration of ancient and new, masculine and feminine, inner and outer, personal and collective well-being. This can not only bring profound release and healing for the Japanese people but also, through its psychic resonance, for our entire collective psyche.

* * * *

At 2.46 p.m. local time on Friday 11 March 2011, Hideki-san and I were on the 10th floor of an apartment building in central Tokyo when the massive magnitude 9.0 earthquake, the most powerful in Japan and the fifth largest in recorded history, struck. For several terrifying minutes the entire building shook violently. Electrical equipment toppled over and ornaments crashed to the floor. All I could do as the mayhem was unleashed around us was to reflect Hideki-san's reassuring calmness and hope and trust in Spirit's higher purpose and Gaia's mercy.

Later, and still shocked, I sat in silence as I saw on TV the incredible devastation wrought on the northern part of the country, not only by the earthquake but by the enormous wave of the tsunami which followed; a 30-foot or more high onslaught of water that swept away everything in its path.

Less than a week before, to link with the publication of the only one of my books not yet published in Japan, I'd been presenting to a large seminar my sense of how Japan had been stuck and its unwillingness but great need to radically change. I shared my sense of the energetic connections between people and places and how the ancient Jomon culture of Japan had lived in harmony with itself and Gaia for so many millennia. And how a fundamental shift was now needed to openly include the voices and views of all Japan's people to innovatively re-gain that harmony and bring its perennial wisdom into the twenty-first century.

As the earthquake and tsunami revealed the release of Gaia's stuck-ness of the tectonic fault-line that runs alongside and under the Japanese islands, I was struck by the poignancy of what I'd been sharing and that fact that the soon-to-be published book that I was there to speak about was called *The Wave*!

I also noted the date and felt an energetic resonance between 11 March in Japan – 3/11 – mirroring the events of 11 September – 9/11 – in the USA.

In the USA, as we've seen, the catastrophic moment of 9/11 re-energized the fear-based national abandonment pattern that still awaits acknowledgement and healing.

The Japanese people, located atop an ever-shifting and fundamentally unstable landscape, have existed in suppressed fear of such an enormous earthquake for many years. The 'big one' has, we trust, now happened. And although its wide-spread devastation spared the Tokyo conurbation, recovery from the aftermath of the tsunami and the nuclear reactor breakdown at Fukushima and their physical and emotional effects on the Japanese people will take enormous effort.

But rather than retreat into fear, it seems to me that the Japanese instead have chosen to take a leap into love. Stoically and with huge resilience, they have been dealing without complaint or selfishness with the practical consequences; caring generously for each other and working without rest to clear the debris and begin the long process of recuperation. And rather than trying to go back, they are already starting to look forward to the birth of a new era for Japan.

To do that they will need visionary, dynamic, innovative and wise leadership across all areas and co-creative communal involvement; not only to rebuild but to reshape Japanese society and its economic and social structures.

One of those potential new leaders is Chief Cabinet Secretary Yukio Edano, who throughout the unfolding calamity has spoken calmly and with honesty and responsibility about what is happening. Another is Yoshito Hori, managing partner of GLOBIS Capital Partners and president and dean of GLOBIS University, who immediately after the earthquake, together with some like-minded colleagues, came up with Project KIBOW, an initiative to support relief and rebuilding efforts and promote change for the future.

KIBOW combines the Japanese word *kibo*, which means hope, and the English word *rainbow*, denoting a project that its founders intend will be a rainbow bridge of hope between people around the world and Japan. Their aim is to raise funds to support not only the reconstruction but co-creative and collaborative initiatives for social and economic change.

I believe the ancestors will join, nurture and give strength and courage to this new generation of community leaders as they and the entire Japanese people strive to midwife a new era for this ancient country; an era of harmony between people and place, and an era of hope.

CHAPTER 18
UK

'If it were not for hopes, the heart would break.'
Thomas Fuller

The United Kingdom has been called a small island with a big history. And the real-ationship between its people and the land is deep and ancient.

It's here, in the white chalk landscape of southern England, that the Neolithic people monumentalized the great sacred precincts of Stonehenge and Avebury ostensibly at the same time that the pyramids were being raised in Egypt.

From these communities of early farmers who lived in peace with each other and the natural abundance of their environment and who aligned their monuments to Sun, Moon and stars, through successive waves of immigration of both people – Romans, Anglo-Saxons, Vikings, Normans and later economic migrants and refugees from across the world – and ideas, the psyche of the United Kingdom of England, Scotland, Wales and Northern Ireland was formed.

The United Kingdom has in turn exported people and ideas. The first industrialized country in the world and home to the oldest parliamentary democracy, it has shared both with the world. Its migrants were some of the first colonists to

America, Australia, Canada and New Zealand. The growth of the British Empire, beginning in the sixteenth-century CE era of Elizabeth I and lasting until the end of World War II, also widely disseminated the English language and the British legal system. Culturally, too, the UK has given the world great literature, from that of Shakespeare and Dickens to Tolkien's *Lord of the Rings* and J. K. Rowling's *Harry Potter* books, and music, from the stirring melodies of Elgar and Britten to the Beatles.

* * * *

Whilst, like the US, the psyche of the UK is diverse, unlike America, its diversity has origins from much further back in history that over time have woven together in an integral way. The successive waves of invaders and immigrants interbred with deep-rooted indigenous people to comprise a mix of attributes that together define what British means to the wider world. And whilst many other cultural strands interweave with that basic thread, it's a fundamental aspect of the UK's psyche that anchors it in a very special connection with the land.

Nevertheless, there are great rifts in that psyche which have been reflected in its history.

It's a nation of Nature lovers: gardeners, birdwatchers, pet owners and walkers. And yet its people were the first nation to be herded from the land and into the dirty, cramped tenements of burgeoning industrialized cities, with their effluent of pollution, to develop an unsustainable capitalist economic model that was bequeathed to the world

It's a nation that values fairness and indeed it was the first country to abolish slavery in 1833. And yet its post-World War II economy has been progressively imbalanced, with real products and services being subsumed by the exponential growth in financial services and speculation centred on the City of London.

It's a nation that's deeply empathetic, giving more per person to charitable endeavours and disaster appeals than perhaps any other nation on Earth. And yet, it is, next to the USA, the most unequal society in the world.

And it's a nation that values honesty. Yet the corruption within its parliamentary system has erupted into a shameful expenses scandal in which two members of the most venerable parliament on Earth have recently been sentenced to jail for fraud, with perhaps others to follow.

* * * *

We shouldn't forget though that the British character is a 'united kingdom'. Made up of four geographical and cultural regions, within its shared history I believe a predominant archetypal pattern has played out which has also spilled out into its relationships with the rest of the world.

One of Britain's most cherished mythologies is of King Arthur, his Queen Guinevere, their Grail knights and the great magus Merlyn. From a child I have loved these stories. But only when I grew up did I appreciate the pattern of betrayal that pervades them.

Betrayal abounds. From Merlyn enabling King Uther Pendragon to shape-shift into the appearance of his vassal Duke Gorlois and go on to betray him by seducing his wife Ygraine, who bore Arthur as a result; Arthur's betrayal of his half-sister Morgan le Fey and the pagan 'old religion' of Britain; his betrayal by Guinevere and her lover Lancelot, and ultimately by his and Morgan's son Mordred. The mythos reverberates subliminally within the British psyche.

And, as for any such pattern, we inflict it on others, they impose it on us and inevitably we embody it within ourselves, as has been the case in the historical conflicts between England, Wales, Scotland and Northern Ireland.

It's not simple to determine the seed-point of the betrayal archetype within the British psyche, but perhaps it energized around the circumstances of England and Wales being subsumed by the Roman Empire. After nearly a century of opposition, in 43 CE the British queen Cartimandua notoriously sided with the Romans and, in betraying her people and the ex-king and resistance fighter Caratacus, enabled the Romans to gain control in Britain. After an occupation that lasted a further three centuries, the Roman legions left, themselves betraying the now rich and vulnerable island to wave after wave of further invasion.

And during the heyday of the British Empire, whilst trade, ideas of parliamentary democracy and justice, education and progress offered benefits, Britain also exported the trauma of its archetypal betrayal. It often arrogantly assumed it knew best – circumstances showed that sometimes it did – but in a number of tragic cases it didn't. And sometimes its betrayal was merely cynical or cowardly.

In the mid-nineteenth century, the British East India Company invested heavily in the drug opium, together with American merchants selling vast quantities of it to Chinese smugglers and resulting in an explosion of addicts. When the Chinese authorities tried to suppress the illegal and immoral trade, the British sent forces that devastated the Chinese coastline and started the Opium Wars. Eventually the imposition onto China of unfavorable treaties, soon followed by similar forced agreements with America and France, led to China's so-called 'century of humiliation.'

In the Middle East, although striving for a fair apportionment of land and justice for the Palestinian people in the face of incoming Jewish settlement after World War II, Britain eventually failed, effectively betraying its custodianship of the land and its people and setting the seeds of ongoing dispute.

In India, although peacefully agreeing to its independence, by the failure to stand firm and help re-soulve the differences between Muslims and Hindus, Britain again effectively betrayed its outgoing imperial responsibility and helped to underwrite the genocide that ensued with Partition in 1947.

And in Africa, the pull-out from colonial territories was sometimes accompanied by unresolved disputes over land, some of which, as in Zimbabwe, remain contentious and the cause of ongoing conflict.

The historic betrayals of others have, however, whether acknowledged or subconscious, sought balance with Britain's generosity and fair-mindedness. Whilst victorious, World War II left the country virtually bankrupt. But rather than trying to hold onto its erstwhile empire, as France attempted to do by force, Britain agreed a process of peaceful disengagement. And since then too, it has welcomed progressive waves of refugees and immigrants, and contributes disproportionately to disaster relief and overseas aid and development.

* * * *

The profligacy of the UK government from 1997, colliding with the global financial crisis that erupted in 2008, has landed the UK with one of the largest national debts in the world. In May 2010 for the first time in some 70 years a coalition government was appointed and this is now pursuing a policy of radical cuts in public spending in an attempt to rein in the excesses of the banks, rebalance the economy and restore a sense of communal, social and ethical values to national life.

To meet those challenges it must get serious about bringing the best of its entire population into decision-making and enactment. The UK, as most of the rest of the world, is still showing that female equality of opportunity isn't being taken seriously. It can't afford to waste so much human potential.

Nor can it afford to let the imbalance of a predominantly male perspective continue to shape its strategic and manifest future.

Here and around the world involvement and inclusion must be authentic and ongoing, not cosmetic and sporadic. National and indeed global perceptions that 'we're all in this together' and a positively motivated and involved citizenry will be crucial in responding to the massive challenges it faces in healing our world.

In World War I, the UK was galvanized by a recruitment poster that declared: 'Your country needs YOU.' It's now time to mobilize to undertake a peaceful transformation – it's time to become the YoUK!

* * * *

But a deeper, more spiritual and more mysterious Britain lies behind today's multicultural society. It guards and embodies a heritage that goes back to the time of Stonehenge, Avebury and the other stone monuments which once proliferated throughout the land and whose wisdom connected its people with the Earth and the Cosmos.

Britain's geomancers, like those of other traditions, sought to create harmony between people and places and also recognized the cosmic connections as defined by the Hermetic tradition of ancient Egypt, 'As above, so below.' The essence of this tradition can now be harnessed to energize the re-membering of our psyche and the reconciliation of our souls. Not only do the land's great Neolithic temples still offer the possibility of transformative experiences for those who go on pilgrimage there, but so do the enigmatic crop circles that have arisen in the fields over the last two decades, though examples were recorded centuries before.

The enigma these temporary temples continue to pose is but one of many in this ancient landscape. Did the 'Lamb of God' also walk this 'green and pleasant land', as poet and mystic

William Blake declared Jesus did in his youth? At Glastonbury, the mystical Isle of Avalon, one of the earliest Christian churches in the world was founded, traditionally by Joseph of Arimathea. And, given the trading routes that archaeologists have shown existed between England and the Middle East and that in the Bible Joseph is described as a merchant, is the legend, like so many, based on a truth that may now be rediscovered?

King Arthur, too, is being revealed by both archaeology and research into arcane texts to have perhaps been real – or at least the honorific name of a war leader or leaders who, when the Roman Empire fell and the legions abandoned Britain in the late fifth century CE, rallied the people and ensured peace for a time.

The ancient temples of stone, whose remnants still pervade the landscape, the perception of Jesus' presence and that of Arthur, the soular hero and the Once and Future King of Britain, and the myriad mystic traditions of Britain are all being re-energized by those who sense the emergence of a New Age here.

The telluric energies of the so-called Aquarian Triangle of Glastonbury, Stonehenge and Avebury in southern England form a nexus that attracts those who are sensing the Shift of consciousness. Pilgrims from around the world flock here, as they are doing in ever-larger numbers to the great sacred sites around the globe.

Regardless of where they are, such sites were constructed to offer experiences that transcend the mundane and offer a glimpse into eternity. Though suffused by different energies, when approached with open minds, hearts and purpose and a willingness to listen, learn and connect with a greater sense of the unity of the Cosmos, all in their unique yet universal way open the portal between worlds and usher the pilgrim through into a new way of being.

* * * *

In late 2003, as I wrote about in detail in *The 13ᵗʰ Step*, at the culmination of the global pilgrimages to activate the 12 multi-dimensional Lemurian soular discs around the world and the unity energy grid of Gaia to support our collective healing and Shift of consciousness, Tony and I returned home to Avebury.

The astrological alignment of the so-called Harmonic Concordance, discovered by astrologer Johnny Mirehiel and embodying the resonance of personal transmutation, was due to occur over the night of 8/9 November. And it was then that we and the many people who were joining us around the world intended to activate the twelfth soular disc energetically centred at Silbury Hill, the nexus of telluric power within the Avebury landscape.

How wonderfully symbolic that the alignment's empower-ment of the unconditional love of the transpersonal 8ᵗʰ chakra of the universal heart and its grounding of that love through the 9ᵗʰ chakra to activate unity awareness within the consciousness field of Gaia took place on the eighth and ninth day of the 'moonth'. The moonth, too, was the eleventh, the number of personal mastery, of the year. And the year itself, 2003, harmonized the numerological numbers two, three and five, representing the complementarity of male and female and the evolution of their resoulution.

In coming home to this beloved landscape, I'd also felt a more fundamental level of awareness ready to emerge. I'd started to sense that interwoven with the Michael and Mary telluric currents that flow across southern England there was now a third current that seemed more playful. Rather like a child, it appeared to energetically stray from its parents within the landscape but return to them at powerful node points where the three energies came together. After attuning to its emerging presence, with grateful appreciation I realized it embodied the essence of the cosmic child, the co-creative force of the Cosmos which was awakening within our collective psyche.

Unknown to me at the time, in 1988 our friends Hamish and Ba Miller, the dowsers who'd discovered and tracked the Michael and Mary telluric leys, had also perceived at the Beltane festival, the early May festival that celebrates the sacred marriage of masculine and feminine on both human and telluric levels, a new energy pattern at the Michael and Mary node point within the Avebury henge. A nested trinity of 12-pointed stars had emerged, centred there. And later, when they investigated other node points where the energies came together, they realized that they too now embedded this new real-ational pattern.

Back in 1987, the Harmonic Convergence had been seen as the start of the period of transformation outlined by the Mayan calendar and beginning the countdown to 2012. So Hamish and Ba's early discovery showed that a Shift of awareness was indeed underway, not only within our human psyche but within the etheric body of Gaia too.

And I too experienced at Avebury, as our global pilgrimages culminated in the activation of the twelfth soular disc, the seeding of the cosmic child within our collective psyche, the activation of Gaia's 12-faced geometric unity field and the beginning of our collective resoulution.

Hamish and Ba had also, again unknown to me until later, perceived the elemental attributes of the Michael and Mary telluric leys as being Fire and Water. As had been revealed during our journeys around the world, these elemental characteristics were also embodied as the primary essence of the soular discs and indeed of the Shift of consciousness itself. For, as we'd come to understand, the highest vibration of Fire is Spirit and that of Water is unconditional love, which is now flowing through our communal psyche.

****

Gaia's unity grid had been activated, but according to the guidance I'd received from the Elohim, the guardians and guides of our Soular System, the 'thirteenth master key' still needed to be 'turned at Avebury on 23 December 2003'. At the time of receiving this message, four years before, I'd no idea what it meant, nor its significance for the Shift. But in the last few months my understanding had grown.

Many geomancers have viewed the great circle of Avebury henge as representing an energetic and symbolic *omphalos*, or navel, for Gaia. It lies in a shallow bowl in the chalk landscape, surrounded by a high bank and a deep inner ditch, and is essentially hidden from outer view. More than 4,000 years ago, priests and pilgrims would have walked between enormous portals of crystallized stone, some of which still stand sentinel, into the interior of this marvellous arena.

21 December is well known as the shortest day of the year, or winter solstice, in the northern hemisphere. But what is less known is that the Latin word 'solstice', which means 'solar stand-still', is named because for a three-day period the Sun rises in the same place on the south-eastern horizon before commencing its new year path to greater daylight.

So, rather than 21 December, which is the date considered by most of those researching the prophecies of the Mayan calendar to be the point of transformation, it is the 23rd that completes the three-day period of the darkness of the labour pangs of the winter solstice and culminates in the rebirth of the solar/soular hero, offering new hope to the world.

This is also the day in the ancient Druidic lunar calendar of Britain of 364 days, comprising 13 'moonths' of 28 days each, that is 'out of time' and reconciles the lunar and solar year – and so the feminine and masculine aspects of our archetypal psyche.

This timing also represents the yearly cycle of the Moon as measured against the stars and so in effect connects our psyche with the wider Galaxy.

And the twenty-third day of the twelfth month of the year 2003 added up to and embodied the numerology of 13 – the number of transformation.

It was on this day we were to turn the thirteenth master key at Avebury.

It was on this day too that the Sun would become conjunct with the foot of Ophiuchus, the thirteenth zodiac sign, and thus the centre of the Galaxy.

* * * *

Ophiuchus is the constellation that shows a human being holding a serpent. I'd first attuned to its energies back in December 2001 when a solar eclipse had occurred there. This had been perceived by some mystics and astrologers as beginning the reawakening of the Lemurian aspects of our hidden heritage. Ophiuchus has been interpreted as representing the Adam Kadmon, the perfected human of the Qabalah, and the serpent as symbolizing our *kundalini* energy and the transformation of our DNA.

To the ancients, Ophiuchus, or, to give him his Greek name, Asclepius, was the god of healing who, though grievously wounded, was as an immortal unable to die. And so he became the cosmic healer, wounded himself but able to help others to heal.

The foot of Ophiuchus 'stands' on the ecliptic, the path of the Sun and planets through the sky that determines the band of constellations known as the zodiac, and so it is legitimately a thirteenth zodiac sign.

The symbolic and energetic power of Ophiuchus is emerging in our collective awareness at this momentous time. The esoteric numerology of 13 is that of transformational wholeness, as represented in numerous spiritual teachings and embodied by Jesus and his 12 disciples and King Arthur and his 12 grail knights.

But even more significantly, the foot of this cosmic healer is conjunct with the Galactic Centre. And after a 26,000-year wave of precession, our Sun and entire Soular System are also now aligned there at the December solstice. So Ophiuchus, the cosmic healer, is supporting us in symbolically and energetically stepping into the manifestation of such unity awareness.

The traditional healing staff of Asclepius, the caduceus, is also embodied in the landscape and psyche of Albion, formed by the Michael and Mary dragon paths curving around the 'staff' of the alignment that links sacred sites across the country.

We finally understood why the Elohim had specified this day and place, and that the 'master key' was humanity itself. We are the ones we have been waiting for, as the Hopi prophecy maintained.

At 9.43 a.m. universal time on 23 December 2003 the Sun and New Moon were conjunct in the sky and, through the archetypal healing essence of Asclepius/Ophiuchus, with the Galactic Centre. And at Avebury, our attunement in the universal heart of the 8th chakra turned the master key within us and energetically opened the umbilical portal between ourselves, Gaia, our entire Soular System and the Galactic Centre.

With nine years to the day until the December solstice of 2012, the time the ancient Maya and many mystics deem offers us the opportunity to give birth to a collective Shift of consciousness, the galactic portal was opened and the cosmic blueprint of galactic and unity awareness activated to support us on our way forward and give us the choice to embody our destiny.

I likened then the nine years to come to the nine months of human gestation. As I now write, it's early 2011 and we are in the last cosmic 'moonth' of the process. It's now that we're really beginning to feel our collective birth pangs.

But as with the birth of a baby, as any mother will know, this is the time to relax, trust the process and breathe!

PART III
HEALING THE WHOLE-WORLD

There are three fundamental aspects to healing on a collective level and completing our evolutionary Shift of awareness.

The first, as we've already noted, is the return of the divine heart-based feminine to the forefront of our collective psyche and her balance with the divine mind-based masculine. This enables the empowerment and manifestation of the divine child — the Christed, Buddhic embodiment of unity awareness that is our fundamental nature and cosmic destiny.

The education of women and girls is an investment in humanity. And the active involvement of women at all levels and in all sectors of societies throughout the world is crucial to developing and implementing policies and principles, strategies and operational functions.

Too often, even in so-called developed nations such as the US and UK, where ostensibly women live lives of equal opportunity, that is still rarely the case, especially in the higher echelons of authority. The inbuilt rigidity of the status quo also militates against full female participation in decision-making, to the detriment not only of women but of our entire societies.

The UN has been a vocal advocate of women's rights for many years, but only now, when that advocacy has been shown to have had limited impact around the world, have the various women's organizations and representations been drawn together under the remit of UNWomen, which was set up on 1 January 2011 under its first head, Michelle Bachelet, the ex-President of Chile.

The second aspect we need to consider is the transformation of our collective worldview. As we've seen, the perspective of western science is that of a solely material world which is random and meaningless and in which consciousness is merely the accidental outcome of arbitrary evolutionary processes.

Such a limited, disempowering and frankly wrong outlook has brought us and Gaia to the edge of destruction.

The new vision that is gaining ground is of the integral reality of the whole-world of the Cosmos. Reconciling science and spirit, it grounds all our experiences in a meaningful and spiritually based awareness of the oneness of All That Is and is a vastly more empowering perception of our co-creative role in the Cosmos.

This scientifically articulated vision of the whole-world offers us a bigger-picture understanding that invites and inspires us to come together in community, to treat each other with honesty and fairness and to literally 'get' that when we hurt someone else, we injure ourselves.

And when we heal ourselves, we heal each other.

The third is that we need to fully realize that we are the ones we've been waiting for. Rather than waiting for someone else to sort out the issues that we need to resoulve, or feeling that somehow they're too big to deal with, by finding the courage within ourselves and overcoming the fear that has held us back, we can fulfil our higher purpose in being here and now. In the universal heart of the 8ᵗʰ chakra, each and every one of us can show up in service to the great transformation of the Shift — it's what we came here to do!

CHAPTER 19
Peace and Resoulution

'Everything that is done in the world is done by hope.'
DR MARTIN LUTHER KING JR

In the twentieth century, commentators estimate that at least 100 million people were killed in wars and genocidal conflicts around the world. Whilst the first decade of the twenty-first century has not seen such mass warfare, humanity continues to be blighted by hostilities and confrontations where civilians, disproportionately women and children, are the victims.

For every dollar spent on United Nations peacekeeping, it's estimated that its member nations spend $2,000 on making war. Of the five nations (the United States, the United Kingdom, France, Russia and China) that constitute permanent membership of the UN Security Council that has the power of veto over all UN Resolutions, four (excluding China) are the top arms dealers in the world.

In 2009, the Stockholm International Peace Research Institute, the SIPRI, estimated that global military spending topped $1.5 trillion. Almost half of that vast amount was spent by the USA. And the next four rankings were held by the other four permanent members of the UN Security Council.

With such an overwhelming focus on so-called defence and its associated military-industrial vested interests, it's hardly surprising that authentic investment in peace, both in effort and, crucially, financial resources, is so relatively minimal.

During this century we are likely to face environmental and resource-stressed challenges far greater that those that catastrophically overpowered our ancestors of 2200 BCE and 1200 BCE. And then, despite the calamities they experienced, they were able to migrate elsewhere and start again. That is not an option for us and our children.

If we persist in spending huge amounts of money and effort on advancing conflict, both in striking at others and ostensibly defending ourselves, rather than on treading the path of peace and co-operation, as Dr Martin Luther King once said, rather than swim together as brothers, 'we shall drown together as fools.'

In the USA especially, the amount of military spending, some $661 billion at least in 2009, is an appalling and dangerous waste of money. Instead of exporting warfare, such monies could be redirected to build up the country's own decaying infrastructure, alleviate the social ills of its people, innovate harmonious technologies, invest in the environment and export humanitarian and peaceful development – a direction far more likely to perpetuate safety for both its own people and the world community.

****

Whilst all five of the Security Council nations could do much more to facilitate peace and resoulution around the world, I know from my own experience that ultimately true peace can't be imposed, it can only arise from the heart.

In November 1993, I asked my then husband Pete if he would like to go away for Christmas. When with a smile he said he'd love to, but where would I suggest, I replied, 'Bosnia.'

The Balkans War was at its height and in my frustration with the apparent apathy and unwillingness of the international community, especially the European countries, to do much to help what was becoming a genocidal conflict, I knew that rather than criticize others, I needed to do something myself. So when Pete said he'd go with me, we liaised with a charitable organization which was delivering aid and managed to raise enough donations to fill a large truck with medicines and supplies for a children's hospital in Mostar, the medieval town famous for its Old Bridge spanning the river Neretva.

Our journey through Europe in January 1994 was blessed by beautiful weather. Bright blue skies and warm winter Sun shone above us all the way into Slovenia and then down the Croatian coast. At first, other than the deserted towns we passed through, there seemed no sign of war. But as we continued southwards towards the city of Split – a good name in what had become a split country – the roads were pock-marked with the mortar bomb craters that the locals, with black humour, called Bosnian roses, and the buildings had been raked by mortar fire and shrapnel.

After Split, our convoy carried on inland. As we did so, we became familiar with the complex history of the torn land we were journeying through.

When the multi-ethnic Yugoslavia broke up in the early 1990s, three elements of the former nation, the Orthodox Christian Serbs, Muslim Bosniaks and Catholic Croats, started battling each other. The small town of Mostar was bombed by Serbian forces, who then gained control over most of it. Soon, however, the Croats had gained enough support to oust the Serbs, who responded by destroying a number of monuments and churches. But with the Serbs expelled, the Croats and Bosniaks then fell to fighting each other, and the Old Bridge over the river Neretva, which had historically symbolized the community of Mostar, was destroyed.

The town's suffering was a microcosm of the horror that engulfed Bosnia-Herzegovina. By the end of it, after massacres, mass rape and ethnic cleansing, the great majority perpetrated by the Serbs, an estimated 100,000 people had lost their lives. It had been the worst conflict in Europe since World War II.

It was both ironic and perhaps an echo of an ancient schism that still resonated through the Balkan states that the conflict had been started by Serbs, the nationality of the assassin of the Austrian Archduke Franz Ferdinand at the Yugoslav city of Sarajevo in 1914, the act that triggered World War I.

While we were in former Yugoslavia, the fighting was still at its height. When we spoke to the teachers and doctors of Mostar, they told us of their concerns that children were being psychologically scarred for life by their experiences. The teachers had closed the local school because of their fears that it would be bombed, as indeed the hospital had been. But away from school, little ones of four and five years old were already wanting to become soldiers and spending their days in pretend battles that emulated the real fighting of the adults. With the kids becoming more violent in their war 'games,' the teachers had reluctantly reopened the school as being a lesser danger than the psychological damage they feared the children were sustaining. But in the couple of days that the school had been open, just before we arrived, a child had been shot dead by a sniper whilst in the playground.

The teachers and doctors we met were heroic and unbearably grateful for the aid we were delivering, but the stories we heard, the destruction we witnessed and the terrible plight of the children we saw broke my heart. My experiences made me realize as never before that the fear and hatred that was being felt by the various factions of what had been a peaceful community was a canker that was destroying its people from within. And that whatever aid could be delivered could only address the symptoms and not the cause.

* * * *

In addition to the small amount of practical assistance we were able to provide, one way of offering help had presented itself the previous evening when we had stayed at the nearby town of Medugorje. It is famous as the site of apparitions of the Virgin Mary. These have been ongoing since 1981 and the town is now one of the most popular Catholic pilgrimage destinations in the world. Just outside it is Krizevac, or Cross Mountain, on whose summit in 1900 the townspeople had erected a huge cross.

On the evening before we went on to Mostar a small group of us from the convoy climbed Krizevac. And at the foot of the cross, with the sounds of gunfire still pounding in the dark night, we prayed for peace to come to this beautiful but war-slashed land.

One concern that had followed us inland from the coast was the continuation of the unseasonably warm and clear weather. We knew that it was encouraging soldiers to perch for long hours in their hillside lairs above Mostar, sniping at anything – or anyone – they could shoot or lob a mortar bomb at.

Leaving Medugorje with a couple of friendly police escorts, our convoy headed the 15 or so miles towards our destination. The round trip, which involved taking the difficult and dangerous route down into the landscape bowl where Mostar was located, delivering the aid to the children's hospital and returning back to Medugorje, would take around six or seven hours. And we would be in sight of potential snipers for most of the time.

But a few miles after leaving Medugorje, just before we began the descent into Mostar, a miracle happened. After literally a week of clear blue skies, rain began to fall, first lightly then more heavily as we continued on.

Under any other circumstances we would have grumbled, but now we were ecstatic. Over the walkie-talkies that connected each truck, we thanked our guardian angels. The rain would deter the soldiers.

In fact the rain lasted the entire time we drove down into Mostar, delivered the aid to the teachers and the medical staff, including toys for the kids, and travelled back up the hill and away from Mostar. Only when we were relatively safe and back near Medugorje did it stop. As the Sun came out and the sky cleared, I said another prayer of thanks and a further prayer for peace.

* * * *

Eventually international governments did intervene in the conflict and NATO troops did prevent further bloodshed. And by the end of 1995 a peace deal had been signed. Now, whilst sectarian tensions are still rumbling, a major reconstruction effort and the fact that some of the worst perpetrators of atrocities are being brought to justice is helping people to move on.

In Mostar, under the monitoring of a European Union envoy, a number of local elections have been held and political control of the town has accommodated each of the factions. The historic area around the bridge is being conserved and restored, and 15 years after the war ended, Mostar is once more being promoted as a cultural and tourist destination. A project to restore the Old Bridge was completed in 2004, and as locals and people of many nationalities now walk over the bridge, not only is it once more the symbol of a community but also of the way in which we can heal the schisms that split us from within.

* * * *

One of the things I noticed whilst in Mostar was the media bias in the reporting of the Bosnian War. The atrocities were all too true. But the reporters didn't relate the way that ordinary people cared for each other in appalling conditions and heroically tried to find ways of reaching out across the divide of hatred.

Years have passed, but if anything the media have generally become more embedded in their unbalanced emphasis on negative reporting. Whilst media coverage is important in bringing the horror of conflict to our collective vision, where peace-building initiatives are occurring but go unreported, such pervasive negativity only serves to heighten fear-based emotions.

During 2010 the Institute for Economics and Peace (IEP) and their colleagues at Media Tenor, based in London, delivered a study, *Measuring Peace in the Media*. Its aim was to analyse television news and current affairs coverage and reference it against the Global Peace Index that measures the levels of peace and conflict in some 149 countries around the world.

Reviewing 37 programmes from 23 networks in 15 countries, including CNN, ABC, CBS, NBC and FOX from the USA, the BBC and ITV from the UK, Al Jazeera from Qatar and others from Europe, the Middle East, China and South Africa, the researchers aimed to see how balanced the coverage was.

The study showed broad inconsistencies in reporting. US broadcasters were identified as being significantly more focused on violence and conflict than their European and Middle Eastern counterparts. Al Jazeera was found to be the network providing the most balanced coverage on Afghanistan. BBC World offered the greatest breadth of coverage, regularly reporting on 67 countries across six continents, which was nearly twice as many countries as the average level of coverage found by the review. And in the media reporting on Afghanistan, the study concluded that a disproportionate amount of coverage was focused on defence and crime, whilst news of progress in other areas that were crucial to building sustainable peace was neglected.

Steve Killelea, the founder of the IEP, said, 'Regardless of whether the tone of the coverage is positive or negative, it is essential for the media to spend editorial time focusing attention on the building blocks of peace. There is always some progress being made, no matter how dire the situation.'

As Killelea and his colleague Roland Schatz, the head of Media Tenor, went on to point out, too much emphasis on violence and security issues reinforces the view that hostile behaviour is the only way to peace. And that given the media's role in shaping and informing public opinion, a balanced perspective and information on what will bring long-term peace and stability are crucial.

* * * *

It's often been said that peace is much more than the absence of war.

Real peace needs to be based on the fairness and justice that are often absent during peace negotiations and their aftermath, leaving a bitter and lingering trauma that continues to scar the psyche of those involved – as is also often the case for personal disputes.

One key way of negotiating authentically peaceful outcomes from conflict situations that dramatically increases the likelihood that the peace will be sustainable is the inclusion of women at the negotiating table. This is now felt to be so important that in 2000 the UN passed a declaration mandating such involvement. But, frustratingly, in the years since there has been little progress in implementing it within member countries and a distressing number of so-called peace treaties have slid back into war.

Another way of negotiating a lasting peace is the imposition of some form of reconciliation process that brings together perpetrators and victims as a form of restorative justice. This was undertaken in the aftermath of apartheid in South Africa, when Bishop Desmond Tutu led the Truth and Reconciliation Committee. And later he advised on the inclusion of similar processes in the aftermath of the Troubles and the Good Friday Peace Agreement in Northern Ireland.

Both the inclusion of women in negotiating settlements and the use of restorative justice can apply to small-scale disputes as well as large-scale conflicts. The inclusion of all voices, a feminine perspective that balances the masculine and an honest and open aim to find a win-win resoulution can then lead to a positive outcome. And instead of being based on compromise, where neither side feels they have got all they wanted, it can be based on a com-promise where new co-creative ways of going forward and generating the benefits of peace can be real-ized.

Lao Tzu, the great Chinese philosopher of 500 BCE, linked outer and inner conflict when he stated that there can be no peace in the world without peace in the heart.

The *ho'oponopono* prayer of the Hawaiian *kahuna* wisdom keepers also takes the ultimate inner responsibility for our outer realities – and crucially without self-blame – when it says simply and from the heart, 'I love you. I am sorry. Please forgive me.'

CHAPTER 20

Nuclear Non-proliferation and Disarmament

'Hope is putting faith to work when doubting would be easier.'
ANON.

At the time of the solar eclipse of 22 July 2009, I was in Japan as the arc of totality cast its shadow over its southerly Ogasawara Islands and significantly the tiny island of Iwo Jima, the site of fierce fighting between the USA and Japan in the spring of 1945.

In 1985, on the fortieth anniversary of the battle, veterans from both sides met to commemorate the conflict. A granite reunion plaque was placed on the site of the US landing on this tiny volcanic blip in the midst of the vastness of the Pacific Ocean. With a memorial in both English and Japanese, it reads '….we pray together that our sacrifices at Iwo Jima will always be remembered and never repeated.'

Sitting in my Tokyo hotel room watching the live TV feed of the eclipse from Iwo Jima, I attuned to the healing of any remaining schism between Japan and America. As I did so, I had a powerful vision of the atomic blasts over the southern Japanese cities of Hiroshima and Nagasaki that had brought World War II to a shocking conclusion.

At my next Japanese workshop, a young man introduced himself as a native of Hiroshima and subsequently shared a horrific psychic vision of being atomized by the detonation, as though the bodies of the citizens of Hiroshima had been proxies for an explosion in our collective psyche.

Only days after the first bomb had exploded, rumours had begun to circulate in the devastated city that the destruction had been unleashed by the energy of splitting atoms, and the victims had begun to describe the weapon as *genshi bakudan*, the root characters of which, as John Hershey wrote in his heart-rending masterpiece *Hiroshima*, mean 'original child bomb'. Given that the bomb had been nicknamed 'Little Boy' by the aircrews that dropped it, I was struck by the poignancy of such a child of terror being born.

It was as if its dropping was the birth of this new nuclear era where we have literally become the first generation of humanity that can also decide whether we will be the last.

* * * *

In Prague, the capital of the Czech Republic, a few months before my Tokyo workshop, the world had heard President Obama give an impassioned speech about his deep commitment to a nuclear-free world.

As the anniversaries again approached of the only dropping of nuclear bombs on people, I could sense that a new era in the drive to release humanity from the existential fear of nuclear war was underway.

But why is Obama so fervent in his quest to rid the world of the nuclear threat?

As an astrologer, when I want to understand the personality and deeper motivations of someone, I'll often take a look at their natal chart. Much has been written elsewhere about Obama's chart, but specifically in regard to his focus on nuclear disarmament, when I looked at his time and date of birth, the connection was clear.

He was born at 7.24 a.m. local time on 4 August 1961 in Hawaii. The Hiroshima bomb was dropped at 8.15 a.m. local time on 6 August 1945. In understanding any resonant connection between the two, the cycles of the years between were less significant than the dates and times.

When I adjusted for the time difference, it turned out that Obama was born almost exactly 36 hours from when the bomb was dropped on Hiroshima. At some subliminal level within his psyche, I feel he is resonating with the suffering that exploded that day and that continues to live on for the so-called 'explosion-affected people', the *hibakusha*, those who survived the initial blast but who progressively over the years have perished from its toxic aftermath.

To enable such symbolism to fully resonate, the US president needed a Japanese partner. But the ruling politicians of the Liberal Democratic Party (LDP), who had been in power in Japan from 1955, had consistently repudiated the mutual apologies and forgiveness that could bring about healing. But on 30 August 2009 their rivals the Democratic Party of Japan (DPJ), led by an unconventional politician called Yukio Hatoyama, whose campaign strategy, as he himself declared, was based on 'love,' won a landslide victory.

Yukio Hatoyama was born on 11 February 1947. The date of his birth, six months apart from Obama's and 18 months after the bombs were dropped, and both leaders coming to power in the ninth year of the twenty-first century continued and balanced the three-fold resonance embodied in Obama's energetic links to nuclear disarmament.

The reforms underway would, in the turmoil of Japanese politics, see Hatoyama ousted within nine months, but his party, continuing in power under another prime minister, the populist Naoto Kan, continues the push for nuclear-free peace and, unlike its predecessors, seems also to be making greater moves to apologize for the Japanese aggression that, whilst not excusing the horrors of Hiroshima and Nagasaki, initiated the conflict that ultimately gave rise to them.

* * * *

After Obama's speech in Prague, when I'd attuned to the unfolding nuclear arms reduction initiative by his Administration and President Medvedev of Russia, I'd had a sense that there would be an important meeting in Washington and that somehow I'd be there for it.

During another visit to Japan in February 2010 I heard early intimations that there would be a meeting in the USA later in the spring to discuss the next steps in nuclear disarmament and non-proliferation.

I'd already planned to be in the USA during April, speaking at the EarthSpirit conference in Vermont hosted by my friends Cameron and Glenn Broughton on the weekend of 10/11 April and teaching classes in Philadelphia the following weekend, staying with my friend Patty Bonner and hosted by my friend Susan Duval. I had a powerful sense that the nuclear meeting would be between those dates, although nothing had as yet been announced.

It was only after I'd confirmed my arrangements for Vermont and Philly that, sure enough, the dates of the Washington meeting were announced as 12 and 13 April!

The week before, Obama and Medvedev had met in Prague and signed a new START, a landmark disarmament treaty to slash both sides' strategic nuclear weapons. And the subsequent meeting in Washington was intended to use that initiative to push for increased security for vulnerable nuclear material and stronger measures to stop nuclear arms proliferation.

On the morning of 13 April, with grateful thanks to Cameron and Glenn for a wonderful conference, I flew down to Washington. Making my way to the motel, I arrived just in time to see a live press conference from the White House that announced significant moves forward in securing dangerous nuclear material: another step towards peace.

Early the following morning, I caught a train into Union Station in the heart of Washington, left my bags and prepared to spend the next four hours until my train journey on to Philly doing whatever energetic work I'd felt called to do here. Walking out into the bright sunshine of a glorious April morning, I felt a call to head first to the Lincoln Memorial. I caught a cab to save time.

I'd last been at the memorial over 30 years before when, on a beautiful summer evening's visit, I'd spent time in Abe's benevolent presence. Amazingly, no one else had been around, and it had been a magical moment.

At that time I was just beginning my career in international business and had been inspired by Lincoln's example of moral strength, honesty and humility. Now, so many years later, as I stood once again beneath his great marble statue that sits looking out towards Washington's Monument and the US Capitol Building beyond, I had the powerful feeling that he was present.

As I looked around, I was drawn to the writing engraved on the memorial, taken from Lincoln's second inaugural address as president in 1865. It clearly shows that at the beginning of the civil war that nearly tore the Union apart, the South wanted to extend slave ownership whilst the North only sought to prevent that happening. The outcome of the war was much more fundamental – the ending of slavery itself.

When Lincoln addressed the crowd on 4 March 1865, the end of the war was only days away. I've since learned that some of his assassins were there listening to his words. That made me wonder how long it was before John Wilkes Booth then killed Lincoln. As I write, I've just checked with Wikipedia and discovered that the date Lincoln was killed was 14 April… Without knowing at the time, the day I'd visited him again after

30 years, the 2010 day I'd stood in the shadow of his memorial again, the day I'd silently thanked him again for his inspirational leadership and for a life supremely well lived, had been the anniversary of his death!

After leaving Lincoln's Memorial I walked alongside the Pool of Reflection and on towards the Washington Memorial, the great obelisk that serves as an acupuncture needle tapping into the energy meridians of the USA, anchoring the intentions of the Founding Fathers. Here, all I felt I needed to do was to attune in the universal heart, re-energize the call for inspiration and love and radiate it outwards.

I felt that the moral valour of both Washington and Lincoln was there – not for me, but for the first black American holder of their presidential office, who, if he were to succeed in his pledge to rid the world of the blight of nuclear weapons, would need all the courage they had embodied.

It then seemed only polite to walk to the White House to personally thank President Obama for leading the way to a nuclear-free world. As I approached, I smiled to myself – perhaps the president would come out into the rose garden and invite me to drop in for a cup of tea?

Stopping by the small gate and guard house, I noticed that further along there were crowds of tourists, but here it seemed quiet and I had a good view of the rose garden outside the West Wing of the White House where the president's Oval Office is.

As I stood quietly gazing at the rose garden, I inwardly thanked the president for his courage in furthering the cause of peace.

As I did so, I noticed a tall marine stand to attention by the side of the French doors that led from the West Wing into the garden. Suddenly the doors opened and a tall slim black man came out. With no one between him and where I was standing, the president walked briskly to the podium set up in the garden and began to speak.

I watched as he dealt gracefully with the media and then walked back into his office.

I'd seen him and energetically thanked him. But I could really have done with a cup of tea!

* * * *

Tadatoshi Akiba, the mayor of Hiroshima, has also worked tirelessly for many years championing a nuclear-free world and, as president of Mayors for Peace, by mid-2010 had signed up the fellow mayors of more than 4,000 cities worldwide. In 2010 he was awarded the Ramon Magsaysay Award for Peace, sometimes called the Asian Peace Prize, in recognition of his work.

No serving US president has visited Hiroshima. But as a first step, on the 6 August 2010 anniversary of the bombings, for the first time the US ambassador to Japan, his colleagues from the UK and France, both nuclear states, and Ban ki Moon, the Secretary General of the UN, all attended the memorial service.

Whilst there, Ban declared that it had been his childhood experience of marching down a muddy road whilst his home village burned that had led him to devote his life to peace and brought him to Hiroshima.

Momentum was building…

Between 12 and 14 November 2010 Mayor Akiba hosted the world summit of Nobel Peace laureates in the city. To ensure that the horrors that had assailed Hiroshima and Nagasaki never happened again, they issued a call of conscience to the leaders of the world's nuclear armed countries to affirm that the use of nuclear weapons was immoral and illegal. Specifically they called on China, the United States, Egypt, Iran, Israel and Indonesia to ratify, and on India, Pakistan and North Korea to sign and ratify the Comprehensive Test Ban Treaty that has already been ratified by 153 nations, so that it can be brought into full legal force.

For months after Obama and Medvedev signed the new START Treaty the Republican senators in the USA stalled its ratification. But in mid-December 2010, in the dying days of the so-called lame duck session of the 111th Congress, with extraordinary bipartisan support, the new START Treaty was passed by a majority of both Democrat and Republican senators and days later by the Russian parliament.

Quietly, too, the USA and Russia, in an initiative co-ordinated by the International Atomic Energy Agency, the IAEA, have been organizing the repatriation of dangerous nuclear material from low-security caches in a number of countries. In mid-December 2010, the latest transfer took place of near weapons-grade nuclear-fuel elements from an ageing nuclear power plant in Serbia back to secure storage in Russia.

These are small steps, but they are crucial. For unless the two biggest nuclear powers are willing to begin to travel the path of nuclear disarmament, how can they and the world community deter aspiring nuclear states, especially the likes of North Korea and Iran, from such calamitous aims?

* * * *

Nuclear weapons were used by the USA to end the worldwide conflict that had originated with the Nazi regime in Germany but expanded thanks to the aggressive military policies of Japan.

To heal, Japan needs to wholeheartedly apologize for its aggression and the USA for the suffering it caused by dropping the bomb, an act which allowed nuclear proliferation free rein.

On 13 September 2010 Japan's foreign minister, Katsuya Okada, formally apologized to a group of six former US soldiers who had been Japanese prisoners of war during World War II. And on 7 December 2010 Prime Minister Kan fully apologized to Korea for the suffering it had endured under Japanese colonization. He added that he wanted to take an honest look at his country's past and have the courage and humility to address its history.

Perhaps 6 August 2011 and 7 December 2011, the sixty-sixth anniversary of the dropping of the atomic bomb on Hiroshima and the seventieth anniversary of the Japanese attack on Pearl Harbor, can be the days when a US president visits Hiroshima and a Japanese prime minister visits Pearl Harbor.

I hope so.

* * * *

At dawn on 16 July 1945 the mushroom cloud of a huge explosion lit for miles around the desolate desert of *Jordano del Muerte*, the Route of Death, in southwestern USA.

J. Robert Oppenheimer, the scientist who'd led the project to develop the world's first atomic bomb had called the test site 'Trinity.' Named most likely from a poem by Elizabethan John Donne that goes; 'Batter my heart, three person'd God', the site was a tragically apt memorial to a poetry-loving friend who'd committed suicide a few months before.

As the Atomic Age was bombed into birth, Oppenheimer, when asked how he had felt at that moment, replied with a line from the ancient Indian epic the Bhagavad Gita that states, 'I am become death, the destroyer of worlds.' And indeed, on behalf of our collective consciousness, I believe he had.

For some 13.7 billion years from the beginning of our universe, evolutionary processes throughout the life cycles of stars eventually led to the creation of the heaviest of natural elements. Their inherent instability results in a progressive and essentially harmless radioactive decay. Nowhere in Nature do they split in the destructive schism that was unleashed that day in the desert.

Oppenheimer's naming of the site of this catastrophic trauma Trinity reflected Donne's 'three-person'd God,' the fundamental trinity of principles and aspects that pervades the Cosmos at all scales. That day it was the atomic trio of protons, electrons and neutrons that instead of co-creating life was forced by humanity into an explosive destruction.

At the core of the cataclysmic power that would be soon unleashed over the Japanese cities of Hiroshima and Nagasaki, was the nuclear fission of uranium, neptunium and plutonium – named respectively after the three outer planets of our Soular System. Each element, resonating with its planetary namesake, archetypally embodies our relationships respectively with revolutionary awakening, the nature of reality, and the death and re-birth cycles of transformation.

Uranium is the heaviest relatively abundant and stable element found in Nature. Whilst minute traces of neptunium and plutonium are naturally present on Earth, both are deemed to be effectively man-made; synthesized for the first time in June and December 1940 respectively.

The discovery of the element plutonium can be accurately placed and timed to 8.00 p.m. on 14 December 1940 at the University of California at Berkeley, whose natal chart was originally drawn up by astrologer Nick Kollerstrom. Pluto's location on the Ascendant and conjunct with plutonium's North Node reveals that the discovery was enormously intentional and represents both the elemental and planetary purpose to serve the transformation of our collective future. The chart's line up of the Sun with the Galactic Centre opposite the Moon at Full and with the Earth centrally located between – dramatically displays the cosmic alignment that in the years leading up to the December solstice of 2012 has become ever more intensely focused as a harbinger of our cosmic destiny.

The schism caused by our choice to originally unleash atomic power for war, co-created the path that has led us to become the first human generation capable of destroying our world – and thus of potentially being the last.

I've shared the now emerging signs for nuclear weapons reductions, but now we also need to consider our so-called peaceful use of nuclear power. For after World War II, whilst nuclear energy was also harnessed for such purposes, the development of other than uranium–neptunium–plutonium nuclear-based technologies wasn't seriously pursued, primarily because they failed to provide weapons-grade fissile material which could be used to manufacture further bombs.

Despite enduring the trauma of being the only nation whose people were victims of atomic bombing – Hiroshima by a uranium bomb and Nagasaki by one whose explosive power was fueled by plutonium, the scarcity of natural energy resources led to Japan by the early 1970s committing itself to nuclear power, based on that same war-focused technology.

And now as I write, the damage to and fallout from the Fukushima nuclear complex that survived the 11 March 2011 Japanese earthquake but was unable to withstand the tsunami that followed has been increased to a maximum Level 7 disaster, equating it with the disaster at Chernobyl.

Virtually all commentators agree that renewable energy technologies are very many years away from being able to fully provide for the world's energy needs. Whilst Fukushima has sounded an enormously important wake-up call to the dangers of uranium-based nuclear energy, environmentalists such as George Monbiot and the father of the Gaia hypothesis James Lovelock recognize that unless the world continues to burn environmentally disastrous oil, gas or coal, at least for the mid-term nuclear energy is and will be crucial to enable the 'lights to stay on.'

So is there an alternative?

Only a few weeks before the catastrophe of Fukushima, the Chinese revealed that they are launching a dramatically safer, cleaner and more abundantly resourced thorium-based rather than uranium-based nuclear technology. Thorium's innate properties and its associated nuclear plant design means that no reactor could run out of control, explode or melt-down as in uranium-based nuclear facilities, and there is also enough naturally occurring thorium to last for thousands of years.

Unlike uranium, thorium is, crucially, utterly unable to provide fuel for bombs. As UK journalist Ambrose Evans-Pritchard puts it, thorium can even 'as a happy bonus ... burn up plutonium and toxic waste from old reactors, reducing radio-toxicity and acting as an eco-cleaner.'

Over the last three years, during my visits to Japan I've experienced three intense elemental initiations, the third at Haruna, into what I feel are the Lemurian roots of the Japanese psyche and which align with a Lemurian past life that I've written about in *The 13th Step*.

Plutonium was discovered on 14 December 1940. As we've already seen, the solar eclipse of 2001 occurring in the constellation of the 'galactic healer' Ophiuchus was deemed by mystics to have re-awakened the Lemurian aspect of our collective psyche. It also took place on 14 December.

So are our Lemurian ancestors who embodied such a profound realationship with Gaia now coming forward through their Japanese descendants to hold a mirror to our collective use/abuse of Nature and nuclear power?

Perhaps, if it evolves to the self-aware stage we've reached, every planetary society at some point comes to an understanding of the universality of elements and the enormous energy they embody. The so-called weak nuclear force is the evolutionary driver of the universe enabling its birth, life and death cycles from the process of nuclear fusion that powers stars to the natural radioactive decay of the heavier elements. Comprehending its secrets offers us a deeper understanding of cosmic life or death.

Some 70 years ago, we chose the route of death. We now need urgently need to change course and collectively choose a path for hope and for life. At this vital moment of choice, I feel the Japanese people and our Lemurian ancestors are offering us a profound gift for the potential healing of our collective psyche, for which I bow my head with a heart-felt *Arigato* – thank you.

CHAPTER 21
W(h)ealth

'Far away there in the sunshine are my highest aspirations.
I may not reach them but I can look up and see their beauty,
believe in them and try to follow them.'
LOUISA M. ALCOTT

As we've already touched upon with regard to the USA and UK, our relationship with money is currently profoundly unhealthy. As the Bible writers of some 2,500 years ago pointed out, it's not money itself but the love – or fear – of it that's the root of the problem.

For money, at its simplest, is energy, whose healthy flow lubricates and eases the processes of trade and acts as a measure of economic activity.

In the 1970s I trained in the UK as an accountant. In those days, cost and management accountants such as myself worked with the real economy of products and services. So-called financial services were limited to lending money and providing insurance that was supportive of the trading of material goods and labour-based services.

But since the computerization and progressive interlinking of the world's financial markets from the 1980s onwards, and particularly the explosion of financial products in the last ten years or so, the global financial market, especially its bonus-driven 'casino banking' aspect, has grown enormously and monstrously.

The 2007/2008 global financial crisis wasn't unexpected or unprecedented. The Wall Street crash of 1929 followed a boom in the new radio stocks. The 1987 crash followed the boom in junk bonds. And the boom in computer-based dot.com start-ups was followed by the bust of 2000.

All of these boom and bust cycles were energized by financial speculation and people with a lot of money wanting to invest to get more – much more.

The latest and largest boom, founded on property speculation and sub-prime mortgages, bundled into complex financial packages that only a few bankers themselves understood, was all too likely to end in disaster.

About a year before it happened I was told by my guides that it would occur, and when. I was also told that it could – if we chose – be the start of a major reformation of our global economies and societies. But I was also warned that the powers that be, the bankers who were making obscene amounts of money and others who were benefitting hugely from the status quo, would do virtually anything to avoid those reforms.

So how the coming financial breakdown would play out would, as always, depend on our willingness to retreat into fear or leap into love.

When the bust came, it was so catastrophic that to save the financial system – or so it was portrayed – governments and taxpayers were obliged to bail out the profligate banks.

* * * *

So, what is the financial market and what is investment banking?

Banking has historically had two arms, retail and investment. Retail banks handle the deposits of personal and business savers and extend personal and small- and mid-sized business credit. For most people, this is the only type of banking they deal with.

Investment banks carry out two very different types of activity. The first is to act as financial advisors, who for a fee use their expertise and contacts, for example to help corporate clients borrow money, raise equity capital funds or take over other companies.

They also, progressively so, trade directly in the financial markets for their own benefit by buying and selling financial assets from one client to another, usually with a large mark-up. It's this trading that has exploded in the last decade with the growth of derivatives, complicated deals that allow the banks to speculate – gamble – on financial markets.

By using their global contacts to make deals, the trading arms of investment banks made huge profits in the boom years. Following the bust of 2007/8 and the bailouts by taxpayers, as there are fewer of them than before to handle the still gigantic opportunity for financial trading, enormous profits are still being made and bonuses paid out.

Until relatively recently, retail and investment banks tended to be operated separately. But over the last few years a number of large investment banks have been bought up by retail banks and other retail banks have grown investment arms. This has created massive universal banks where our retail deposits have been used to fund the much more risky trading activities.

Splitting these big banks, whilst at least preventing depositors' money being used to collateralize financial gambling, is only one step of much larger reform. For neither Lehman Brothers, which collapsed in 2008, nor Goldman Sachs, which is facing legal action in the USA for knowingly selling its clients toxic assets, was involved in retail banking.

It is such banks' abuse of their clients' interests that raises another issue for this type of trading: with the vast amounts of money to be made, insider trading of ostensibly confidential corporate information is rife – but very difficult to prove.

And finally, because bankers' bonuses are paid upfront on the assumed profit of a deal – often maximized by clever accounting and with the estimate of future risks minimized – the reported 'profits' of complex deals whose true profit – or loss – can only be gauged when they run their course, sometimes years later, is distorted.

My husband Tony is an architect. When he designs a building he has to take out insurance that covers up to a further 12 years ahead. In contrast, when the final accounting is done for many derivative deals it's far too late to claw back the bonuses on their overstated upfront profit – the banker is paid and usually long gone!

* * * *

Before we move on to how such an incredibly dangerous and unsustainable situation might be healed, let me share a little more about the rise of the financial derivatives market, which is the 'elephant in the room' of the global economy.

Derivatives and their like began innocuously as insurance for unforeseen trading circumstances. But deregulation has freed the market to grow exponentially to become the core of the so-called 'casino banking' culture.

The market for ever-more complex financial products, increasingly based not on real assets but more and more on a pack of financial cards founded on investment quicksand, has grown to dwarf that of 'real' economic behaviour based on the trading of goods and services.

The latest estimate, which may well be an underestimate, is that the derivatives market is worth an annual $1.2 quadrillion – that is 1.2 thousand trillion dollars – 20 times greater than global GDP! And it is a market that is essentially unregulated and effectively untaxed.

It is as though someone purchased an asset, for example a car, for $1,000 and then spent $20,000 on insurance. In itself that's crazy. But the present-day global derivatives market is literally a gambling house that will gamble on virtually anything, so, to follow our example, the insurance, as well as covering a possible crash or the theft of the car, would extend to such notions as whether the car might change colour or happen to sprout wings and fly to the Moon.

During the last decade the derivatives market progressively bundled virtually worthless or even toxic assets that were revalued artificially and with the risk often knowingly understated due to corporate pressures. And through financial sleight of hand, deals were tied up in such complexity that even now they are unable to be unravelled leading to these financial gambling chips being termed by investor Warren Buffett 'financial weapons of mass destruction'.

The nature of the derivatives market has one further and crucial danger that has progressively increased until it actually threatens global stability, and that is the speculative gambling on commodities and resources from foodstuffs to oil. In the last few years there have already been examples of where hedge funds and market traders have speculatively 'bought' entire crops or quotas of such products, without any other reason than for financial gain, and have thus added artificially to world prices which are already rising due to population and developmental pressures. Unless such abuses are curbed, and urgently, this gambling could prove disastrous.

These global financial markets in greed and fear, partnered with dangerously inadequate economic measures and continuing pathetically lax regulations and oversight and a woeful lack of moral good sense, have brought us to the brink of global economic disaster.

****

Currently, any attempt at reform is being fought tooth and nail by the bankers, especially investment and hedge-fund bankers, who personally make vast amounts of money by gambling with other people's money.

Quite apart from addressing this greed-based culture, radical reforms of the banking and financial system are crucial, especially a dramatic and regulated reduction in the speculative nature of derivatives. What is also little understood is that the financial models that underpin the system and purport to stabilize it actually do the opposite. They're based primarily on the dangerously incorrect perception that they can maximize stability by increased connectivity and by acting in similar ways. The problem is that in reality the global system is a man-made ecosystem. And, like the ecosystem itself, it's what scientists call 'a complex system in a critical state.' As I wrote in *CosMos*, such systems are 'inherently nonlinear in that a small event can trigger either a similarly small dislocation or a catastrophic upheaval.' So, complexity models need to be introduced that put in place checks and balances to buffer such nonlinear interaction. In addition to regulation, this is also key to future stability.

But as I write, the G20 governments are still balking at introducing such reforms and very few bankers yet understand the innate inadequacy of their models. This makes another crisis almost inevitable. And next time, after the taxpayer bailouts of banks that were deemed to be 'too big to fail', those banks will be 'too big to save.'

As Dominique Strauss-Kahn, the managing director of the International Monetary Fund, told the German magazine *Stern* in November 2010, in the next crisis, 'It would be impossible to persuade taxpayers to fund bailouts. It would be a crisis of democracy.'

* * * *

I was invited to give a keynote speech on economic trans-formation at the Women Leaders' Summit at the G20 meeting in Seoul in November 2010 and the following is an extract from that talk. As I pointed out, beyond the reformation of financial markets, fundamental economic issues also need to be tackled:

The first is the tools that are in use globally to define, describe and measure economic activity. The primary economic measure worldwide is GDP, or Gross Domestic Product, that aims to measure the value of goods and services traded across the globe. However, even its economic architect, Simon Kuznets, viewed GDP as inadequate, stating that a nation's welfare 'can scarcely be inferred' from such a measurement.

On the principle of 'what gets counted counts,' GDP measures all goods and services activity, whether beneficial or not. Increases in GDP are viewed as being good, regardless of sustainability. And its greatest drivers are conflict and consumerism, rather than co-operation and creativity.

GDP excludes numerous 'externalities.' So a process that diminishes the Earth's resources and pollutes her environment is currently counted as being 'cheaper' than a process that is sustainable and operating in harmony with natural principles.

And, as Kuznets himself noted, GDP neither includes nor even recognizes any measure of well-being for people or planet.

As many social studies have shown, beyond a certain level of material provision, increased 'wealth,' even when measured by GDP, not only doesn't buy increased well-being but actually reduces it, especially where there's significant inequality between the most and least moneyed within a society.

It needs a major and urgent overhaul to become fit for purpose in a world where rampant materiality is devouring the Earth's natural resources, obliterating her planetary capital and continuing to drive a widening gap between the haves and the have-nots of our global community.

As recognition is growing that the current model that measures economic activity is deeply flawed, there are some encouraging signs that moves are underway to include within it the real costs of production and trade and to move towards a healthier system that also measures well-being and quality of life.

The Himalayan country of Bhutan was the first to introduce such measures with its Gross National Happiness (GNH) index, which is now built into strategic social and political planning. Every significant decision is reviewed to ensure it is aligned with GNH's four pillars: promotion of sustainable development, promotion of cultural values, conservation of the natural environment and the establishment of good governance.

And in his coronation speech on 7 November 2008, King Khesar, fifth Druk Gyalpo of Bhutan, reiterated their importance:

...we must always remember that as our country, in these changing times, finds immense new challenges and opportunities, whatever work we do, whatever goals we have – and no matter how these may change in this changing world – ultimately without peace, security and happiness we have nothing. That is the essence of the philosophy of Gross National Happiness. Our most important goal is the peace and happiness of our people and the security and sovereignty of the nation...

A measure known as triple bottom line, standing for people, planet, profit, where social and environmental benefits rank alongside monetary profits, has been adopted by the United Nations for public sector projects and accounting, and goes some way towards offering a more balanced perspective. Leading companies are also progressively using its principles to show their strategies for sustainable operations.

In France, President Nicolas Sarkozy appointed Nobel Economics laureate Joseph Stiglitz to develop new measures and, in November 2010, announced that it was time to put the well-being of the French people above that of the GDP.

In the UK, too, the new government has been pushing for such reform, while in the USA, the creation of a new Key National Indicator System aims to help Americans better understand and assess the country's progress and overall well-being.

One of the most important shifts we need to make in the developed nations is to move from seeing that 'more is good' when it comes to economic activity to 'enough is good.' In doing so, we can set a far better example to developing nations on how to balance economic progress whilst retaining traditional values.

Healing our psyche of its collective fear of loss will involve developing policies and technologies that conserve resources and ultimately, as in Nature, waste nothing.

And we also need to aspire to a w(h)ealthy real-ationship with money and adopt a steady-state approach to our overall global economy where once material needs are met, further expansion comes from co-creativity and a sense of well-being and community rather than from accumulating more 'stuff.'

****

As the Shift gathers pace, there are a growing number of initiatives that are embracing this new paradigm.

One example comes from Jessica Jackley, who in 2005 asked herself what she could do to improve the lives of some of the poorest people on the planet. Three years before, she'd been inspired by a talk by Dr Mohamed Yunus, Nobel Peace Prize laureate and founder of the Grameen Bank. He had spoken of his then new concept of offering micro-finance to budding entrepreneurs and Jessica heard her calling.

With co-founder Matt Flannery, Jessica set up www.kiva. org. This micro-finance initiative offers a 'hand up' rather than a 'hand-out.' And thanks to $25 individual loans, by late 2010 it had raised over $160 million from some three-quarters of a million lenders for nearly a quarter of a million entrepreneurs in developing nations around the world.

With a repayment record of around 98 per cent, this extraordinarily positive project is inspirational. PayPal, the online e-commerce website, agrees with me, for it's the only charity that it supports by waiving its fees.

Another example emerged in the summer of 2010, when billionaires Bill and Melinda Gates and Warren Buffett announced the Giving Pledge movement, where they committed to giving at least half of their wealth away to charitable causes before or at the time of their death. By the end of 2010 some 40 moneyed families in the USA had signed the pledge.

As Mark Zuckerberg, the co-founder of Facebook and the youngest person so far to have taken the pledge, says, 'People wait until late in their career to give back. But why wait when there is so much to be done? With a generation of younger folks who have thrived on the success of their companies, there is a big opportunity for many of us to give back earlier in our lifetime and see the impact of our philanthropic efforts.'

* * * *

Even in times of austerity, most of us in developed countries are still vastly better off than the other members of our human family around the world. In my own life, I grew up as the daughter of a coal miner in the north of England. When Dad died, I was ten years old, we had virtually no money and I helped Mum by working evenings and weekends from then onwards. Many years later I became a very successful businesswoman and earned what most people would see as an enormous salary. I then left the corporate world to do something I felt I was really here to do: to prepare and empower people for the Shift. So I've had very little, then a lot and then a lot less money in my life and have learned how to maintain an emotionally healthier real-ationship with what is, after all, merely a mechanism for exchange and an energy which, like all others, needs to flow if it's not to become stagnant.

I've learned that what money I've made doesn't define me as a person.

I've learned to value both spending and saving – and doing without sometimes.

I've learned that being rich is about far more than having money.

And I've learned above all that unless there is already an inner sense of well-being, money doesn't make you happy.

* * * *

With Neptune transitting the USA's tenth house of government and national esteem since 2002/3, emphasizing underlying deceit and corruption, and then Pluto transitting its eighth house of money from 2008, it was primed for the toxic financial bubble that it had fed to burst. But the long-term nature of those planetary influences mean not only that the bankers and government have not yet fully acknowledged let alone dealt with the fundamental issues, but that their fear and greed, unless checked, are highly likely to trigger an even worse meltdown.

And such are the fear-based patterns and the desperate outer search for security in our collective psyche that to get to the point of releasing and healing this deep-rooted dysfunctional and dangerous behaviour, we need another push of cosmic support.

This is already emerging in 2011, especially with the beginning of the transit of Neptune into the altruistic sign of Pisces, where, after a few months retracing his steps into Aquarius, as though to ensure we're really ready to evolve, he'll remain until 2025.

It is the younger generations who are leading the revolutions, whether in the Arab and developing world or the developed economies of the USA, Japan and Europe. It is they who are perceiving an interconnected world where co-creativity and communities can be harnessed to overcome the global challenges that we face.

It is primarily they who are articulating a hopeful message for the future. And it's our job as their elders to support them in every way we can, not only to retain that hope but to ensure it achieves its full expression.

CHAPTER 22
Me to We

'Hope is the companion of power and mother of success;
for who hopes strongly has within him the gift of miracles.'
SAMUEL SMILES

Happiness surveys consistently show that we're happiest when we're serving something beyond and bigger than ourselves. And other research demonstrates that the level of our social capital, our feeling of belonging and the strength of community networks improve our health and well-being on both individual and group levels.

In developed societies, studies have shown that spending on healthcare *per se* is unrelated to life expectancy or level of health. As the editors of the *British Medical Journal* commented in 1996, 'What matters in determining mortality and health in a society is less the overall wealth of that society and more how evenly wealth is distributed. The more equally wealth is distributed, the better the health of that society.'

Kate Pickett and Richard Wilkinson, in their 2009 book *The Spirit Level*, were able to show that with regard to health, living in a more equal society benefitted *everyone*, not just the poor. They related the experience of the UK during the two world wars. Increases in life expectancy for civilians during the war decades were twice those seen throughout the rest of the twentieth century, increasing by more than six years for both men and women, whereas for the decades before, between and afterwards, the increases were between one and four years.

Material living standards reduced during both wars, but both eras had full employment and significantly narrower income differences – the result of deliberate government policies to promote co-operation with the war effort. In World War II, the British slogan was: 'We're all in it together' – the very theme promoted by the government now. But then it was demonstrably true, while now, as we've seen, levels of inequality have ballooned and are as yet unrestrained.

But beneath the surface turmoil, something more profound and more hopeful is gaining strength.

* * * *

Around the world during the last few years, the expansion of grassroots initiatives has been exponential. Numerous individual projects have arisen, energized by passion and concern for the environment, social justice, human rights and peace. As environmentalist and entrepreneur Paul Hawken notes in his book *Blessed Unrest*,

> *Although the six o'clock news is usually concerned with the death of strangers, millions of people work on behalf of strangers. This altruism has religious, even mythic origins and very practical eighteenth-century roots. Abolitionists were the first group to create a national and global movement to defend the rights of those they did not know.*

Such initiatives are about empowering people rather than leaders and about ideas rather than ideologies, but ideas that have a common but often unstated fundamental assumption: that essentially we're all part of an interconnected whole.

Hawken goes on to say, 'Healing the wounds of the Earth and its people does not require saintliness or a political party [thank goodness!], only gumption and persistence. It is not a liberal or conservative activity; it is a sacred act.'

This sense of an interwoven web of life and sustenance finds another voice in poet Gary Snyder, who discerns, as I too have experienced, a current of human empathy whose lineage can be traced back through generations of healers, philosophers, priests, poets, artists and indigenous elders who, in Snyder's words, 'speak for the planet, for other species, for interdependence, a life that courses under and through and around empires.'

That deep heritage is evolving to a new level of collective consciousness.

But, perhaps because we are as yet unable to name or even imagine our emergent transpersonal self, its arrival is unheralded.

* * * *

As we've seen, revolutionary leaps forward in our collective consciousness have been taken in the past. Between 800 and 200 BCE, a pivotal period in our history termed the Axial Age by German philosopher Karl Jaspers, innovative thinking in China, India, Greece and the Middle East simultaneously and independently laid the spiritual foundations for the succeeding two millennia.

Religious historian Karen Armstrong considers that a second Axial Age was that of the Enlightenment, which encompassed the birth of the scientific method and the development of the technologies that form the basis of our current global society.

At the time, no one named these Axial Ages. Only in hindsight were they identified as axes in our evolution.

We're now living in the transformational process of a third Axial Age that I believe is far greater and more revolutionary than any we've been through before. We're in the turmoil of an intense moment of transcendence during which the schism that arose from the dislocation of the spiritual and scientific worldviews arising from the first and second Axial Ages can be reconciled – resolved – within our collective psyche.

And as they are, we are literally empowered to re-member ourselves and undertake an evolutionary Shift into an entirely new way of being.

****

Our global interconnectivity through the internet is transitioning us, I believe, through an electronically based technosphere into an even greater level of in-to-greation that is based far more on an inner expansion of our collective consciousness. We are moving into what the spiral dynamics model calls the eighth holographic level of global interconnection. And what I describe as the 8th chakra of the universal heart.

We're waking up to an emerging understanding that *all* we call reality is integrated and manifested as a cosmic hologram where every facet reflects every other at all scales of existence.

The expanding social activism that's surfacing as fractal patterns within the hologram is supported by the connections of the technosphere, of which the internet social activist site Avaaz is an example.

Only three years after its start-up, by the end of 2010 Avaaz had some five million members. Its campaigns have already achieved the reversal of government policies in Brazil and Japan, raised substantial amounts of money for direct life-saving actions in Haiti and Burma and helped win victories on international treaties that include banning cluster bombs.

The Economist has described Avaaz as 'poised to deliver a deafening wake-up call to world leaders.'

Avaaz's model of campaigning is resolutely people-powered. Its activities are directed by regular polls of its members, who decide where the greatest needs and opportunities for change are and have the responsiveness to be flexible and focused, co-operating with other campaigns to have the maximum effect in any given situation.

Because Avaaz takes no funding from governments and corporations and offers no tax deductibility for donations, it is fundamentally free to say and do whatever its members around the world advocate.

Joining Avaaz is free and at the end of 2010 all the work of its network was organized by only 15 full-time campaigners and funded by fewer than 5,000 'sustainers,' each donating only a few dollars or euros each week. With such minimal bureaucracy and regular independent and published auditing of their finances, Avaaz is determined to be fiscally responsible to both its members and the causes they advocate.

Avaaz is, in my view, a great example of a global opportunity to interconnect for good. And proof that when we do so, our results are far greater than the sum of our parts.

* * * *

Another example of a technologically empowered initiative is the whistle-blowing organization WikiLeaks.

WikiLeaks could only have come into being and had the massive impact it has in the last few years for a number of reasons. First is the recording and archiving of vast amounts of previously hard copy information, including that marked 'Top Secret,' onto electronic databases that can be accessed by increasing numbers of people, especially in the US government and military. Second is the amazing capacity of the internet, which enables the provision of huge amounts of information at a moment's notice. And third is the increasing desire for greater transparency and honesty, for access to the truth and for previously held secrets to be exposed.

My own sense is that the Shift is bringing a progressively greater transparency to our collective psyche and therefore the diminishing ability for people to lie and get away with it.

An article in the *Los Angeles Times* of 15 October 2010, co-written by Coleen Rowley, *Time* magazine's Person of the Year in 2002 and former special agent/legal counsel for the FBI, and Bogdan Dzakovic, a federal air marshall who used to co-lead the USA's Federal Aviation Administration's Red Team investigating airport security vulnerabilities, posed the question: 'If WikiLeaks had been around in 2001, could the horrific events of 9/11 have been prevented?'

Their view is that if WikiLeaks *had* existed in 2001, the large number of people who had seen warning signs that something devastating was being planned would have had a quick and confidential means of exposing their concerns.

It's an indictment of the mainstream media that investigative journalism has in many instances been dismissed by the owners of media outlets. As we've seen, too, the media are generally biased in terms of 'negative' rather than 'positive' reporting.

The emergence of WikiLeaks and other Wiki-based online resources where large numbers of people submit and edit information to consensual standards is a step along the path for HOPE, as it reflects the healing within us that is taking us from loneliness to aloneness to all-one-ness.

Such enterprises are signs of our guru-ing up. As we do so, we inevitably begin to activate the awareness of the universal heart and discover our own inner guru and higher wisdom and enact the empowerment of our higher purpose.

With such wisdom, not only the fulfilment of human rights but also their balancing with human responsibilities becomes paramount as we realize, as does the Hawaiian *ho'oponopono* prayer, that we are ultimately the co-creators of all our realities.

CHAPTER 23
Healing our Real-ationship with Gaia

'Hope is the thing with feathers that perches in the soul and sings the tune without the words and never stops at all.'

Emily Dickinson

Over many years I've had the most incredibly wonderful opportunities to experience some of the most beautiful areas of our blue-green planet, from the summits of mountains to the depths of the oceans and from the wildness of Africa, Alaska and Australia to the gentle joys of my own back garden. The abundance of the natural world and the apparently chaotic but deeply ordered opportunism of life in inhabiting every niche of every environment are extraordinary and inspiring.

But, to my great sorrow, I've also seen at first hand the untold damage we've done to our Earth. I've experienced how our limited and ignorant worldview and selfishness as a species have resulted in our progressive abuse of Gaia. We've pillaged her resources as though they were unlimited or replaceable and polluted the environment as though someone else would come and clear it up.

In Alaska in 2002 I saw the tar balls that still scarred the beaches after the *Exxon Valdez* oil spill there in 1989. I've scuba-dived in the Mediterranean and seen plastic bags littering the bottom of the sea. And walked in far deserts and seen the same plastic litter spoiling the landscape. I've seen the aftermath of indiscriminate logging and the soil depletion and erosion that follow. And I've seen toxic sludge ruin waterways and destroy wildlife throughout eastern Europe.

But Gaia is amazingly resilient in her capacity to regenerate. And, as we're exploring in *HOPE*, the fact that cosmic mind explores itself at all scales of existence as a hologram means that by undertaking our own personal inner healing and healing the schisms within our collective psyche, we're also able to heal our real-ationship with Gaia.

To do that, instead of seeing the Earth as a passive backdrop to our lives and merely the source of the resources we need to survive, we urgently need to begin to perceive her as a living being and a co-evolutionary partner.

I've also come to understand that the Shift isn't only an expansion of consciousness for ourselves, but for Gaia and indeed our entire Soular System, one that's playing out on many levels of perception and existence.

To complete the Shift, we need to heal our real-ationship with Gaia in both mundanely practical and profoundly spiritual ways.

On the physical level, whilst climate change is likely to be the greatest environmental challenge we face, it's by no means the only concern, as Ervin Laszlo and I described in *CosMos*. Increasing resource depletion, disease and pollution, mass extinctions of animals and plants and soil deterioration and erosion are but a few of the issues that threaten global breakdown.

Whilst there are numerous grassroots initiatives and some corporate and governmental progress towards addressing these, much more needs to be done and much more quickly if we're to avert worldwide catastrophe.

Rather than go into the specifics of both the problems and the potential solutions of such environmental issues here, I've given details of resources at the back of the book. Here we'll focus on how we transform our worldview of Gaia to commune with her at a deeper level and heal our real-ationship with her and all her children.

But before we do, let's just take a brief look at our collective approach to climate change, how hope may be emerging and how environmental regeneration can restore our sense of well-being, not only physically but also emotionally.

* * * *

Regardless of the extent to which climate change is man-made or driven by solar cycles or, as I suspect, a combination of both, and other factors we're not yet aware of, I do believe it's happening.

So what are we going to do about it?

The disappointing outcome of the much-heralded climate change summit in Copenhagen in December 2009 was merely an agreement to aspire to limit climate temperature to no more than 2° above pre-industrial levels and to establish a bottom-up undertaking and review process.

However, responding to this lack of government action, a People's Declaration from the many environmentalist organizations there began to empower a newly co-ordinated movement.

In April 2010, Evo Morales, the president of Bolivia, called for a World People's Conference on Climate Change. Thirty-five thousand people from over 100 countries, including environmentalists, indigenous leaders and social activists, answered that call and took part in the conference at Cochabamba, Bolivia.

The resulting Cochabamba People's Accord acknowledged, for the first time on a collective level, Mother Earth as a living being with inherent rights, and tasked human beings with fulfilling innate obligations towards her and fundamentally respecting and living in harmony with all beings. It demanded the creation of an International Climate and Environmental Justice Tribunal and proposed a Universal Declaration for the Rights of Mother Earth.

On a governmental level, little progress was made in the run-up to the following summit in Cancun, Mexico, a year later. But then something extraordinary and completely unexpected happened. Spurred on by the increasing activism of developing countries and with the Cochabamba Accord submitted to its leaders, the United Nations achieved almost global consensus that 'climate change is one of the greatest challenges of our time' and an agreement to urgently step up actions to radically curb greenhouse gas emissions, with developed nations funding and supporting developing nations through the process.

What the Cancun summit did was show that through co-creating a process that included everyone and involved listening as well as talking, the foundations of a comprehensive and urgently needed agreement could be laid.

There is still an enormously long way to go before we arrive at worldwide implementation of environmentally sustainable policies. But at the end of the summit, as the delegates were preparing to leave, a few headed to the beach and in the sand wrote the word 'Hope.'

* * * *

Whilst I was in Seoul for the 'Dialogue between Civilizations' initiative at the G20 summit of November 2010, my wonderful hosts WON Buddhist International took a group of delegates to their lovely campus at Incheon in the north-west of South Korea.

During the three-hour drive we passed through beautiful rolling countryside covered by a lush array of trees. The landscape had been utterly transformed from the state it had been in at the end of the Korean War in 1953, when the hills had been left barren and scarred by the conflict. When hostilities ceased, the South Koreans decided to replant the hills. Entire communities undertook this wonderful project together; men, women and children, from the youngest to the oldest, planted millions of trees that now have grown to become one of the most poignant legacies of peace.

In Africa deforestation isn't only caused by commercial logging but also by rural communities who've traditionally used wood for cooking. The introduction of solar ovens that use the Sun's energy for cooking is gathering ground and will reduce the pressure for wood.

Reforestation throughout the continent, pioneered by Nobel Peace Laureate Wangari Maathai in Kenya and groups in Ethiopia and elsewhere, is inspirational, involving local communities in the restoration of their environment. Such projects aim not only to ensure the regeneration of the landscape but also to educate the people, especially the children, who will be the greatest beneficiaries, in a wholistic appreciation of nature.

Donna Goodman of the EarthChild Institute's aim is to support the planting of some two billion trees – one for every child on Earth under the age of 18.

And in the UK the Coalition government announced in 2010 a major tree-planting project in towns and cities, especially deprived areas. Whilst beautiful and also beneficial for the climate and biodiversity, the main aim of the Big Tree Plant campaign, which aims to plant one million trees by 2015, is to enhance people's well-being.

Studies in the USA, Holland and elsewhere have shown that trees in our urban environment have a positive impact on our mental, emotional and physical health, especially when local communities are involved in the choice of trees and their planting

* * * *

As we continue our journey of HOPE, the Shift in our awareness calls us to expand our perceptions of the whole-world to experience its holographic reality. As we activate the 8th chakra of the universal heart within us, we pass through a portal that connects our personality-based sense of self with a far greater transpersonal vision of who we really are. We liberate our perception from the constrictions of space and time and not only begin to know that all we call reality is connected, but also to feel and *live* the synchonicities and miracles of that realization.

More and more people are communicating with angels, elementals and devas, ascended masters and other non-physicalized beings and discovering for themselves their guidance and wisdom. Exploring these 'extraordinary' new realms of consciousness whilst grounding their revelations in our 'ordinary' lives is, I feel, crucial to the transformation offered by this cosmic moment of evolution.

As we're seeing in the unfolding events in North Africa, the Middle East and elsewhere, we are entering the realms of what the ancients would have recognized as the mythic reality of solar/soular heroes. Rather like Sam in the *Lord of the Rings* trilogy, we are the everyman – or every-hobbit – who by his very ordinariness becomes the ultimate hero of the saga.

Our journey of self-discovery doesn't need to be an outer epic that takes us around the world, however. Instead it's an inner pilgrimage that takes us the greatest distance of all: that between the head and the heart.

* * * *

As we activate the 8th chakra of the universal heart, as I've shared in *The 8th Chakra* and my CD of attunements *Heart, Mind and Purpose*, we also begin to connect with the 9th or earthstar chakra. As we expand our awareness into larger transpersonal levels, grounding that perception through the 9th chakra is key to balance. But, as ever more people are discovering, the 9th chakra offers an even greater gift, for it connects us with the consciousness of Gaia herself.

When I was first guided by Thoth and the Elohim to energetically work in this way and began to share it with others, a great number of complementary therapists participated in my workshops. They found that by connecting with Gaia through the 9th chakra, regardless of their modalities – crystal healing, flower remedies, homoeopathy and many others that utilize Earth-based resources and resonance – they gained far greater intuitive insights than before. Indeed, many began to actually hear the guidance of the elemental beings of Earth, Water, Air and Fire and the plant devas, much as high adepts have done for millennia.

Indeed, communicating with Gaia in this way, I believe, holds the key to our resoulution of myriad environmental and resource-based issues. Even ecologists and bio-engineers who are discovering the amazing abilities of bacterial life to literally eat toxins and convert sugar to diesel, processes that could have major benefits for us, are treating these wonderful beings as merely disposable resources. If, instead, they're willing to expand their awareness and honour the bacteria as fellow beings, I feel that co-creative insights will offer an even greater ability to meet the challenges we face.

And as more of us come to expand our awareness, we gain a deeper communion with Gaia and understanding of the Shift that she too is undertaking.

* * * *

Communing with Gaia and her panoply of elemental, devic and angelic beings is rather like getting to know new friends who at the beginning may be shy but are willing to engage if we're prepared to listen to them.

I first began to sense the presence of such beings when I came to live within the Avebury landscape about 16 years ago. Living on the path of the energetic St Michael ley line for the first four years, I shouldn't have been surprised that his angelic presence was amongst the first that I encountered.

Over time I energetically attuned to the elemental beings that pervaded the landscape and gradually became more and more sensitive to their presence and able to differentiate between the beings that embodied the archetypal essences of Earth, Water, Air and Fire. For years, our relationship became that of teachers and pupil; my willingness to listen and their loving willingness to share their wisdom enriched my life enormously. And when it came to my garden, their tips and mere presence ensured that the vegetables I grew were bursting with life.

St Michael is traditionally associated with the element of Fire. Again over time, I began to be aware of his fellow archangels, Uriel, Gabriel and Raphael, who are associated respectively with Earth, Water and Air and whose presence, along with that of other angels, continues to enlighten and nurture my inner journey of discovery of the incredible nature of the Cosmos.

And both within the Avebury landscape and around the world, I've encountered and learned from many discarnate guardians of sacred sites and the spirits of place. At each site I visit, I stand at the threshold. Attuning in the universal heart and grounding my intention through the 9th chakra, I then link my consciousness with the highest realms of Spirit and the heart of Gaia, inwardly expressing that I'm there with an open heart, an open mind and an open purpose to listen to the wisdom of the guardian and to be in service to whatever healing the guardian, any ancestors whose energies pervade the place and any elemental, devic and angelic beings whose voices I may perceive should ask of me.

* * * *

Many researchers and mystics have warned of cataclysmic Earth changes to come, and indeed as climate change accelerates, the incidences of extreme weather and other environment events are ramping up.

Just as we are activating transpersonal chakras within our energy field, so too is Gaia. And just as we need to balance the higher energies and levels of consciousness that are flowing through us, so does Gaia.

During my pilgrimages between 2001 and 2006 to facilitate the Shift by activating the 12 Soular Discs around the world and thus a grid of unity consciousness for both humanity and Gaia, my understanding grew that the degree of grace with which we go through the Shift will bring forth an equivalent response from Gaia. The activation of the grid, as already explained, was completed at the 23rd December solstice of 2003 and ushered in a nine-year gestation process that's due to complete at the end of the Mayan calendar at the December solstice of 2012. We're now entering the birthing process itself and, whether we feel ready or not, as for a human birth, the more we can go with the unstoppable process of transformation that is in train, the easier that birth will be. So, the sooner and more collectively we wake up to the real-ization that Gaia is also a living being and that we are profoundly interconnected, the greater the ease with which she will go through the Shift too.

The sheer numbers of people now on Earth and our devastating need for Gaia's resources are pushing her to her limits. Like an overwhelmed mother with too many children screaming for her attention, she is on the brink of being unable to cope. And tragically, like some mothers, her exhausted response may be to destroy her children before they destroy her.

It doesn't have to be like that.

My own experience over many years of communing with Gaia and helping others to do so is that when we are ready to listen to her wisdom, she's more than ready to commune with us.

In late August 2005, I watched at home in the UK as Hurricane Katrina devastated the Gulf coast of America and the city of New Orleans, killing over 1,800 people and leaving an estimated $81 billion of damage in her wake. It eventually became clear, though, that the main fault lay not with Katrina herself but the insistence on building in low-lying areas, the clearing of the mangrove swamps that would have dissipated her energies and the inadequacies of the system of levees built around the stricken city.

A few weeks later, I was in Austin, Texas, to teach a weekend class at the wonderful Crossings Center founded by my friends Joyce and Ken Beck. But as the weekend approached, so did a second hurricane, named Rita.

As Rita bore down on the coast, I guided my class to attune with her and Gaia and ask that her path be less dangerous and damaging than her sister's had been. As I tuned into her energy, I envisaged her becoming gentler and altering her path to one that would essentially pass over that of Katrina rather than cause fresh devastation. Our intentions were added to the many prayers offered throughout the USA before Rita hit land.

Rita had been an even more powerful storm than Katrina. But when she hit the coast, sure enough, her effects were significantly less severe than feared. Her storm surge, which had been expected to hit the cities of Galveston and Houston, unexpectedly struck farther east. Winds blowing offshore in Texas actually flattened out, limiting the surge to well below Galveston's sea wall. And the strong rain that was expected to fall on New Orleans, adding to its misery and the pressure on the levee system, didn't materialize.

My class and I breathed a sigh of relief and were overwhelmed by an enormous feeling of gratitude – thankfulness that I aim to express every day to Gaia and all her beloved children with whom we share this miraculous world.

****

Within our energy field we have meridians and chakras, and so too does Gaia. After many years of geomantic attunement and research, whilst I've come to the view that certain places do hold the primary essence of certain chakric aspects, I've seen that different people interact differently with the various levels of Gaia's energy field. And so I tend not to be specific but suggest everyone finds their own connection and communion with places and their guardian spirits. The only thing I do suggest is to approach, as I've learned to do, all such sites with an open heart, an open mind, an openness of purpose and a willingness to listen and learn.

But, as we've seen with the Rift Valley which reaches through Africa and upwards through the Middle East, there are areas that both energetically and symbolically embody a resonance between the psyche of humanity and the psyche of Gaia.

To many geomancers, the boundaries of the tectonic plates that continually recycle the cellular skin of the planet are such regions. The so-called Ring of Fire that circles the Pacific Rim is one of them. The Afar Depression of Ethiopia, where the remains of both Lucy and Ardi were discovered, is a geomantic hotspot. And the continuing turmoil of Afghanistan and Pakistan is taking place over a triple junction of plates.

As we've discussed in relation to Pakistan and Afghanistan, such areas heighten the visibility of the underlying tensions within our psyche – and when we're able to authentically resoulve our differences, the release of those tensions then has a disproportionately beneficial effect both on ourselves and Gaia.

With such a geomantic linkage, resoulution of the schism playing out between Israel and the Palestinians and also within Afghanistan will almost certainly have dramatic benefits for our entire collective psyche.

* * * *

As in New Orleans, in many cases the damage done by natural events has been worsened dramatically by our stupidity and ignorance.

In Turkey, for example, seismologists have known for years that the major faults that thread beneath its capital Istanbul will one day, probably very soon, unleash an enormous earthquake. Yet the authorities' acceptance of inadequate building regulations has allowed enormous numbers of people to live in homes, be taught in schools and work in buildings that in an earthquake will immediately collapse into rubble.

The earthquake that rose up from the geological and geomantic hotspot beneath Haiti in January 2010 was powerful. But again the awful number of deaths, estimated by the Haitian government to be more than 300,000, was primarily caused in this desperately poor country by the collapse of badly constructed and located buildings.

As both the Shift and its collective and environmental birth pangs intensify around the world, we need to work in harmony with Gaia on all physical and spiritual levels to mitigate her dis-stress and dis-ease. Communing with her in the unconditional love of the 8th chakra and through the perception of the 9th chakra offers us a profound understanding that we've as yet hardly begun to access. When pharmaceutical company executives have asked indigenous shamans how they've gained their encyclopaedic knowledge of plant remedies, they've responded that the plants have communicated with them. When we start to really attune with Gaia, I believe we can learn how to rectify and resoulve much of the damage we've done to our environment, optimize her resources and generate energy in radically new and sustainable ways.

She is ready, I believe, to teach us, but we must be ready to listen and learn.

* * * *

We've already seen how elemental symbolism and resonance may be perceived and experienced in the holographic interaction between people and places and between our collective psyche and that of Gaia.

We've also seen how the archetypal elements of Fire and Water predominate in the energetic transformation of the Shift, as I first discovered during our Soular Disc journeys.

In April and May 2010, both elements were to the fore as two eruptions, one natural and one man-made, hit the news.

In mid-April, on Iceland's southern rim, the volcano Eyjafjallajökull erupted from beneath the ice-cap of the glacier above it, spewing a vast cloud of gas and dust that rose high into the air. The glassy debris was then caught by the jet stream and carried over much of Europe, where it grounded planes and resulted in mayhem for travellers.

Far to the south, less than a week later, on 20 April, BP's Deepwater Horizon oil-drilling rig in the US Gulf exploded, killing 11 people and causing the largest marine spill in the oil industry's history at nearly 206 million gallons of crude oil. And whilst the wellhead leak was capped in July, the spill continued to cause enormous environmental damage.

In January 2011, tar balls were still washing up, the wake of fishing boats was still showing trails of oil sheen, crude oil still remained in deep water and coastal marsh grass was still polluted and dying. There were gigantic underwater plumes of dissolved oil that weren't visible on the ocean's surface and an 80 square mile 'kill zone' now surrounds the blown well, where everything on the seafloor appears dead.

Let's look at the archetypal symbolism and cosmic influences that interconnect the two events, noting that both occurred as Chiron entered Pisces for the first time in over 40 years – the oil spill on the exact day.

As my friend, fellow geomancer Sarah Bisby, put it when writing of the Icelandic eruption, 'As water is classically symbolic of emotion, frozen water then represents suppressed emotion, under which the fire of passion in this case is quite literally exploding.'

Both Sarah and I sensed that the Icelandic north, the 'head' of Gaia, where the powers of the mind are prominent, was literally exploding both through the volcano and, previously, the explosive meltdown of the country's financial system.

The Gulf of Mexico, in contrast, is a classic grail, a watery basin lying at the heart of the planet, whose heartbreak was now pumping the fiery life-blood of its oil into the surrounding water.

The symbolic presence of Fire and Water – head and heart – resonated through both Icelandic and Gulf eruptions.

The presence of the Earth element was the foundational elemental womb against which the events played out. But the element of Air also played a role in linking the two.

As Sarah noted,

The reason the Icelandic eruption had such an impact on all our lives was because the power of the explosion (denial of suppressed emotion) *was enough to eject the ash directly into the Jet Stream, which then brought toxic clouds over much of Europe. If the deeper symbolism of the eruption was about how our minds/thoughts* (air) *have been distorted by the denial of our emotions –* our frozen hearts – *then it also represents a denial, or at least disconnection from, our lower three chakras, representing our relationship with our primal selves and ultimately with our planet, Gaia.*

Our addiction to oil and another aspect of our 'frozen hearts' – our arrogant attitude towards Gaia – caused the oil spill.

Sarah and I also agree that, as she says,

*If we allow our frozen hearts to thaw and take
responsibility for our emotions rather than continue
to suppress and deny them (Icelandic eruption),
then we can anchor our higher energy centres in the
compassion of the heart and make decisions from the
mind involving the heart connection (the essence of the
re-energized divine masculine). And we must continue
to acknowledge, awaken and integrate our lower three
centres, through which we can connect to the newly
empowered divine feminine energies, and therefore
to the heart and womb of the planet. Then we too can
dance in harmony with the winds and the water, pulse
to the fire and the rhythms of the Earth. Once fully in
tune, it will become inconceivable for us to destroy these
delicate mechanisms, as we will fully understand how in
doing so, we destroy ourselves.*

The entry of Chiron into Pisces, the twelfth zodiac sign, represents the completion of an entire astrological cycle. And the eight-year sojourn of this wounded healer in this most spiritual of Water signs offers us insights into how to heal our real-ationship with Gaia and to empathize with her suffering and that of all her children

Paola Emma, an Australian astrologer, also warned back in December 2009:

*On the negative side this position of Chiron may increase
the risk of serious pandemics, because the medium
of Pisces, with its openness and fluidity, is ideal for
the spread of infections, the absorption of poisons
and the lowering of our collective immunity. Tears and
powerlessness, with the loss of control are some of the*

*traditional attributes of mystical Pisces when its energy
is mishandled. The Earth may become more susceptible
to illnesses brought about by pollution and neglect, the
same applying to all the beings that populate it, animals
and humans. The situation on our planet may worsen
before the healing can begin.*

But, as she went on to note,

*One way or the other, this long transit will make us
realize that, if any member of the human family suffers,
the whole of humanity suffers. The potential for collective
healing through this configuration is self-evident, but only
via spiritual surrender of ego-centred attitudes. Chiron in
Pisces basically suggests that to cure the body (ours, the
Earth's) we need to heal the soul.*

I began writing *HOPE* as the miners in Chile were beginning their epic inner journey underground. But what can their experience offer us on a larger symbolic level?

As a prelude to the journeys of *The 13th Step*, I discovered that two of the twelve Lemurian Soular Discs that anchor the unity energy grid of Gaia were located in Antarctica and Akutan Island off Alaska, both positioned on the meeting of tectonic plates around the Pacific Rim, the Ring of Fire that is marked by volcanic and seismic activity.

Some geomancers have sensed the arising of new energies – the planetary *kundalini* – in the Andes. My own sense is that the energetic Water activation of the Antarctic soular disc and its connection with Tierra del Fuego, the land of Fire, combine these two elemental forces, which, as we've seen, are the archetypes of the Shift, at the symbolic 'root chakra' of these new energies.

They continue up through the geological and geomantic 'Ring of Fire' where the waters of the Pacific meet the volcanic mountain ranges of South America. Shaped like a vast geomantic serpent, the *kundalini* energies then rise up through Central America and on to the western coastal area of North America, passing through Mount Shasta until they reach the 'head' of the serpent at the soular disc at Akutan in the Aleutian Islands.

The heroic story of the Chilean miners at the 'sacral' chakra of the *kundalini* Earth serpent was energetically resonant with this enormous awakening *kundalini*.

As we've seen, the numerology embodied in their 'initiation' was mythic – 33 miners, 33 days for the rescue, 69 days in all below ground, rescued as the twelfth day became the thirteenth day of the tenth month of the tenth year of the millennium.

The men underwent, within the womb of the feminine, as they perceived and described it, a process of rebirth.

The timing was immaculate, too, with Venus, the planet of real-ationship and love, going through the darkness of her retrograde period before re-emerging into the sunlight of a new dawn.

****

As we collectively awaken the transpersonal 8th chakra of the universal heart and, through the 9th chakra, connect with the heart of Gaia, our intentions become more coherently focused. In prayer and in service to healing, we can progressively discern and address the causal seed-points of the remaining schisms that fragment our psyche.

And in doing so, we're able to heal our real-ationship with Gaia and all her children too. For no longer can we perceive her as separate and passive, but as an essential aspect of the cosmic hologram through which the infinity of cosmic mind explores itself.

CHAPTER 24
Our Cosmic Destiny: 2012 and Beyond

'The moment that God created hope was the first moment of creation.'
JUDE CURRIVAN

Some five billion years ago our Sun began to shine and the matrix of consciousness that is our Soular System started its incredible evolutionary journey. We've now come to a cosmic crossroads that offers us the chance to move to the next stage of our collective evolution.

So what is our higher purpose for being here and now at this vital moment? And what may our cosmic destiny be if instead of retreating into the old patterns of fear, we choose to travel the path for HOPE and take a collective leap into love?

* * * *

We've explored how the holographic consciousness of our Soular System affects our psyche at all scales, from the personal to our human collective to that of Gaia, including all the archetypal planetary influences that shape us and our experiences of life.

Our expansion of consciousness is also embodied by Gaia, not only by such processes as climate change but by changes in her electromagnetic field.

A geomagnetic reversal, often referred to as a pole shift, is a change in the direction of Gaia's magnetic field that switches the polarity of magnetic north and south. Such reversals have occurred many times in the past, the last one being about 780,000 years ago. As a precursor to such a shift, a process that in the past has lasted from a matter of weeks to tens of thousands of years, the magnetic field undergoes a period of wandering about and becoming weaker before its polarization finally flips and then settles down once more.

Over the last 150 years, records show that the overall field has reduced by 10–15 per cent, a decline that has accelerated in the last few years. The north magnetic pole has been moving from northern Canada towards Siberia, a process that has also accelerated in the last few years. Over the last 100 years or so it has moved from a rate of around 6 miles per year to now nearly 40 miles per year.

We and Gaia are electromagnetic beings and affected by such fields on both obvious and more subtle levels. From the fossil record, such geomagnetic reversals in the past seem not to have caused any major biological problems. Whilst we can't tell from those records if evolutionary processes were enhanced or triggered, my own sense is that they were and that what is now happening is energetically an important aspect of the Shift. And whilst it may be that the field's current alteration in position and strength may be causing distressing phenomena such as whales and dolphins beaching themselves, I would contend that this is more likely to be caused by the cacophany of underwater sonar and other telecommunications being used by the world's military and fishing fleets disorientating these beings.

A further electromagnetically linked phenomenon that is currently due to peak in late 2012/early 2013 is the Sun's sunspot cycle. NASA has recently warned that with our society's dependence on technology, a large solar flare could cause blackouts to satellite communications and a geomagnetic storm on Earth that could bring down Earth-based energy grids. The effects of such potentially severe space weather events can, however, be mitigated by orbital satellites offering early warning and a network that can disconnect and buffer the electrical systems that power the grid.

Combining prosaic and practical prevention and protection measures is of course appropriate and sensible. But I believe that a far greater awareness of the fundamental interconnections between ourselves and our Soular System family is a more profound and ultimately beneficial means of ensuring that we live in harmony within a planetary system that for billions of years has ensured that the evolution and abundance of biological life has been nurtured and sustained.

* * * *

Now, we'll consider the real-ationship of our entire Soular System with our Galaxy and how the Shift may be about to usher us into the real-ization of our cosmic destiny.

As yet we have a very limited perspective of how our Sun and Soular System's electromagnetic field interacts with our Galaxy, or indeed the energetic characteristics of the spiral arm of the Galaxy within which our system is embedded.

What is beginning to be realized, though, is that just as the atmosphere and oceans of Gaia have calm and turbulent regions, so it is eminently likely that as we hurtle through space, either on a cyclic or irregular basis we encounter different levels of energetic turbulence within the interstellar medium. And whilst our Sun's electromagnetic field extends way beyond Pluto, there are galactic phenomena so energetic that even the heliosphere which surrounds and protects our planetary system might be unable to withstand their effects.

But again, over the duration of billions of years, even when cataclysmic events have occurred, whether arising from circumstances on Earth or visited out of the sky, Gaia and the life she has borne have endured.

And, just as Chiron, the wounded healer within the consciousness of our Soular System, is aligning to support our inner healing, so the constellation of Ophiuchus, the archetype of the cosmic healer and in mythology the pupil of Chiron, is embodying the archetype of the enlightened human and connecting us with galactic consciousness.

The increasing 'visibility' within our collective consciousness of the human-god Ophiuchus, depicted holding the healing serpent of the caduceus, is a sign to me that the transpersonal 11th chakra within our soul-level energy field is now being activated.

From the 23rd December solstice of 2003, the Sun and Earth have been energetically aligned with the Galactic Centre. As we journey towards 2012 and beyond, at each December solstice the Sun is between the Earth and the GC, and at the June solstice, the Earth is between the GC and the Sun.

Energetically anchoring these alignments from opposite sides of the sky are the 'cosmic twins' of Ophiuchus and Orion.

The ancient Egyptians associated the constellation of Orion with Osiris, the cosmic principle of regenerative life and divine masculinity whose life, death and resurrection correlated with the constellation re-emerging into view, after 70 days of 'death', at the time of the Egyptian new year in late July and the new birth the annual Nile floods gifted to the land.

The area above the head of Orion is known esoterically as the silver gate, the cosmic gate of ascension. Its position is the equivalent of the 11th chakra above our heads.

Interestingly, in late 2010 astronomers announced that the star nearest to the silver gate, the red giant Betelgeuse, is ready sometime soon – although in astronomical terms this could be anytime from next week to 1,000 years hence – to explode as a supernova. In their turmoil, such explosions seed into the interstellar medium the heavier elements such as carbon, nitrogen and oxygen that are essential for biological life as we know it.

It's estimated that, at over 800 light years away, Betelgeuse going supernova would shine as brightly in our sky as the full Moon for a short while, but would be too far away to be a danger. But should it occur within the coming few years, what an incredible symbol of the birth of the Shift it would be!

Exactly opposite Orion in the sky stands Ophiuchus, whose foot, as we've seen, correlates with the GC and the point known as the golden gate, whose position is equivalent to the 9th chakra beneath our feet. And so galactic consciousness streaming from the GC and through the archetypal cosmic healer and enlightened human is now energetically being anchored in the heart of Gaia.

The association of Ophiuchus with healing also links the constellation with Isis and the divine feminine, embodying another aspect of its cosmic mirror with Orion/Osiris and the divine masculine.

At the December solstice, the birth date of archetypal and mythic soular heroes, the Sun now conjoins the galactic golden gate of Ophiuchus, revealing that it's the reintegration of the divine feminine and her resoulution with the divine masculine that's vital to the Shift.

Synchronistically, at 3.30 on the morning of 19 October 2006, when Tony and I and two companions began the walk from the Mount of Olives to the golden gate of Jerusalem, as I've described in *The 13th Step*, but unknown to me at the time, at this exact moment Ophiuchus and the golden gate of the 9th chakra were directly beneath us in the sky at the opposite side of the Earth. And Orion and the silver gate of the 11th chakra were directly above us, so enabling the cosmic consciousness of the Galaxy to holographically resonate and ground through us as we began the process of resoulution of the divine feminine and masculine within the ancient holy of holies of the Jerusalem Temple.

Uranus and Neptune undertook transits of Ophiuchus in the 1980s, energetically preparing their energies for the transformation of the Shift. And Pluto, who transited Ophiuchus in the years to the end of 2003, when we activated the portal to the Galactic Centre at the December solstice when the Sun too was conjunct with the GC, continues to be our way-shower through the transition and on to the fulfilment of our cosmic destiny.

****

The fact that the Sun and Moon are exactly the same size as seen from Earth should astonish us. The Sun is about 400 times as big as the Moon. But he is exactly the equivalent distance further away and so their cosmic dance with the Earth enables the miracle of total eclipses, especially one of the most awesome sights in Nature, a total solar eclipse.

Solar and lunar eclipses that come in pairs a couple of weeks apart at times of the New and Full Moon realign the archetypal energies of the Sun and Moon within our psyche and that of Gaia and offer opportunities to move on from old patterns and co-create new ones.

As the energies of the Shift increase, so does our sensitivity to eclipses. These occur in related so-called Saros and Metonic series of 18- and 19-year spirals, so offering us the opportunity to complete the issues of the previous cyclic turn, release them and move on to the next level.

Through to the end of 2014, there are a number of partial eclipses, just three total lunar eclipses and one total solar eclipse, on 13 November 2012.

The astrological chart of this total solar eclipse, visible over the vast expanse of the South Pacific ocean, is especially potent, as it is located in the intense water sign of Scorpio and its date numerologically resonates with the transformational harmonics of 12 and 13, with the master number 11 and the Sun and Moon conjunct at the time with the North Node of higher purpose.

A review of the chart elicits its energy as being that of inspirational visionary truth, the compassion to heal and release residual karma and aspire to the full embodiment of higher purpose. It's a wonderfully suitable astrological portal to usher in the final days of the Mayan calendar and the hoped-for breakthrough to a new enlightened era.

And it may energize a further profound real-ization within us.

Having witnessed four total solar eclipses, one of the most incredible aspects for me is the absolute blackness within their rim. For the minutes of totality everything is physically and energetically silent, as though being wiped clear. And as a cosmologist, I know the closest cosmic phenomenon in appearance to this unique Soular System marvel is a black hole.

Whilst no black holes have yet been seen through a telescope, the total absorption of all light within their circular event horizon renders astronomers' perceived appearance of them virtually the same as the moments of solar eclipse totality.

The emerging vision of the nature of our universe being in essence a cosmic hologram originally came from the understanding of how the information held within a black hole is proportional not to its 3-D volume but, remarkably, its two-dimensional surface.

And the centre of our Galaxy, which is thought to be a gigantic black hole, is also perceived by mystics as embodying the information of galactic consciousness.

So does a total solar eclipse, with its appearance of a black hole, energetically link our psyche to that of the Galactic Centre and the cosmic hologram that is the fundamental nature of all that we call reality?

* * * *

As I've discovered and experienced for myself over many years, we have incredible cosmic support for the Shift from ancestors, the entirety of Gaia herself, the elemental, devic and angelic realms, ascended masters, guides and extraterrestrials. Our expanding awareness and the opening of the universal heart within our collective psyche are enabling us not only to communicate with these multi-dimensional realms but also to re-member our divine nature and the eternal wisdom of our own higher selves. And, above all, to embody the unconditional love of unity consciousness.

As the Shift accelerates, we're beginning to commune through the 10th chakra with the matrix of consciousness that is our Soular System and through the 11th chakra with that of our Galaxy.

As 2012 approaches, we are literally re-membering the wholeness of all that we are and of All That Is. Level by level, our awareness is expanding beyond the limits of our personal sense of self and we're beginning to explore the transpersonal realms of the Cosmos.

And crucially, the 9th chakra is grounding our expanding awareness within the ordinary/extraordinariness of our human experience.

By choosing love in every thought, feeling and action, we're progressively in-to-greating into the 12th chakra level of universal consciousness and ultimately the 13th oneness of unity awareness.

The great spiritual teachers and mystics that came before us told us this would be so for us all one day.

What if, as singer Joan Osborne asked in 1995, God is one of us?

S/he is. And we all are.

Continuing to HOPE...

In the late summer of 2010, uncharacteristically, I was feeling hopeless. The news was full of negative stories, people around me were feeling low and I felt I'd come to the end of a long cycle of my life and was empty and bereft, with no sense of excitement about what was to come.

And I'd just signed a deal to write a book called *HOPE*!

For weeks I couldn't write. How could I write on such a subject when I felt so hopeless myself?

And that's when I began to realize Spirit was offering me a great opportunity.

When all seemed darkest, I forced myself to go deep within to find that tiny spark of hope that never dies as long as we live and can love.

I searched for the memory of when I'd felt most hopeful. And when I found it and re-membered how I'd felt then, I could sense once more a glimmer of hope beginning to glow at the very core of my being.

Over the coming days, even though everything around me continued to seem bereft of hope, I gently nurtured its optimism within me. Gradually as I re-membered other hopeful times, I began to see signs of hope all around me.

And with a renewed sense of hope, my sense of purpose was in turn empowered. Months later, as I was about to complete HOPE, I experienced in Japan the catastrophic shock whose enormous scale of destruction and aftermath are still unfolding as I write. Despite the devastation and tragic loss of life, the stoicism, resilience and extraordinary care shown to each other by the Japanese people, and their determination for this to be a new beginning, is inspiring and incredibly hopeful. As I left Tokyo for home, the trees were bringing forth their first blossom, traditionally seen in Japan as the harbinger of spring, ushering the promise of warmer days and the renewal of life. This year, the blossom also signifies the power of love and hope to succeed against all odds.

Around the world, too, that promise, nurtured by Spirit and the cosmic support we have at this incredible moment of transformation, is flowering in the peaceful revolutions that are empowering people to overcome their fears and fulfil their hopes of a better future.

When the Fire of the infinite flame of cosmic mind and the Water of the eternal ocean of its heart individuated into the fiery sparks and watery droplets of our personal selves, our exploration of that apparent separation began to take us further and further away from the unity awareness of All That Is.

At that first moment of co-creation, I believe God – and we as co-creators – hid a tiny spark of hope deep within us. For that ember of hope gives us the courage to find our way home to the unconditional love and wholeness of all that we really are, have always been and ever will be.

As we approach 2012 and the potential of a new era, the opening of the universal heart within us is calling us to reconcile the divine feminine of our hearts and divine masculine of our minds to give birth to the divine child of our higher purpose. Now is the time for all of us to re-member the hopes of our highest dreams for ourselves and Gaia and to envisage and together co-create their realities.

Jude
Avebury, England
April 2011

Resources

A number of websites are now enabling group healing attunements to be focused, including:

- www.pathforhope.com, which also has links to other websites. You can also join its attunements through Facebook at www.facebook.com/Path-for-HOPE and through Twitter at www.twitter.com/pathforHOPE.

- www.glcoherence.org, a science-based initiative uniting people in heart-focused intention to shift global consciousness.

These online resources invite you to add your unique voice to group intentions and healing attunements, enable unfolding news of the Shift to be shared and support an interactive forum to continue to spread the message and co-creative aims of *HOPE.*

- Online activism is rapidly increasing and there are many websites detailing specific areas for you to add your voice. The website www.avaaz.org covers a wide range of campaigns chosen collectively by its millions of members around the world.

- Friends of the Earth provides information and action on climate change, food and biodiversity on its website www.foe.co.uk.

- www.faircompanies.com offers information and resources for sustainable living.

- www.treehugger.com has sustainable design and ecological news and solutions.

- You can find information on new and emergent 'good ideas' on www.ted.com.

- www.idealist.org is a global clearing house website for ngo and volunteering resources and opportunities.

- www.kiva.org is a globally based microfinancing initiative where you can invest your money via PayPal.

- Jude Currivan, *The 8th Chakra*, Hay House, 2006

- —*The 13th Step*, Hay House, 2007

- — *Heart, Mind and Purpose*, CD, Hay House, 2008

- Jude Currivan and Ervin Laszlo, *CosMos: A Co-Creator's Guide to the Whole World*, Hay House, 2008

- Paul Hawken, *Blessed Unrest*, Penguin Books, 2007

Index

abandonment 61–7
abuse 67–8
  Pakistan 216–17
  Russia 138, 140, 141–4
Afghanistan 214–15
  abuse 68
  geomantics 301
  level of awareness 92
Africa
  and China 198–200
  deforestation and
    reforestation 295
  South Africa 257
  see also Ethiopia
Age(s)
  of Aquarius 42, 104–5,
    107–9
  of Aries 106
  Axial 287–8
  Bronze 47–9
  of Pisces 106–7
  of Taurus 105–6
Ahmad Shah Massoud 215
airline crashes 9, 144

Akiba, Tadatoshi (Mayor of
    Hiroshima) 267
Alcott, Louisa M. 273
Alioso, Francis 43–4
all-one-ness 58, 87
Amiel, Henri-Frédéric 83
ancestors 18–19, 54
Annunaki (Enki and Enlil) 22,
    25–7, 28, 32–3, 34, 37,
    49–50
anxiety and relaxation 64–6
Arab world
  protests 177–83
  see also specific countries
archaeology 17, 19–23
  Ethiopia 5–6, 9–10
  evidence of environmental
    change 18, 28–9, 45–7,
    48, 203–5
archetypes
  healing patterns 61–74
  Neterw pantheon 179
  see also Fire and Water
Ardi 5–6, 6–7, 9–10

Armstrong, Karen 287
Ashkenazi Jews 161, 162
Ashoka, Emperor of India
      205–6
Asian tsunami (2006) 32
astrology 98–104, 109–10,
      283–4
   Ages 104–9
   Chiron 98, 101, 102, 157–8,
      212, 303, 305–6
   Harmonic Concordance
      239–43
   influence on nations
      India and Pakistan 211–
         13, 216
      Iran 173–4
      Israel and Palestine 157–
         8, 169–71
      Russia 137
      USA 115–16, 118, 133,
         283
   Barack Obama, birth chart
      262–3, 264
   Ophiuchus (Asclepius) 242,
      245, 246, 312, 313, 314
   Solar/Soular System 15–16,
      85–6, 97, 109–10, 309,
      311–14
Attis, cult of 164–5
Auschwitz 145–6, 150–1,
      152–3, 169
authoritarianism 92–3
   Russia 139–40
Avaaz campaigning model
      290–1

Avebury, England 85, 239–46,
      300
awareness see chakra system;
      self-awareness; spiral
      evolution of awareness
Axial Age 287–8

Ban ki Moon 267
Beck, Don and Cowan,
      Christopher 89–90, 91
Begin, Menachim 158
Berossus 30
Betelgeuse 312–13
betrayal 68–70, 237–8
Bhutan 280
Bible
   Armageddon 8
   Judas 68, 69–70
   Lucifer 11
   and Sumerian texts 21, 22,
      23–4, 25, 27, 28–9, 30,
      50
   see also Christianity; Jewish
      history and Judaism
Bisby, Sarah 304
Black Madonna 144, 153–4
Black Road 13, 15
Bond, Gerald 46
Bosnia 252–4
   media reporting of wars
      256–8
   Medugorje and Mostar 255–6
   peace deal (1995) 256
BP Deepwater Horizon
      explosion (2010) 303

Breathnach, Sarah Ban 219
British Medical Journal 285
Bronze Age 47–9
Brown, Dee 126
Buck, Pearl S. 115
Buddhism 64
    India 205–6
    Tibet 192–3
Buffet, Warren 277, 282
Bush, George W. 118–19, 131

chakra system 44, 69, 83
    Gaia (8th and 9th chakras)
        296–7, 298, 301, 302,
        307
    8th (universal heart) 56, 74,
        80, 83, 84, 90–1, 195,
        240, 242, 318
    9th (earthstar) 10, 85, 224–
        5, 240, 296, 307, 316
    10th (Solar/Soular System
        awareness) 85–6, 97, 316
    11th (galactic awareness) 86,
        312–13, 316
    12th (universal
        consciousness) 86–7, 316
    13th (oneness of unity
        awareness) 316
child aspects 33, 41–2, 195–6,
    223–4
childhood trauma *see* healing,
    archetype patterns
Chilean mining disaster and
    rescue xv–xvi, 306–7

China 187–8
    and Africa 198–200
    Confucianism
        revival and political reform
            201–2
        traditional beliefs and
            196–8
    Cultural Revolution (1960s)
        189, 191
    eclipse 195–6
    Olympics (2008) 188, 190,
        191
    Tiananmen Square 202
        and human rights
            movement 190–1,
            200–1
    and Tibet 188–9, 190,
        191–4
    war with Japan 226
Chiron 98, 101, 102, 157–8,
    212, 303, 305–6
Christianity 17, 146
    Jesus 148, 163–4, 243
    Saint Paul 163–5
Clinton, Bill 116, 118
Cochabamba People's Accord
    293–4
Cohen, Andrew 94
Cohen, Roger 183
compassion 6, 54, 56, 59
consciousness/collective
    consciousness
    Axial Age 287–8
    schism 4

Shift 18, 42, 43, 51, 56–7, 70, 74, 77–8, 81–2, 83–4, 85, 109–10, 184
  see also cosmic hologram
cosmic hologram
  emerging vision of integrated reality 78–9, 80, 81–2
  scientific view 75–7, 78, 79, 81
  WorldShift2012 movement 75–6, 77–8
CosMos 221, 278, 292

Dalai Lama 189, 193
Day of Atonement 164, 169, 172
denial 70–3
  Israel and Palestine 165–6
Dickinson, Emily 291
Drews, Robert 48
drug addiction 68

EarthChild Institute 295
earthquakes 302
Ebionites 164
eclipses 195–6, 314–15
The Economist 288
ego-minds and self-awareness 57–8
Egypt 32–4, 37, 38–40, 46, 178–82, 203–4, 210
Einstein, Albert 79, 89
Eisenhower, Dwight 130
Elohim 241, 243, 297

empathy 6, 58, 59, 91, 287
Encke comet 32, 34
Enki and Enlil 25–7, 28, 32–3, 34, 37, 49–50
environmental change
  archeological evidence 18, 28–9, 45–7, 48, 203–5
  see also Gaia
environmentalist movement 293–4
Epiphanius of Salamis 165
Ethiopia
  archeology 5–6, 9–10
  archetypal patterns 68, 73
  Rift Valley (Gate of Tears and Afar Depression) 3–6, 13, 301
  spiritual and healing journey 3–13
  tree-planting project 7, 295
Ethiopian Airlines crash 9
extraterrestrials
  Annunaki (Enki and Enlil) 22, 25–7, 28, 32–3, 34, 37, 49–50
  UFOs 70–2, 86

Fagan, Brian 46
fear-based behaviours *see* healing, archetypal patterns
feminine–masculine aspects 8, 40–2
  Bronze Age 47–8

and child 33, 41–2, 195–6,
    223–4
Chilean mining disaster
    306–7
Japan 223–4, 231
personal and collective
    balancing 58–9
Shekinah 148–50, 153–4
Sun and Ophiuchus
    313–14
wars/conflict 49
feng shui 196–7, 223
financial markets/banks *see*
    under w(h)ealth
Fire and Water 9, 144, 148,
    150–2, 153, 154, 178,
    207–8, 209, 211, 216,
    222, 223, 241, 297, 298,
    303, 304, 305, 306–7
Flood stories 23–4, 27, 28–32,
    43, 44
France 281
Fuller, Thomas 235

Gaia 291–3
    8th and 9th chakra 296–7,
        298, 301, 302, 307
    communicating with 297–8,
        299–300, 302
    devic and angelic beings
        150–1, 296, 297–8
    electromagnetic field and
        reversal 309–11
    natural and man-made

disasters 303, 304–7
Soular System 309, 311–12
tree-planting projects
    294–5
UN and activist measures on
    climate change 293–4
see also geomantics
Galactic Centre (GC) 312, 313,
    314
Gandhi, Mahatma 52, 209,
    210
Garden of Eden 21–2, 27, 50
Gates, Bill and Melinda 282
genetic studies 4–5, 25–6
geomantics 37, 196–7, 211,
    216–17, 238, 301–2,
    303–5, 306–7
    nexus points and unity grid
        43–4, 154, 171, 239,
        299, 306
    telluric currents 240, 243
German Americans 121
Germany
    and Soviet Russia 135–6
    Zionist Jewish agenda 161
Giffords, Gabrielle 131–2
Giving Pledge movement 282
Goblecki Tepe, Turkey 20–3,
    24, 40
Goodman, Donna 295
Gorbechev, Mikhail 136, 137,
    138, 143
Gozo 44
Greenland 46

Hamas 159–60, 167, 168
Hancock, Graham 19
Hansen, James 142
happiness
    surveys 280, 285
    see also w(h)ealth
Harmonic Concordance
        239–43
Hatoyama, Yukio 263–4
Hawken, Paul 286, 287
healing
    archetypal patterns 61–74
    hope and love 51–9
Herodotus 173
Hershey, John 262
Hiroshima/Nagasaki bombings
        and nuclear disarmament
        226–7, 261–4, 267,
        268–9, 271
Hogan, Craig 77
Hu Jintao 188
human rights movement 190–
        1, 200–1
humanistic viewpoint 93
hurricanes 299–300
hyenas 12

Icelandic volcanic eruption
        (2010) 303, 304–5
Iles, George 15
immigration see under USA
India
    caste system 206–10
    current situation 213–4

drug addiction 68
Emperor Ashoka and
        Buddhism 205–6
Hinduism 205, 207–10
and Pakistan
        and Afghanistan 214–15,
        301
        astrological charts 211–
        13, 216
        Partition (1947) 210–11,
        239
    trauma and healing
        216–18
Pushkar 207–9
Vedic era 41, 204–5
Indus river basin 203–5
inequality 279–80, 285–6
    USA 119, 128–9
information 77, 79
Institute for Economics and
        Peace (IEP) 257
integrated reality, emerging
        vision of 78–9, 80, 81–2
internet
    Avaaz 288–9
    Wikileaks 16, 289–90
Iran 172–4, 183
Ireland
    and Irish migration 121–4
    Northern Ireland 258
Islam 107, 146, 147, 154
    Hamas, Palestine 159–60,
        166, 168
    Iran 173–4

and Jewish festivals 169
Israel
  and Arab protests 182–3
  and Iran 172–4, 183
  and Palestine 156–7
    astrological influences
      157–8, 169–71
    attack on aid flotilla (*Mavi
      Marmara*) 154, 160
    conditions for sustainable
      peace 166–8, 172,
      174–5
    conflicts and peace
      process 158–60
    denial 165–6
    geomantics 301
    rejection 158
    see also Jerusalem; Jewish
      history and Judaism

Jagland, Thorbjørn 201
Japan
  cultural values, trauma and
    healing 228–31
  earthquake and tsunami
    (2011) 232, 271, 317–18
  Edo period 225
  Fukushima nuclear reactor
    breakdown (2011) 232,
    271
  Hiroshima/Nagasaki
    bombings and nuclear
    disarmament 226–7, 261–
    4, 267, 268–9, 271

Jomon culture 219–20, 221,
  225, 231, 232
Meiji Restoration 226, 228,
  230
militarism 225, 226, 230
sacred sites 221–5
western technology and
  trade 225–6, 227–8
Yayoi culture 220, 221
Japanese in Egypt 180–1
Jasna Góra monastery, Poland
  153–4
Jaspers, Karl 287
Jerusalem 8, 168, 169, 171,
  173, 313–14
  Shekinah 148–50, 153–4
Jesus 148, 163–4, 243
Jewish history and Judaism
  Auschwitz 145–6, 150–1,
    152–3, 160, 169
  Covenant 146–8, 151–2,
    154, 155, 171–2
  Day of Atonement 164,
    169–70, 172
  exile mythology 160–5
  Shekinah 148–50, 153–4
  Yahweh 146–7, 148, 149,
    150–1, 153, 154, 171,
    173
  see also Israel
Johnson, Samuel 37
Judi Dagh, Zagros Mountains
  30–1
Jung, Carl 70–1, 97

Kan, Naoto 263, 268
Katyn massacre, Poland 143–4
Kean, Leslie 72
Khazaria 162
Killelea, Steve 257, 258
King Jr, Dr Martin Luther 187, 251, 252
King Khesar of Bhutan 280
Kramer, S. M. 24
kundalini Earth serpent/energy 41–2, 306–7
Kuznets, Simon 279

Lao Tzu 106, 259
Laszlo, Ervin 75–6, 77, 221, 292
Lazarus, Emma 116
Lin Yutang 3
Liu Xiaobo 200–2
loneliness 58, 63, 64, 290
loss, sense of 63–4

Maathai, Wangari 295
Malta 40–5
Marx Hubbard, Barbara 75–6
masculine aspect *see* feminine–masculine aspects
Matheno 26
Mattawa, Khaled 184
Mayans
  Black Road 13, 15
  calendar 29, 104, 240, 242, 243, 244, 299

Mayewski, Paul 46
media reporting of wars 256–8
Mediterranean region 43, 46
Medvedev, Dmitry 141
  START nuclear arms reduction talks with Obama 258, 260–1, 262
Mesopotamia/Syria 24–5, 45–7, 203–4
Michael and Mary telluric currents, England 240–3, 243
micro-finance initiative 282
Middle East *see* Arab world; *specific countries*
military spending/military-industrial complex 130–1, 252
Milky Way Galaxy 13, 15
Miller, Hamish and Ba 240–3
Mirehiel, Johnny 239
Miura, Hideki 221, 222
Mohamed Bouazizi 177–8, 180
money issues *see* w(h)ealth
Morales, Evo 293
movements 286–7
  environmentalist 293–4
  Giving Pledge 282
  human rights 190–1, 200–1
  WorldShift2012 75–6, 77–8
Mubarak, Hosni 178, 179, 180, 181, 210

Nakaya, Shinichi 221, 222, 223
Napoleon I 203
national psyches 95, 96
  see also specific countries
Native Americans 117, 120, 126–7
Netanyahu, Binyamin 168, 170–1, 182
Netherlands 93
New Zealand 34–5
Ningishzidda 34
Nobel Prize winners 137, 200–2, 267, 281, 282, 295
non-local phenomena 79
Northern Ireland 258
Nottale, Laurent 77
nuclear non-proliferation and disarmament
  Comprehensive Test Ban Treaty (2010) 267
  Hiroshima/Nagasaki atomic bombs 226–7, 261–4, 267, 268–9, 271
  US–Russia START talks 264–7, 268
nuclear weapons, Pakistan 216

Obama, Barack 127–8, 132, 133
  nuclear-free policy and birth chart 262–3, 264
  START nuclear arms reduction talks with
    Medvedev 264, 266–7, 268
Okada, Katsuya 268
Ophiuchus (Asclepius) 242, 245, 246, 312, 313, 314
Oppenheimer, J. Robert 269
Orion 312–14
outcasts 11–12, 73–4

Pakistan see under India
Palestine see under Israel
Paola Emma 305–6
past secrets 16–18
philanthropy 282
Poebel, Arno 24
Poland 143–4, 153–4
  Auschwitz 145–6, 150–1, 152–3, 169
  and Russia: Katyn massacre 143–4
Putin, Vladimir 138, 139–40, 143, 144

Rabin, Yitzhak 159
Rajaram, Dr N. S. 204
Ramadan 169
re-membering 2, 13, 18, 56–7, 83–7, 316
Reeve, Christopher 51
rejection 73–4
  Israel 158
relaxation, anxiety and 64–6
religion

Age of Pisces 106–7
see also specific religions
Rift Valley (Gate of Tears and
    Afar Depression) 3–6, 13,
    301
'right'- and 'left'-brain
    perception 4
rock art 38–9
Rohl, David 22, 29, 30
Rowley, Coleen and Dzakovic,
    Bogdan 290
Russia
    abuse 138, 140, 143–4
    astrological chart 137
    Katyn massacre, Poland
        143–4
    resurgent authoritarianism
        139–40
    Soviet era and subsequent
        reforms 135–9
    Soviet forces in Afghanistan
        214
    and USA
        and EU relations 141
        START nuclear arms
            reduction 264–7, 268
    war with Japan 226
Russian Jews, Israel 159,
    175

sacred marriage 41–2, 49, 59
sacrifice 8–9, 23
    animal 30–1, 147
    Jesus 164

Jewish Covenant and
    Auschwitz 145–8, 150–3,
    154, 155, 168, 171–2
Saint Paul 163–5
Salas, Robert 72
Sand, Shlomo 160–2, 165
Sarkozy, Nicolas 281
Saudi Arabia 141, 214–15
Schatz, Roland 258
Schmidt, Klaus 21, 23
scientific view
    and cosmic hologram 75–7,
        78, 79, 81
    and non-local phenomena
        57
Seidenberg, Abraham 204
self-awareness and ego-minds
    57–8
self-esteem 64–5
Sennacherib 30
Shekinah 148–50, 153–4
Shift *see* consciousness/
    collective consciousness;
    cosmic hologram
Sipkins, Dr Penny 6
Smiles, Samuel 285
Smith, George 28
Snyder, Gary 287
solar and lunar eclipses 195–6,
    314–15
Solar/Soular System 15–16,
    85–6, 97, 109–10, 309,
    311–14
South Africa 258

South America 38, 50
  Chilean mining disaster and
    rescue xv–xvi, 306–7
  World People's Conference
    on Climate Change 293–4
South Korea 294–5
spiral evolution of awareness
  model and levels 89–90,
    92–4
  multi-disciplinary approach
    95–6
Stalin, Josef 135–6, 143
Stiglitz, Joseph 281
Stockholm International Peace
  Research Institute (SIPRI)
    251
Strauss-Kahn, Dominique 278
Sumerians 11, 21, 22, 23–9,
    30–1, 32–3, 34, 37, 38–
    40, 49–50
sunspot cycle 310–11
Susskind, Leonard 77

Tarnas, Richard 97
Taurid Complex meteor shower
    32–5
Taylor Green, Christina 132–3
The 13th Step 8, 25–6, 32, 83,
    90, 146, 239, 306, 313
Thoth 34, 57, 96, 179, 297
Tiananmen Square see under
    China
Tibet 188–9, 190, 191–4
tree-planting projects 7, 294–5

tribal communities 92
Tunisia 177–8
Turkey 20–3, 24, 28, 46
Tusk, Donald 143

UFOs 70–2, 86
United Kingdom (UK) 235–6
  Big Tree Plant campaign 295
  level of awareness 93
  Northern Ireland 258
  paradoxes of national psyche
    236
  reform of wealth/well–being
    measurement 281
  sacred sites and mythology
    238–9
  Avebury 85, 239–44, 298
United Nations (UN)
  climate change and
    environmental summits
    293, 294
  Declaration of Human Rights
    201
  Israel–Palestine conflict 167
  peace negotiation role of
    women (2000) 258
  Secretary General 267
  Security Council 251, 252
  triple bottom line measure
    281
underwater ruins 19–20, 205
United States of America
    (USA)
  and Afghanistan 214–15

astrological influences 115–
    16, 118, 133, 283
BP Deepwater Horizon
    explosion (2010) 303
challenges 131, 133
domestic politics 128–30
economy 119, 130–1
healing workshop, Texas 69
hurricanes 300
immigration 116–17
    colonial period 119–21
    Irish 121–4
    Italian 124–5
    Mexican 125–6
    Vietnamese 125
inequality 119, 128–9
and Japan 225–7, 261–4,
    268–9
level of awareness 93
Lincoln and Washington
    Memorials 265–8
military
    spending 130–1, 252
    UFO sightings 72
Native Americans 117, 120,
    126–7
and Pakistan 217
reform of wealth/well-being
    measurement 281
and Russia 141
    START nuclear arms
        reduction 264–7, 268
September 11th 2001 117–
    19, 132–3, 215, 290

shooting of Congresswoman
    Gabrielle Giffords and
    Christina Taylor Green
    131–3
slaves 117, 120, 127–8
White House 265–6

Virgin Mary
    apparitions 255
    Black Madonna 144, 153–4
vulture 11–12

wars/conflicts
    Afghanistan 214–15
    Africa 199–200
    archetypal patterns 68, 74
    Bronze Age 47–8
    China 187
    feminine–masculine aspects
        49
    media reporting of 256–8
    military spending/military-
        industrial complex 130–1,
        252
    peace negotiations 258–9
    September 11th 2001
        terrorist attacks 117–19,
        132–3, 215, 290
    Vietnam 125
    World Wars 124–5, 135–6,
        156, 226–7, 261–2,
        268–9, 286
    see also Bosnia; Israel, and
        Palestine

Weinberg, George 61
Weiss, Harvey 45–6
Wen Jiabao 188
w(h)ealth 285–6
    astrology and healing
        283–4
    author's experience of 283
    developing countries 282
    financial markets/banks
        273–6
        bonuses 276
        boom and bust cycles
            274
        derivatives 276–7
        prospects for reform 278
    GDP and alternative
        measures of 279–81
Wigram, William and Edgar
    30–1
Wikileaks 16, 289–90
Wilbur, Ken 94
Wilkinson, Richard and Pickett,
    Kate 64–5, 285–6

women
    Christian peripheralization
        of 164
    peace negotiation role of 258
    UK 237
    see also feminine–masculine
        aspects
Woolley, Leonard 28–9, 31
WorldShift2012 movement
    75–6, 77–8

Xi Jinping 188

Yahweh 146–7, 148, 149,
    150–1, 153, 154, 171,
    173
Yeltsin, Boris 137, 139

Zeilinger, Anton 77
Zeilinger, Michael 227
Ziusudra 27, 28, 30, 37
Zoroastrianism 173
Zuckerberg, Mark 282

Also by Dr Jude Currivan

The 8th Chakra: What It Is and How It Can Transform Your Life

The 13th Step: A Global Journey in Search of Our Cosmic Destiny

CosMos: A Co-Creator's Guide to the Whole World (with Ervin Laszlo)

Heart, Mind and Purpose: Teachings and Attunements
to Awaken your Divine Potential (CD)

Hay House Titles of Related Interest

The Biology of Belief: Unleashing the Power
of Consciousness, Matter & Miracles,
by Bruce Lipton

Cellular Awakening: How Your Body Holds and Creates Light,
by Barbara Wren

The Contagious Power of Thinking:
How Your Thoughts Can Influence the World,
by David R. Hamilton PhD

How Your Mind Can Heal Your Body,
by David R. Hamilton PhD

The Secret of 2012 and a New World Age:
Understanding Fractal Time,
by Gregg Braden

ABOUT THE AUTHOR

Dr Jude Currivan is a cosmologist who was previously the most senior businesswoman in Britain. She now works worldwide as a planetary healer, internationally acclaimed author and inspirational speaker.

Jude has researched consciousness and metaphysics since childhood. She holds a PhD in archaeology from the University of Reading researching ancient cosmologies, and a master's degree in physics from Oxford University specializing in cosmology and quantum physics.

From the age of four she has experienced multi-dimensional realities. Throughout her life she has worked with a multitude of wisdom keepers and has led many sacred journeys worldwide.

She is the author of *The Wave* (O Books, 2005), *The 8th Chakra* (Hay House, 2006), *The 13th Step* (Hay House, 2007) and *CosMos: A Co-creator's Guide to the Whole-World* (Hay House, 2008) co-authored with Dr Ervin Laszlo.

She was presented with the 2010 CIRCLE award for Business and Science by Won Buddhism International and sponsored by the United Nations, cited for her 'outstanding contribution towards planetary healing and expanding new forms of consciousness.'

Her global work reconciles leading-edge science, research into consciousness and spiritual wisdom, and aims to raise awareness and empower practical and sustainable harmony and wholeness on personal and collective levels.

www.judecurrivan.com